Here Are My People

SINCE 1970
Histories of Contemporary America

SERIES EDITORS

Lynn Itagaki, *University of Missouri*

Daniel Rivers, *Ohio State University*

FOUNDING EDITORS

Claire Potter, *The New School*

Renee Romano, *Oberlin College*

ADVISORY BOARD

Mary Dudziak, *University of Southern California*

Devin Fergus, *University of Missouri*

David Greenberg, *Rutgers University*

Shane Hamilton, *University of Georgia*

Jennifer Mittelstadt, *Rutgers University*

Stephen Pitti, *Yale University*

Robert Self, *Brown University*

Siva Vaidhyanathan, *University of Virginia*

Susan Ware, General Editor, *American National Biography*

Judy Wu, *Ohio State University*

Here Are My People

LGBT COLLEGE STUDENT ORGANIZING IN CALIFORNIA

David A. Reichard

The University of Georgia Press
ATHENS

© 2024 by the University of Georgia Press
Athens, Georgia 30602
www.ugapress.org
All rights reserved
Set in Kelpler Std by Rebecca A. Norton

Most University of Georgia Press titles are
available from popular e-book vendors.

Printed digitally

Library of Congress Cataloging-in-Publication Data

Names: Reichard, David A., author.
Title: Here are my people : LGBT college student organizing in
    California / David A. Reichard.
Identifiers: LCCN 2023053898 (print) | LCCN 2023053899 (ebook) |
    ISBN 9780820366333 (hardback) | ISBN 9780820366760 (paperback) |
    ISBN 9780820366883 (epub) | ISBN 9780820366890 (pdf)
Subjects: LCSH: Sexual minority college students—California—
    History. | Homosexuality and education—California—History. |
    Student movements—California—History. | College environment—
    California. | Education, Higher—Social aspects—California.
Classification: LCC LC2575.5.C3 R45 2024 (print) | LCC LC2575.5.C3
    (ebook) | ddc 378.1/9826609794—dc23/eng/20231229
LC record available at https://lccn.loc.gov/2023053898
LC ebook record available at https://lccn.loc.gov/2023053899

CONTENTS

ACKNOWLEDGMENTS   vii

INTRODUCTION   1

CHAPTER 1. CREATING CAMPUS ORGANIZING HOMES   13

CHAPTER 2. NAVIGATING STRUGGLES FOR RECOGNITION   27

CHAPTER 3. CLAIMING A QUEER EDUCATION   37

CHAPTER 4. OPENING UP PEOPLE'S EYES   48

CHAPTER 5. FOSTERING QUEER CREATIVITY   60

CHAPTER 6. FORGING CROSS-CAMPUS ALLIANCES   74

CHAPTER 7. ENGAGING POLITICS   85

CONCLUSION   97

LIST OF ABBREVIATIONS   101

NOTES   103

BIBLIOGRAPHY   161

INDEX   179

ACKNOWLEDGMENTS

This book has been many years in the making, and I benefited from advice and support from more colleagues, archivists, librarians, and friends than I can possibly name. Nevertheless, I extend my deepest thanks to everyone who supported the project, gave advice, or pushed me to ask new kinds of questions. This is a better book because of it.

The people who generously shared their experiences with me through oral histories were especially important to this project. Those interviews filled in gaps, raised new questions, and inspired me to move forward, and I thank all the folks I interviewed. Several of them have passed on since I interviewed them, reminding me just how tenuous documenting LGBTQ+ history is—and how much we must continue to do so to preserve those histories. I am forever grateful for the willingness of all these folks to share their experiences not only with me but with future generations.

Staff, archivists, and volunteers at LGBTQ+ community-based organizations do the tireless work of preserving and making accessible invaluable materials essential for any historian attempting to understand the LGBTQ+ past. At ONE Archives at USC, I especially thank Michael Oliveira, Michael Palmer, and Loni Shibuyama; at the GLBT Historical Society in San Francisco, many staff, volunteers, and organizational champions supported this project. I especially thank Daniel Bao, Paul Boneberg, Marjorie Bryer, John Fagundes, Isaac Felman, Aimee Forster, Rebecca Kim, Terence Kissack, Gerard Koskovich, Bill Lipsky, Ruth Mahaney, Glenne McElhinney, Martin Meeker, Jacob Richards, Craig Scott, and Amy Sueyoshi. And I offer special thanks to Ron Grantz and Buzz Haughton from the Lavender Library in Sacramento, California.

Equally helpful were the many archivists, librarians, and student workers at libraries and university archives across California. In particular, I thank Kathleen Hansen at CSU Monterey Bay; Lynne Drennan, Brianna Loughlin, and Julie Thomas at Sacramento State; Meredith Eliassen at San Francisco State; Kathryn M. Neal and William Benemann at UC Berkeley; Charlotte Brown and Julie Jenkins at UCLA; and Danelle Moon, Daniel Jarvis, Diana Kohnke, and Carli Lowe at San José State. The collection documenting LGBTQ histories at

Stanford, originally organized by alum Gerard Koskovich, is especially rich, so I am thankful for all the archivists and librarians who have made these materials accessible. And I thank Jason Baxter at the Daniel E. Koshland San Francisco History Center at the San Francisco Public Library.

Among colleagues, scholars, and friends who supported and enhanced this project, I especially thank Rina Benmayor, Warren Blumenfeld, Nan Alamilla Boyd, Deb Busman, Deborah Cohler, Juanita Cole, Karin Cotterman, Jacqueline Dewar, Andrew Drummond, Ilene Feinman, Susan Freeman, Marcia Gallo, Francine Graff, Jon Graff, Nelson Graff, Robin Guthrie, Emily Hobson, Kristen La Follette, Amanda Littauer, Craig Loftin, Colleen O'Neill, Joseph Plaster, Tim Retzloff, Daniel Rivers, Don Romesburg, Ronni Sanlo, Gerald Shenk, Marc Stein, Ernest Stromberg, Tomás Summers Sandoval, Maria Villaseñor, and Barbara Voss. A special thank you goes to my History Writing Group at CSU Monterey Bay, whose members have read much of this work along the way and provided invaluable feedback and even more support—Chrissy Lau, Kyle Livie, Frederik Vermote, and Dustin Wright.

The research for this project was supported by grants from the Southwest Oral History Association and the Historical Society of Southern California and sabbatical leaves from California State University, Monterey Bay. At the University of Georgia Press, I thank Jared Asser, Jon Davies, Ellen Goldlust, Mick Gusinde-Duffy, Lynn Itagaki, Lea Johnson, Matthew O'Neal, and Daniel Rivers for shepherding the manuscript through the publishing process. I also thank the anonymous peer reviewers who provided invaluable feedback and helpful suggestions from the initial book proposal to the final manuscript. I am ever grateful. And I appreciate Jordan Gonzales's work on the book's index.

I offer a very special thanks to my amazing husband, Nelson Graff. He has seen me through this project from start to finish, reading and commenting on many, many, drafts; celebrating the milestones; calming the anxious moments; and always cheering me on. Through ups and downs, he has always been there, my biggest supporter. I could not have done this without you.

Here Are My People

INTRODUCTION

Beginning in the late 1960s and continuing throughout the 1970s, a new generation of LGBT students and their allies began to come together and organize publicly on college campuses across California. They formed student organizations, participated in creating new women's studies programs, sponsored educational and cultural events, advocated for policy changes, and engaged local, regional, and national gay liberation and lesbian feminist politics. George Raya, a first-generation Mexican American college student and one of the organizers of the Society for Homosexual Freedom at Sacramento State College, the first such LGBT organization on that campus, wrote to a friend in 1974 that he and his allies were "doing un-heard of things. . . . . [P]eople were coming out left and right, straights and gays were mixing and great dialogues were developed."[1]

The utopia that Raya described was in practice more complex. LGBT college students longed for connection, inclusion, and belonging. "Finding one's people," or variations on that theme, became a common refrain. Lisa Orta, who attended UC Berkeley in the early 1970s as an undergraduate, recalled "looking for my people" and teared up at her memory of first meeting a gay man in one of her courses. In 1975, one student described a gathering of the Gay People's Union at Stanford as an opportunity to be "around gay people like me." And former UCLA graduate student Don Spring recalled that his involvement in the Gay Student Union made him realize that "here are my people, people that I could relate to."[2] These testimonies suggest not only that LGBT students recognized a need to connect with others like them—to find their people—but also that the process required movement as they sought connections and in many cases joined with others in very public ways.

But how and why did this shift happen? And how did LGBT college-student organizing connect to the wider gay and lesbian movement of the late 1960s and 1970s, especially in California? As scholars have amply demonstrated, college students were crucial players in the labor, progressive, peace, and antifascist movements of the 1930s as well as in the African American civil rights and Black Power movements, the Chicano movement, women's liberation, and antiwar and other movements of the 1960s and 1970s.[3] Only recently have scholars taken up the history of LGBT student organizing. Most have focused on the history of such organizing on particular campuses, providing rich insights into how students came together and broke institutional barriers to create new queer spaces.[4] Some scholars have included LGBT student-organizing histories within wider community or regional studies, increasingly beyond the United States, offering a sense of how location and the presence (or absence) of queer communities near campuses influenced such organizing.[5] A few scholars have taken a cross-campus view, comparing LGBT student histories on different campuses in Florida, across a region like the U.S. Midwest, at particular kinds of institutions (such as Christian colleges and universities), or through an analysis of denials of recognition for LGBT student organizations.[6] In addition, history-of-education scholars have explored LGBT curricula, identity development, and faculty experiences.[7] All of these studies have greatly informed our collective—and my particular—understanding of the ways in which LGBT college students navigated their shifting identities, campus climates, and local communities.

Despite this rich body of work, the history of California's LGBT college student organizing has garnered surprisingly limited scholarly attention. Oral history and/or public history projects at the University of California, Santa Cruz; the University of California, Berkeley; and Stanford have led the way. And while these projects have generated invaluable archives of materials documenting campus-specific histories of LGBT student, staff, and faculty experiences, to date there has been no comparative analysis of LGBT student organizing across California's many geographic regions, various postsecondary institutions, and diverse student populations.[8] Here Are My People fills this gap, focusing on the years between 1967, when a small group of students and allies attempted to organize a "student homophile league" at Stanford, and 1979, when activists from across the United States (including college students and others from California) organized the first National March on Washington for Lesbian and Gay Rights, an event some described as a national coming out for the gay and lesbian movement.[9]

The timing of this student organizing is significant. *Here Are My People* frames such activism within recent scholarly reconsideration of the 1970s. As Beth Bailey and David Farber argue, that decade saw the impact of various social movements of the 1960s—including a more visible gay and lesbian movement—become even "more concrete in American communities and in Americans' daily lives," a shift evident in other parts of the world as well.[10] While care should be taken in designating the 1970s as particularly distinct, many scholars have documented the ways in which economic crisis as well as changing ideas about race, ethnicity, gender, and sexuality defined much of the decade.[11] The result has been a recognition that the 1970s was in many ways defined by significant social movement organizing.[12] By focusing on local and statewide LGBT student organizing, Here Are My People documents how such organizing was deeply connected to broader shifts.

In addition, LGBT college students organized in many communities shaped by California's rich queer histories across race, class, gender, and nationality as well as by important social, economic and political institutions with national influence.[13] In San Francisco, Nan Alamilla Boyd argues that queerness was "sewn into the city's fabric," the result of its transformation from a "frontier" space defined by Native conquest, colonial rule, and overlapping diverse cultures and communities to a "wide open town" with a "live and let live sensibility," defined by military presence and rapid economic development, especially after World War II.[14] Similarly, Los Angeles, a city also defined by histories of conquest, colonial rule, immigration, cross-cultural interaction, conflict, and rapid transformation, became home to a variety of social spaces and institutions—entertainment venues, bars, cafes, private clubs, and personal networks.[15]

Such queer place-making prompted various efforts to suppress LGBT visibility, fueled by the construction of homosexuality and challenges to gender norms as pathology.[16] Anti-cross-dressing laws in San Francisco, crackdowns on gender inversion in Los Angeles, and police raids on LGBT bars and other social spaces in the early to mid-twentieth century illustrate these efforts to suppress visibility.[17] By the 1950s, as Daniel Hurewitz argues, California's political culture came to treat "gender inversion and homosexual behavior as dangerous," demanding, in Cold War fashion, "containment."[18] In response to such oppression and alienating social conditions, members of California's queer communities created important and groundbreaking homophile organizations, including the Mattachine Society, ONE, Inc., the Daughters of Bilitis (DOB), and the Society for Individual Rights, all of which sought to educate, inform, lobby medical practitioners and politicians, and provide self-support.[19] At the same time, bar-based queer communities challenged police crackdowns at the local level through lawsuits and direct resistance, supported by organizations like the Tavern Guild in San Francisco.[20] Patrons fought back against such harassment at the Black Cat in Los Angeles and Compton's Cafeteria in San Francisco, among other venues.[21] Gay men, lesbians, and allied clergy in San Francisco formed the Council on Religion and the Homosexual in 1965 after a police raid on a drag ball prompted outrage. And youth began to organize as well: San Francisco's Vanguard became one of the first LGBT youth organizations in California.[22]

By the late 1960s and early 1970s, the rise of Black Power and the movement to end the war in Vietnam had radicalized many younger gay men and lesbians across the United States, posing a challenge to the liberal politics of inclusion that Martin Duberman argues was "broadly radical."[23] This "gay revolution," as Josh Sides suggests, gained quick momentum in California.[24] Some of this new militancy predated the June 1969 Stonewall Rebellion in New York. The Committee for Homosexual Freedom, founded in the spring of 1969 in the San Francisco Bay Area, "blended left radicalism and militancy with exuberant gay pride," as Christina Hanhardt describes, leading to protests at local businesses that had fired homosexual workers and to assertions of new rights claims.[25] Gay liberation front organizations sprung up in Los Angeles and San Francisco as well as elsewhere across the state.[26] In the San Francisco Bay Area, some activists on the left moved beyond rights claims, demanding a liberation that, as Emily Hobson argues, would produce a "fundamental transformation in the meanings of sexuality" and in solidarity with other liberation struggles—anticolonial movements, feminism, and Black Power in particular. Such sexual liberation "could only be won through a broader social revolution," as Hobson contends, a "necessary part of revolutionary change." For lesbian feminists, this change took the form of organizing for community protection through what Hobson calls "collective defense," manifested through shared housing, separatism, and alliances with the struggles of communities of color.[27]

By the mid-1970s, many activists shifted toward a reform agenda, sometimes mindful of gay liberation's more radical origins. As Hanhardt argues, some activists combined a "countercultural performativity of gay liberation with a gay focused reform agenda," shifting to "militant gay liberalism."[28] For others, especially cisgender white gay men, the "mainstreaming of sexual dissidence" in the 1970s, as Jonathan Bell argues, provided opportunities to align with mainstream political parties, revealing the "power of whiteness as an organizing force" for those organizers.[29] The shift toward a gay and lesbian liberalism, as Marc Stein suggests, included the formation of advocacy organizations and political clubs as well as lobbying for housing, access to health care, antidiscrimination legislation, policing, and other services and running for elected office.[30] This complex political climate—from liberation to liberalism—provided the vibrant context in which California's students organized on college and university campuses.

California's unique higher education system also shaped student organizing contexts. As a consequence of the Master Plan of 1960, California boasted a large, relatively accessible, high-quality, and multicampus public university structure, with junior colleges (community colleges), California state colleges (later renamed universities), and the University of California offering students various pathways and distinct options. Alongside private colleges and universities, these systems enhanced the ability of LGBT students to form webs of connection across campuses and within regions. Some LGBT student activists began their organizing at one type of campus and transferred to another before attending graduate school at a third. Such connections facilitated mutual support for individual students and campus groups, formalized as alliances of LGBT students across campuses and student organizations.[31]

California's vibrant political environment also shaped the issues LGBT students engaged as well as the campus and community contexts they navigated. Between the end of World War II and the late 1960s, the relationship of California's residents to government was transformed, translating, as Jonathan Bell argues, into increasing union power, prosperity for more Californians, and changing attitudes about the role of government and the merits of social programs. The rise of the Democratic Party in the 1960s provided fertile ground for the state to benefit from expanded federal programs. Yet a growing conservative shift against higher taxes and government regulation took root in some parts of the state, including Orange County in Southern California and the suburbs south of San Francisco.[32]

These changes occurred just as LGBT student organizations began to gain footing on campuses. By the late 1970s, as in other parts of the country, a backlash by religious conservatives had reframed feminism and gay rights as threats.[33] In California, the struggle over Proposition 6 (also known as the Briggs Initiative, after State Senator John Briggs of Orange County), illustrates that backlash. The Briggs Initiative would have prohibited teachers and other employees of public schools from "advocating, soliciting, imposing, encouraging, or promoting" homosexuality.[34] The ballot measure's defeat thanks to a widespread grassroots campaign and the subsequent assassination of San Francisco supervisor Harvey Milk in the fall of 1978 constituted a watershed in California's queer history. These events were especially important in mobilizing LGBT college students to become more aware, more involved, and more visible in the face of vocal reactions against gay rights, and these struggles played out on campuses as well.

While electoral politics and ballot initiatives were important aspects of this political landscape, other kinds of grassroots community organizing provided LGBT students with role models, experience, and analytical tools. Vibrant civil rights, labor, antiwar, identity-based, feminist, and campus-based student movements made visible the promises, challenges, and political possibilities of such organizing.[35] Some LGBT students participated directly, engaging in organizing around civil rights, free speech, the war in Southeast Asia, women's liberation, and struggles for ethnic studies before turning to LGBT issues.[36] For others, models developed by their peers provided examples of how to engage. For San José State College student Warren Blumenfeld, involvement in antiwar and civil rights became his entrée to gay liberation on campus. Raya's high school experience with the Mexican American Youth Organization laid the groundwork for his participation in the Society for Homosexual Freedom.

And for UC Berkeley student Barbara Bryant, who grew up in a left-leaning politically active household in Berkeley, the campus was a place "where protest happened."[37]

For these and other students, this organizing played out in several key ways. Creating spaces on campus was an early priority. LGBT students created what I call organizing homes—primarily student organizations—where they could find each other and form connections, create institutional structures that built bridges between the campus and the local community, and engage the gay and lesbian and feminist movements. After gaining such institutional bases, these students embraced education as a tool of liberation for themselves and for the campus community. They invited local LGBT activists and others to organizational meetings to share knowledge and experience. Student groups sponsored public programming to educate the campus community about LGBT-related issues and concerns. Seeking to challenge the heterosexism of their academic programs, LGBT students advocated for LGBT-focused courses in student-run experimental colleges and women's studies programs.

LGBT student organizers also advocated on behalf of their needs and those of other LGBT students. They provided services such as peer counseling and hotlines where little or none existed. They claimed and/or created spaces on campus—organizational offices and other places to gather and socialize as well as dances to celebrate and connect. They linked movement activists to campuses for discussions, lectures, panels, awareness weeks, and sometimes protests. They showcased LGBT creative practices, among them poetry, theater, and film. And some challenged existing norms of gender expression through the embrace of drag, genderfuck, and other transgressive forms of expression not only to express their own sense of self but also to challenge peer assumptions about gender. LGBT students worked together across campuses to form regional and statewide alliances linked through newsletters, conferences, self-help trainings, and social events, enhancing the capacities of one campus with the power of many.[38]

Politics became the glue that animated most of this organizing. Most LGBT student organizers of the late 1960s and early to mid-1970s initially saw their work as deeply connected to gay liberation and lesbian feminism. In ways similar to other LGBT activists, they frequently constructed their campus organizing as aligned with other liberation struggles.[39] By the mid-1970s, as LGBT students claimed campus space, some organizers shifted their focus to sustaining that space and building new kinds of communities.[40] Efforts aimed at organizational sustainability and community formation, however, did not preclude political engagement, with some activists framing their organizing in civil rights terms and others sustaining a vision for social transformation that moved beyond assimilation.[41] As *Here Are My People* documents, students framed most of their organizing as in service of gay liberation, lesbian feminism, gay rights, and/or human rights. On-campus organizing became a critical bridge to communities off-campus, including local, regional, and national political movements. Some LGBT student organizers threw themselves into local issues—protesting police harassment, engaging local school boards, creating speakers' bureaus to visit K–12 schools, and challenging elected officials. By the end of the decade, many LGBT student organizers in California framed campus organizing as deeply connected to a growing national gay and lesbian movement, spurred on especially by Anita Bryant's crusade against gay rights and the battle over the Briggs Initiative.[42]

All of this organizing was not without challenges. LGBT students worked alongside LGBT faculty and cultivated allies among their peers but sometimes faced reactionary resistance—pushback from administrators, trustees, some faculty, other students, and alumni—that occasionally led to struggles for formal recognition, sometimes including legal action.[43] Some LGBT students found common cause with their peers around other issues. Some lesbian students worked closely with feminists, including in women's studies programs, finding such spaces more welcoming than campus-based LGBT student groups. And LGBT students of color were not as well represented on some campuses as on others. As with many movements, LGBT student organizing was fractured by race and gender, with leadership often trending white and male despite efforts to be more inclusive.[44]

Despite these challenges, the LGBT student organizing of the 1970s paid dividends years later, preparing the way for a more diverse group of activists in the 1980s, 1990s, and beyond. Shaped by the advent of HIV and AIDS, greater sensitivity to and involvement of bisexual and transgender students, and more vocal calls to attend to the ethnic, racial, class, age, gender, and ability dimensions of queer campus life, this next generation continued the tradition started at San José State, Sacramento State, San Francisco State, Los Angeles City College, UC Berkeley, Stanford, UCLA, and other campuses.[45] Here Are My People explores how this organizing started, who was involved, the challenges organizers faced, and the impact they had—on students themselves, campus climates, and the wider gay and lesbian movement of the 1970s.

The LGBT students who organized in the late 1960s and 1970s were not the first to attend college and find each other. From the romantic friendships of the nineteenth century to women's colleges in the 1920s, students formed same-sex relationships, experimented with challenging gender norms and identities, and formed small but important communities.[46] However, the risks were many, including potential expulsion.[47] Changes in higher education after World War II and the Cold War created new opportunities as well as numerous challenges for LGBT students to find each other. As John D'Emilio argues, the shift toward state attempts to contain and control homosexuality "represented but one front in a widespread effort to reconstruct patterns of sexuality and gender relations shaken by depression and war," producing what he describes as a "congruence between anti-Communism in the sphere of politics and social concern over homosexuality."[48] College campuses became important sites where these "lavender scares" played out.[49] LGBT students and faculty were caught up in periodic purges designed to root out homosexuals alongside other Cold War targets—leftists, communists, and other "subversives."[50] Some students, including those at UCLA, UC Berkeley, and Stanford, were funneled into college health systems to be "treated" for their "sickness" rather than condemned for moral infractions or outright expelled.[51] Others, especially male students, were harassed by law enforcement on and off campus, sometimes getting caught up in the legal system.[52] Moreover, for many students as well as faculty, fear, loneliness, and alienation defined the campus experience.[53] Others formed close attachments with roommates, hallmates, fraternity brothers, or sorority sisters. Through such networks, gay and lesbian students formed a semblance of community in semiprivate ways, creating what Craig Loftin calls distinct "gay social worlds" including "campus literary clubs, culture clubs, drama clubs or secret societies."[54] Students at times gathered off campus at private house parties, bars, or popular cruising places. Graduate students may have had more opportunities to find gay or lesbian campus networks, even if they were underground.[55]

Homophile organizations provided new opportunities to gather, form communities outside of bars and clubs, and advocate for civil rights claims but also had policies prohibiting membership to anyone under the age of twenty-one and were not always welcoming to students.[56] Some older students became members, volunteers, guest speakers, or attendees at events, however, and some organizations did try to support students. In 1962, for example, the Daughters of Bilitis created a scholarship to honor Blanche Montgomery Baker, a San Francisco psychiatrist and homophile supporter.[57] As Marcia Gallo notes, this and other scholarships were intended to "promote the organization in academic and scholastic circles as well as provide a way for DOB to make concrete contributions to the education of individual women."[58]

By the late 1960s, young queer people began to assert themselves publicly and claim their own spaces. Charles Thorp, a student at San Francisco State College and an organizer with the Committee for Homosexual Freedom, chastised organizations like the Society for Individual Rights in 1969 for "copping out" on teens by refusing to accept members under twenty-one, drawing inspiration from the African American civil rights movement: "The Negroes are saying 'I'm black and I'm proud,' and 'Black is beautiful.' Well what are our people saying? Inside, I know I'm saying 'I'm homosexual and I'm proud.'"[59] Some homophile activists took notice. "What teen aged homosexuals (male and female) are looking for is a means of socializing," noted Del Martin, a founder of the DOB, in 1968. "They want to meet their peers. They want to hold dances and other social functions.... They have looked to the homophile organizations for help, but to no avail." Youth, Martin argued, "should be part of the homophile community where they can attain a sense of belonging and where they can be guided into constructive and creative channels."[60] College students, like other LGBT youth activists, took up this call on their own.[61]

Who were these students? Despite California's racial and ethnic diversity, most of the state's LGBT student organizers appear to have been white, as was the case for such student organizations across the United States during this era. Where possible, I highlight the voices of students of color to shine a light on how their experiences compared to those of their mostly white peers. And while the enrollment of women at California's colleges and universities increased in the 1970s, many LGBT campus student organizations were predominantly male.[62] However, such general assessments require important qualifications. Some lesbian and bisexual women felt unwelcome in an environment created by gay male students and preferred to organize separately, either by themselves or in collaboration with feminists on campus. Some lesbians found women's studies programs a more conducive space in which to organize as lesbians.

In this volume, I generally defer to the terms historical actors used to describe themselves—primarily gay, lesbian, and occasionally bisexual—mindful that to the students of the late 1960s and 1970s, such terms were more expansive than they are today.[63] However, I have also chosen to use the umbrella terms queer and LGBT. The term queer has a distinct and political history and is now commonly used in academic and activist circles: in Don Romesburg's words, it does a good job at "capturing all this unruly field has to offer."[64] And while LGBT raises challenges for historians of this period, as Stein points out, it also signals a more inclusive and fluid representation of gender identity that some college students at the time attempted to model.[65] Moreover, even though the groups and activists covered here are arguably not transgender in the ways we might use the term today, including T in the umbrella term LGBT captures the spirit of what some student organizers attempted to represent in themselves and the gender identity issues they engaged.[66] My goal is to contextualize how students described themselves in terms of sexual orientation and gender identity, using umbrella terms as needed.

Researching the histories of LGBT student organizing has required a multifaceted approach. At the beginning of this project, I cast a wide net, looking for anything I could locate about the subject, digging into university archives and student newspapers. What I discovered was an inconsistent archival record that challenged the kind of comprehensive cross-campus comparisons I originally envisioned. While some university archives contain a wealth of source material, others barely scratch the surface of LGBT student histories.

Most helpful were campus newspapers and records of student government, academic departments, and university administrators, though some campus collections are more comprehensive than others.

Archives with roots in queer communities were essential to my research. Collections at the GLBT Historical Society in San Francisco, the ONE Archives at USC in Los Angeles, and the Lavender Library and Archives in Sacramento were especially critical, providing the bulk of archival sources related to some campuses. Records of LGBT students and their organizing are scattered throughout these archives—in ephemera collections, subject files, personal papers, organizational records, periodicals, and oral histories. Most if not all of these materials are absent from official college and university collections. As has been the case for many scholars of queer history, oral histories were exceptionally important to my work, expanding and enhancing the limitations of the archives in rich and powerful ways.[67] I began with a core group of five interviewees, an effort that snowballed to include dozens of others, most of whom were affiliated with the same or similar campus groups. I identified some interviewees through archival research, tracking down folks to see if they wanted to speak with me. Most graciously agreed. I also drew on many oral histories collected by other scholars and institutions. These firsthand accounts often constituted the main record of LGBT student organizing on a campus, highlighting the limitations of archives as a source for understanding the queer past.

After considering the availability of source material, I chose to focus primarily on five campuses—Sacramento State, the University of California at Berkeley, San José State, Stanford, and the University of California at Los Angeles. The sources available in university and LGBT-specific archives as well as campus newspapers provided an especially rich record of LGBT student lives on these campuses. Furthermore, these campuses presented opportunities to conduct original oral histories or draw on those completed by other researchers. Finally, through the list favors Northern California, these schools represent different types of institutions. I have supplemented my examinations of these campuses histories with those of other institutions—especially San Francisco State, the University of Southern California, Cal State Long Beach, and Los Angeles City College—where available archival records and/or oral histories significantly enhanced a topic. Community colleges are not as well represented here even though they are much more numerous than other sorts of campuses. Community college newspapers were especially enlightening—and sometimes the only archival record available. Despite such limitations, *Here Are My People* offers a nuanced understanding of LGBT student organizing in California during the crucial formative period of the late 1960s and 1970s.

The chapters are organized thematically, a contrast with how most other scholars have approached these histories.[68] This structure allows me to synthesize and draw connections across campuses, exploring patterns of organizing as well as distinctions of location, type of institution, social identities of student organizers, and varied impacts on campus and local communities. I also highlight the voices of student organizers themselves, allowing them to frame their own experiences and to do so in their own words.

In the fall of 1999, during my first full year of teaching at CSU Monterey Bay, I became an adviser to the campus LGBTQ student organization, All in the Family, which had been founded three years earlier.[69] In the spring of 2000, All in the Family was named Club of the Year, in part for its work in the unsuccessful effort to defeat Proposition 22, an anti-gay-marriage initiative.[70] That campaign had increased student involvement in the club and raised its profile on campus. The following fall, I was chatting with one of the group's organizers, who was lamenting the slim attendance at recent meetings and events but who nevertheless took a long view of the situation: it was just the "ebb and flow" of student organizing at CSU Monterey Bay. Sometimes an organization was swamped with active members, and sometimes it wasn't. The organizer concluded that student groups had a life cycle: students entered, participated, sometimes pulled back, and then graduated.

After researching the history of LGBT student organizing in California, I see things a little differently now. In the 1970s, students moved in and out of such organizations for many reasons. A group was too political or not political enough. Lesbians could take leadership in some, while gay men dominated the scene in others. Some organizations drew hundreds of students to events and received support from student government, while others had to fight tooth and nail to just exist. Many students found joy and exhilaration in this work, but it could also be as difficult as it was life-changing. Perhaps the students in All in the Family had similar experiences: at the time, I was too new to being the club adviser to understand fully.

Moreover, while a remarkably large number of LGBT students took California's campuses by storm in the 1970s, becoming the first highly visible generation, that visibility sometimes came with a cost. Administrators resisted the activists' presence. Peers criticized them in student newspapers. And alumni wrote angry letters to campus presidents. Fast-forward to 2000. The members of All in the Family had seen the passage of Prop 22, the harsh treatment of LGBTQ folks in the media, and the challenges of being out on campus. Without knowing anything about LGBT student organizing histories, how were they—or I—to know that they were part of a longer history of similar struggles and could learn much from past organizing efforts?[71]

Understanding the ebb and flow of LGBT student organizing requires great sensitivity to historical context—the very different kinds of campus communities in which students (came) come together and (claimed) claim space, whether organization members created (create) inclusive environments, the importance of student leadership, and the synergy of time and place. Students are and have been a key critical audience for this project, reflecting my dedication to the idea that if today's LGBTQ+ students know these histories, they will understand more fully the challenges, persistence, and joy that their queer student ancestors found in, brought to, and gained from this work. This book provides today's LGBTQ+ student organizers and their allies with some perspective on the historical context of their work—insight into why some queer students participate(d) while others do (did) not, into why some campuses are (were) more welcoming than others, and into the connections between campus organizing and wider social movements. Such insights will give today's activists a better picture of whose shoulders they stand on. Given the current climate in which many LGBTQ+ youth, including college students, live, an understanding of how a prior generation of organizers "found their people" could not be more important.

CHAPTER ONE

Creating Campus Organizing Homes

Shortly after students formed the Student Homophile League at Columbia University, the first such organization in the nation, there were reports that a similar one was in the works at Stanford.[1] In 1967, donor Lee Narver contacted the university in protest, prompting one administrator to note in an internal memo that Narver was "livid about it," though "no one knows anything about a chapter of these queers being formed at Stanford."[2] The following January, a student using the pseudonym Wendell Anderson arranged to have the Reverend Richard Roe of United Campus Ministries serve as sponsor for the new Student Homophile League. Formed by a few students and faculty, the group had two meetings in the spring of 1968 and one public event focusing on "Homosexuality and Ethical Choices."[3]

In response, the president's office received a letter from Mrs. William A. Mudgett enclosing a news clipping about the event and asking whether the university should keep Rev. Roe on the staff. "It is difficult for us working on class funds for money to meet up with this kind of thing," wrote Mudgett, suggesting that Stanford should "make entering requirements to keep out deviates!! Let's not be the second group in the nation."[4] Andrew Doty, associate director of university relations, replied that the group had few interested members and was not a "social organization for introductions of any kind."[5] By spring, Mudgett's concerns were moot: the organization had fizzled.[6]

A year later, Bear Capron, a freshman who had arrived at Stanford in the fall of 1968, placed an advertisement in an alternative newspaper, the *Berkeley Barb*, seeking gay friends.[7] While Capron received a number of responses, the one from Anderson, a Stanford senior, stood out. He asked Capron to "carry the torch," and Capron "flat out said yes." After collecting a "pile of stuff" from the earlier effort, Capron booked a room in Tresidder Memorial Union for a meeting of the Stanford Homophile League, arrived early, placed a sign on the door, sat down at a table, and waited. No one stopped by. Not until the

13

fall of 1970 did an LGBT student organization finally take root on the Stanford campus.⁸

The process through which LGBT students created what I call organizing homes on California's college and university campuses in the late 1960s and 1970s was at times fractured. Primarily through student organizations and within women's studies and other academic programs, organizers engaged in queer place-making that was both conceptual (representing a perceived shared affiliation to work collectively in support of LGBT people and issues) and actual (gathering spaces on campus). Such organizing homes became important bases where students could form connections with each other and with local communities, create queer campus space, foster creative expression, and engage politically.⁹ Organizing homes offered many students a refuge but were also complex, shaped in particular by the specificities of race, class, gender, and gender identity. And LGBT students faced numerous challenges to their very public presence. While the students' goals varied—educating the campus community, supporting self-understanding, working for social change, and providing peer support, among others—all of these activist students sought to stake a claim for a visible and viable campus home. As Glenn Erickson of UCLA's Gay Student Union (GSU) suggested, one of their goals was to "simply be. To exist as a reminder to the campus as a whole that we are here, we will not be invisible."¹⁰

Origin Stories

Students began organizing efforts for a variety of reasons and chose a variety of approaches. Sometimes, informal networks and off-campus connections were of prime importance, particularly in the earliest days, when no queer presence was generally visible. Lee Mentley formed friendships with two other gay students at the Los Angeles Gay Community Services Center, and after they discovered that they all attended Cal State, Long Beach, they moved to organize on campus.¹¹ Some gay men met at local bars, through shared housing, or in campus tearooms (informal spaces where gay men met, sometimes for sexual encounters).¹²

For others, involvement in off-campus political communities, especially those related to gay liberation and women's liberation, shaped the move to campus organizing. Journalist Leo Laurence recalled that student involvement in both the Committee for Homosexual Freedom and the Gay Liberation Front (GLF) in San Francisco provided early inspiration for organizing at San Francisco State.¹³ And the earliest organizers of the Los Angeles GLF included at least two UCLA students, Randy Schrader and Greg Byrd (one of the few African Americans in the GLF), both of whom were instrumental in forming the first GLF at UCLA.¹⁴ In some cases, among them Los Angeles City College, community-based gay liberation activists came to campus. In May 1970, the Los Angeles GLF organized a gay liberation conference and protest against campus police entrapment of gay men in bathrooms.[15] By the spring of 1973, Jesse Crawford, a self-described gay activist and candidate for the "councilman of minority affairs" on Associated Students, the campus's student government, called for the formation of a gay student union to fight "unjust oppression against homosexuals," to help gays and lesbians "band together so that they don't have 'to wear masks,'" and to increase public visibility.[16] By November 1973, Los Angeles City College's GSU was planning educational events and socials, and it survived for the rest of the decade, albeit with a few name changes.[17]

Campus and community fluidity was especially important for many lesbian students. In Sacramento, lesbian faculty and college students involved in the women's movement helped create of the campus Women's Caucus, which became an early organizing home.[18] Freda Smith attended Sacramento State in the mid- to late 1950s and eventually became involved in the city's women's movement. Returning to campus in 1971, Smith connected with other lesbians in the Women's Caucus, which she described in 1974 as a "place to meet other women with the same concerns that you have. A place to talk, to share, and to listen."[19]

Some students announced the intention to form an organization via advertisements in campus newspapers. At Cal State Los Angeles, a large, diverse, urban, and mostly commuter school, a small ad in the campus newspaper announced the formation of the GSU, urging, "Gay sisters and brothers come home!"[20] LGBT students on other campuses used similar tactics.[21] New groups were also announced via flyers posted on campus: at San Francisco State College, organizers posted flyers promoting a meeting of the "Liberation Front for Gay Students to form a counter-culture and change the straight-orientation of this college"; the GLF "is survival for all gays."[22] The presence of such advertisements and flyers drew students in, announcing the presence of LGBT students and offering opportunities for them to gather.[23]

On other campuses, LGBT students wrote letters to the editor or authored opinion pieces in campus newspapers seeking interested others. After publishing an October 1970 letter from someone identified only as a "gay woman" reflecting on her discovery of both gay liberation and women's liberation, the *Stanford Daily* received a response from "Steve," who praised the student newspaper for being "liberated enough to print materials on Stanford gays" and called on "the gay community at Stanford" to "get itself together."[24] As a result, the pair organized an initial conversation, billed as a "Stanford Gay Lib or GSU rap," in November, and by January 1971, the university's new GSU had about one hundred members.[25] At UC Santa Barbara, the campus newspaper published a series of columns, "Out of the Closets," authored by members of the newly organized GLF. One column described the challenges of finding a faculty adviser, securing space for a dance, and gaining official recognition.[26] The school's newspaper later published a letter to the editor in which Cynthia Palmer, Joan Weir, and Jill Wilkowski expressed concern "about the apparent lack of community among lesbian women" and invited interested individuals to a potluck.[27]

Organizing homes sometimes drew members of local LGBT communities. The constitution of Stanford's Gay People's Union (GPU) declared that the group was open to students, staff, and community members.[28] Such openness sometimes prompted administrative scrutiny. One 1973 GPU meeting, addressed concerns that the organization was too community-oriented and consequently "might be getting in trouble with the university because of our low # of Stanford people." The group sought ways to reach more students, "even if they are too frightened or disinterested to come in now," and soon thereafter hosted a session for Stanford students on how to develop more campus activities.[29] Similarly, the campus newspaper at San José State described its GSU as one of "the only student organizations in the area meeting the needs of gay college students, both male and female"; it and the Lesbian Feminist Alliance also drew students from "surrounding schools."[30]

On some campuses, students faced many obstacles to creating organizing homes. At Bakersfield College in the early 1970s, a group began to discuss how to create a space for homosexual students on campus. In 1972, a student using the pseudonym Susan suggested that coming together "like other minorities" would provide a path to acceptance, a recognition "for what they are and what they can be together." Despite noting that the "homosexual ... has always been abnormal with respect to society," the editors of the college's student-run newspaper supported the effort, asking, "Where else can they achieve security and peace of mind other than in the company of their own like?" By that fall, however, attempts to form a gay student union sparked the ire of campus president John J. Collins, who blocked the effort despite strong backing from the student government. The combination of administrative pushback and mixed reactions from their peers, despite support from student government, effectively prevented such an organization from forming for the remainder of the decade.[31]

At West Los Angeles College, however, the presence of institutional allies led to a different outcome. Organizer Preston Reese approached Nina Terebinski, a favorite cultural anthropology professor, to serve as adviser for that campus's GSU when it was founded in 1977, and she became a "trusted ally."[32] Women's centers—both on campus and in local communities—also became important sources of support, providing spaces for students, particularly lesbians, to meet and host programs.[33] San José State's Women's Center, which opened in the fall of 1972, provided space for a group calling itself Radical Lesbians (which included students and community members) to meet weekly and publicized those meetings on the center's calendar.[34] Similarly, the Women's Center at UC Santa Barbara hosted the "Gay Women's Group" and became a venue for other lesbian-themed programming.[35] The Sacramento Women's Center, whose organizers and volunteers included numerous lesbian students, hosted lesbian raps and mothers' groups and shared news of local events.[36] The center also included a bookstore with titles focused on lesbianism and women's herstory, among other topics.[37]

While women's centers became key allies, lesbian student involvement sometimes prompted pushback from student government and/or other women involved in such centers. At San Francisco State, a 1978 struggle over leadership of the campus women's center, which had opened in 1973, erupted over accusations that the center's supervisor and Associated Students president had criticized the "lesbian concentration" among the center's volunteers.[38] Lesbian students responded with accusations of homophobia and raised concerns about the center's importance as a lesbian-friendly space. As one volunteer suggested, lesbians were especially active in the center "because they have more at stake than the straight women do."[39] Sometimes, concerns about lesbian involvement in women's centers led critics to embrace overblown rhetoric: Theresa Corrigan, who taught women's studies classes at Sacramento State, told the *Sacramento Bee* in 1977 that concerns about lesbian involvement "really hurt the center. People were seeing us as a group of radical raving feminists and lesbians—using that scare word, so that people would freak out and assume we were doing weird things"; in reality, however, "we are of different ages, races, classes, and sexual preferences."[40] Regardless of such conflicts, women's centers provided early support for LGBT students, especially lesbians, on many campuses.

Gender, Race, and Ethnicity

The forms that these organizing homes took reflected organizers' many intersectional identities and experiences, especially race, ethnicity, and gender identity. On some campuses, lesbians and gay men worked together in one unified organization. On others, they worked in one group but formed separate caucuses. And elsewhere, gay men and lesbians organized separately, intersecting only occasionally. While many campus-based student students organizations were started by and sometimes predominantly served white gay men, others were more diverse. Campus conditions, location, and size as well as the overall diversity of the student population all played roles.

Most organizations generally had less participation from bisexual men, lesbians, bisexual women, and students of color than from white gay men. David Strachan, a bisexual student at San José State in the late 1970s, recalled that the school's GSU primarily comprised gay-identified men who had little interest in bisexuals or lesbians.[41] Such divisions were not unusual nationally. Warren Blumenfeld of the National Gay Student Center noted in 1972 that many lesbian and bisexual women chose to create separate spaces, unwilling to "tolerate the chauvinistic and racist attitudes of the white Gay males in the groups."[42] Some lesbian students of color also navigated potential conflicts between their home communities and their campus organizing. CSU Long Beach GSU president Marguerite Silicero, who identified as Mexican American, did not use her last name in one campus newspaper interview because "she has a family to protect." According to Silicero, getting women to join the GSU was challenging because "stating you're a lesbian is a very political act."[43] The need to navigate these nuances of experience and context led students to choose different organizing models.

Creating separate caucuses for lesbians and gay men was more common on larger and/or more elite campuses, especially if those campuses also drew participants from local communities. At Stanford for much of the 1970s, the GPU included both a Men's Collective and a Women's Collective (also known as the Lesbian Collective), recognizing that "the needs of gay men and women do not always coincide," according to organization's constitution.[44] The Gay Student (later People's) Union at UC Santa Barbara developed a similar structure, with a Gay Women's Collective that met separately and planned its own events.[45]

On some campuses, gay men and lesbians worked more closely together. West Los Angeles College's GSU was nearly 70 percent women, among them a significant number of African Americans.[46] When campuses had separate gay and lesbian caucuses, collaboration could occur. At Cal State Long Beach, GSU leader Giovanni DiLuzio told the student newspaper in 1975 that the group was "more effective" because it had its gay men's and women's caucuses "working together," though such collaboration was often not present on some other campuses.[47]

Such collaboration could also be challenging. When Sacramento State students and faculty formed the Society for Homosexual Freedom, it primarily comprised gay men, and Matrisha Person (known at the time as Patricia One Person) found that meeting attendees "were not receptive to lesbians": "I don't think they understood at that time what feminism was about and what we were talking about, so we just retreated. We went back to women's liberation."[48] In 1972, gay men and lesbians sought to "break down the barriers" through a "fish bowl" conversation between Professor Martin Rogers and student Freda Smith. Nevertheless, the separation between gay men and lesbians on campus lasted well into the decade.[49]

Some gay men in San Francisco State's first LGBT student organization, the GLF, were "condescending and chauvinistic" toward their lesbian peers, according to a 1970 campus newspaper story about the organization.[50] Paula Hamilton was one of the few lesbians involved in a successor organization, the Gay Academic Union, which was run primarily by students with faculty support. In 1975, Hamilton appealed to other lesbians on campus to join the union, adding, "If there is anything I, personally, can do to assist better communications among lesbians, the GAU, the Women's Center, other campus organizations or private individuals, please contact me."[51] By the latter part of the 1970s, such collaborations became more common. At Cal State Los Angeles, a Gay Student Union was reorganized in 1975 after a brief hiatus, and the group's twenty-five members consciously sought to include both men and women, an approach the *Los Angeles Times* described as "unusual in campus organizations." As the group's president, Julie Heckman, noted, one goal was to "improve relations between female gays and male gays ... to work together as men and women."[52]

On other campuses, lesbian students organized separately. San José State's original GLF (organized in 1969 but unrecognized by the university) had included both men and women, but the successor GSU, formed in 1974, served primarily as an organizing home for gay men.[53] At around the same time, lesbians at the school organized the Lesbian Feminist Alliance, which bridged campus and community.[54] One former GLF member recalled that the separation had been necessary because women in the earlier group were "relegated to menial work—looked over." In addition, the opening of the San José State Women's Center, which many lesbian and bisexual women helped organize, the group gained a meeting space.[55] By the late 1970s, however, gay men and lesbians at San José State were again working together, perhaps as a consequence of the increasing national hostility to gay-rights gains as epitomized by the Briggs Initiative. By 1979, the GSU adopted the caucus model, with the Lesbian Caucus meeting at the Women's Center.[56]

In the fall of 1972, lesbians at UCLA created the Gay Sisterhood, which sponsored two events hosted by the feminist-oriented Women's Resource Center: a "gay-straight" dialogue that drew about 150 people, and a coffeehouse. When the *Daily Bruin* published an early 1973 article about the new "lesbian organization," some students welcomed the prospect of a place to meet "other gay women at UCLA" but at least one interested person feared "having to be a militant lesbian."[57] The group, which soon changed its name to the Lesbian Sisterhood, sought "to have a place to get together, be comfortable, and have fun" as well to reach out to other women on campus.[58] While some lesbians had attended GSU meetings, they were more likely "gay-identified," according to cofounder Jan Aura, rather than feminists. Rather than stay in the GSU and struggle, many lesbians just decided to "do their own thing." Further, as Aura explained, lesbians found "vitality" in the feminist movement. For Aura, women-only organizing was "not about rejecting men for me but was about the need to organize, to separate, build a positive identity, affirm self, and then re-engage." After the Lesbian Sisterhood organized, the GSU became "almost totally male."[59]

Most campus-based organizations were dominated by white cisgender men, with only a small minority of students of color. According to Wiggsy Sivertsen, who served as a member of the counseling faculty at San José State, Latinx students chose not to become involved in LGBT student organizing because coming out was "very frightening for them" as they feared a "potential loss of family." Some students nevertheless became activists. Larry Duplechan was the only Black student involved in UCLA's GSU in the mid-1970s: though he did know of other Black gay men on campus, they had no interest in joining the group. Though he never recalled experiencing outright racism, Duplechan "was a lot of people's first Black person," and according to a 1975 *Daily Bruin* article, "both sexism and racism existed in" the GSU.[60]

Some students of color occupied leadership positions in campus-based LGBT organizations. In addition to CSU Long Beach's Silicero, Zelima Williams, of Nicaraguan heritage, was a founder of the San José State GLF. And George Raya, who had been active in the Mexican American Youth Association while in high school, helped to organize the Society for Homosexual Freedom at Sacramento State.[61] At schools with more diverse student bodies, LGBT students of color were more likely to participate. By the 1970s, Los Angeles City College served nearly nineteen thousand commuter students and was very racially and ethnically diverse.[62] A spring 1979 photo of the school's GSU suggests the involvement of a significant number of Latinx students, among them Vice President Tony Lopez, who was slated to speak at a press conference regarding Gay Pride Week.[63] A photo of the contingent from Los Angeles City College at the summer 1979 Christopher Street West Parade shows a number of students who appear to be African American. And one Black "non-gay" member, theater major Freda Marshall, ran for Homecoming Queen and listed her affiliation with the GSU in her candidate profile.[64]

New Queer Spaces

Organizing homes established, LGBT students began to use these new platforms to create new kinds of queer spaces.[65] In particular, organizational meetings—held in classrooms, women's centers, and other campus buildings—offered a mix of business, peer support, and socializing; in the days before social media, these meetings constituted a lifeline for many LGBT students.[66] On some campuses, dozens or more students would show up. Early meetings of Students for Gay Power (SGP) at UC Berkeley drew upward of one hundred attendees, similar to the numbers at the GPU at Stanford and the GSU at UCLA.⁶⁷ For many LGBT students, a meeting constituted their "first experience meeting other gay people and seeing what they're like," as one UCLA GSU member noted in 1977, as well as "a place where they could seek out others of their own kind without fear of rejection, harassment or ridicule."⁶⁸ The GSU at Cal State Long Beach became a significant hub for peer-to-peer support: "If we go into this thing with positive feelings," Steve Berman, acting chair, told the campus newspaper in 1972, "then everything will turn out positive. Just sitting around rapping is going to be a super experience." At Long Beach, it was "often hard for gay students to talk to heterosexual students on campus," and a "lack of meaningful conversation makes many gay students feel alone." An account of one GSU meeting in the fall 1973 described it as "disorganized, unstructured and activities are left unscheduled. No one cares, though. Just being together for an ho[u]r is almost all that is necessary."⁶⁹

Attending such meetings could be transformative. Barbara Bryant, an undergraduate at UC Berkeley in the late 1960s, remembered that her "heart would beat a little faster about connecting with this in a public way" when attending GSU meetings.⁷⁰ Paul Wysocki recalled that an early meeting of the San José State GLF "was packed. There were five speakers, all members of the Gay Liberation Front, to talk about being gay. 'Wow!' I remember thinking. 'These are normal, everyday people.'"⁷¹ Scott Beardsley was awestruck at his first GPU meeting at Stanford and experienced a feeling of freedom, of no longer being alone. Beardsley later became involved in the UCLA GSU.⁷² One community college student found a 1975 GPU meeting equally transformative: he "ended up talking about myself to a really honest gay person for the first time in my life. I was around gay people like me, and it felt great. That day, I finally accepted myself as a homosexual and I felt higher than I had ever felt before. It is wonderful to be gay. I am normal. I am okay. I am finally happy! I thank Stanford GPU for this self-awareness."⁷³

Some students had less positive experiences, however. Lisa Orta saw a poster advertising a "gay" meeting on the UC Berkeley campus in 1973 but arrived to discover formally dressed men discussing literature in paneled room with heavy furniture. "They all got quiet" when she entered; she sat in the back of the room, feeling unwelcome, and never returned.⁷⁴ When Jack Fertig told his roommate at UC Berkeley that he was going to a GSU meeting, "I never saw him again. I got back to the room that night, and he was out." By the next day, the man's belongings were gone, and his place was assigned to Dave Cash, an openly gay man later served as president of the GSU and ran for office in Associated Students.⁷⁵ Don Spring's first GSU meeting at UCLA was underwhelming: "Silence pervaded the room with everyone turning around to see who just entered. . . . I felt miserable at that first meeting, leaving after a few hours . . . knowing no one and caring little for this cold group of people."

Spring tried again, however, and eventually became a very active member of the organization.[76]

Some LGBT student organizations—especially those that had been denied or were struggling to gain official recognition—preferred or needed to gather off-campus.[77] The first meeting that Warren Blumenfeld attended of the San José State GLF was held "in a little greasy spoon on a dingy side street," with fifteen men and women present.[78] Though tenuous, that coffeehouse was "a truly meaningful thing," declared the GLF newsletter, "a bridge between us and the rest of the community. A place where we can truly be ourselves, walk in with dignity and self-respect, share our talents, and enjoy our worth. A place where we can enjoy being our complete selves."[79] In May 1971, while the GLF was seeking recognition as an official student organization, members met at a bar near campus.[80]

Office spaces were equally important for sustaining LGBT student organizing homes, serving as sites for event planning, peer counseling, newsletter production, telephone conversations, and socializing. In the fall of 1972, the GSU at UC Berkeley designated a "Gay Lounge" from eight o'clock in the morning to seven in the evening.[81] At Stanford, the GPU office in the Old Firehouse hosted meetings and many other events. As Arthur Corbin recalled, the organization visibly claimed the space by hanging a large GPU banner on the front of the building.[82] According to Gary Steele, with the establishment of the GSU office, "gay people at UCLA at last had a place where they would meet and work together and get away from the 'only on Thursdays' syndrome"—a reference to the organization's regular meeting day.[83] Students unwilling to stop by the GSU's table on Bruin Walk could just drop in to the more discreet office.[84] When the office furniture was rearranged in April 1975, the GSU newsletter reassured readers that "the same friendly faces will still be there to comfort the weary student."[85] GSU member Larry Duplechan fondly recalled that the office "kind of became where I hung out between classes," the "social and political hub for at least my first year of college." In addition, the office's phone, typewriter, and mimeograph machines were essential to the production of its newsletter.[86] UCLA GSU member Joy Toy described the group's office as "the beginning of a home": he was there "so much they made me the office manager."[87]

At Stanford, a GPU logbook noted the many reasons visitors stopped by the office. One Stanford student was "lonely and wanting to meet gays" but was not "sure about his gayness." Another "guy came by to talk. He's bisexual and wants to get into spending time with gay people and get more into his own gayness." Similarly, another student sought "to know other gay people for the first time," leaving "after a lovely talk": "This was the first time he had ever talked to another gay person and he plans to come to our meetings." Other visitors did not speak to staffers, instead just hanging out, studying or doing homework, or browsing flyers and other materials. Some sought information for research projects or were from other LGBT student organizations visiting the campus. Some students came by looking to meet other gays and lesbians or to see their friends who were staffing the office. For some lesbian students, finding other lesbians staffing the office was especially important for feeling connected. On April 11, 1973, several people stayed after the GPU meeting to read, talk, browse literature, and do horoscopes.[88]

Access to space sometimes caused challenges. San Francisco State's LGBT student organization had some "rough goes" when it sought office space in the new student union, as John Blackburn recalled. "We had a lot of educating to do ... to make them understand how important it was for there to be an office for the gay students, like the Black students, like the Asian students": "Every group had to have their place on campus."[89] Recognition as an official group was required to secure such space. The Lesbian Sisterhood at UCLA did not seek affiliation with the Student Legislative Council, the vehicle for official status, and consequently faced consistent challenges in securing space. The group partnered with the Women's Resource Center, but when the center lost its space in Powell Library in 1975, the Lesbian Sisterhood did so as well.[90]

LGBT organizations created other venues for gathering, including potlucks, parties, social hours, coffeehouses, dances, game nights, and picnics. Some took place at private homes, some on campus, and others at public venues with members of the local community joining in.[91] Social events at times accompanied organizational meetings. A UCLA GSU general meeting was held at the Sunset Canyon Recreation Center in conjunction with a party that featured a potluck, dancing, and socializing.[92] Such social events supported group cohesion, allowing students to make new friends, find sexual partners, and form connections. At a February 1970 SGP meeting at UC Berkeley, attendees agreed that "the esprit de corps engendered by a party ... is worth more than seven group discussions."[93]

Dances were especially popular, drawing attendees from beyond the campus community.[94] The flyer for a February 1973 celebration of the San José State Women's Center, where lesbian students gathered for meetings, noted, "Sisters, this is women only, so come with a lot of energy: women's dances are the wildest time around!"[95] Some dances had themes: a medieval/renaissance Dance at UC Berkeley, a Gay '70s Dance hosted jointly by gay student groups at CSU Northridge and UCLA, Halloween dances at UCLA and CSU Long Beach, a Valentine's Day dance at UC Santa Barbara, and an Oscar Wilde dance at San José State.[96] At CSU Long Beach, the GSU organized a "Roll Me Over in the Clover Rock" event, a "Celestial Hop," and dances on the Queen Mary.[97]

Dances also became opportunities to engage politically. The San José State

GLF planned a June 1971 dance that coincided with the wedding of President Richard Nixon's daughter, Tricia, dubbing it the "White House Reception West" and planning to invite Nixon, California governor Ronald Reagan, and Glenn Dumke, chancellor of the California State University System, none of whom were friends of LGBT students.[98] At UC Berkeley, administrators withheld approval for a spring 1970 GSU dance until the group agreed to advertise it as a "people's dance" and not just "for gays."[99] When Reagan told a local television station that he had not yet received an invitation, the GSU sent the governor and his wife, Nancy, a letter assuring them that "the members in no way meant to slight you" and extending a "personal invitation for you both to attend, with sincere apologies and a promise that it won't happen again."[100] The dance was a success, drawing attendees of many sexual orientations and even making money, which the GSU donated to local organizations such as the Gay Switchboard and the People's Alternative Coffee House.[101] "Not only have we demonstrated the effectiveness of our publicity efforts," the GSU newsletter proclaimed, "but we have also shown the university that there is an enormous, occasionally cohesive, gay community eager to show its face."[102] By the end of the 1970s, LGBT students used dances to drum up awareness of antigay activists such as Anita Bryant and opposition to the Briggs Initiative. More than just social gatherings, dances created spaces for community and political organizing.[103]

Creating an Infrastructure

Organizing homes also enabled LGBT students to begin creating peer support systems and structures, which had previously been virtually nonexistent. The Lesbian Feminist Alliance at San José State offered weekly raps, social events, concerts, dances, and support services "for women of all ages, races, backgrounds, and beliefs," including a telephone referral line and a lesbian mothers' group.[104] Some of these efforts crossed campuses. The GPU at Stanford organized a "Benefit Gay Show" with drag performer Charles Pierce for a member who had sustained injuries in a bar fight. The event, held at nearby Foothill Community College, raised nearly seven hundred dollars.[105]

LGBT student organizations also supported each other through raps, discussions which offered opportunities to address conflicts within groups and provided discussion space for a range of topics, including politics, religion, sexuality, and "gay-straight dialogues." In 1974, after the founding of the Lesbian Sisterhood at UCLA, the organization hosted a "lesbian rap group" at the Women's Resource Center. Topics included "coming out, monogamy, peer pressure, our politics."[106] Raps for lesbians at the Sacramento State Women's Center addressed political differences, which some attendees found alienating while others found refreshing. "Sacramento Lesbians are trying to create a sense of community as well as offer an opportunity to exchange ideas," noted one participant. "This can only be accomplished if we deal with divergent viewpoints among ourselves."[107] Some students preferred raps to organizational meetings. In 1976, when the UCLA GSU hosted a series of "Closet Crackers"—informal off-campus events designed to "help UCLAers who think they may be gay or bisexual to meet in small groups"—Alan Turri attended, hoping "that at last I would meet somebody, ANYBODY, who would alleviate that sense of isolation which had beleaguered me for so long." He found the event "a pleasant alternative to meeting gay people vis-à-vis the cold turkey method in bars, baths, or (unfortunately) GSU meetings."[108]

Because campus counselors could not be counted on to provide support for LGBT students, many of these groups—among them the GSU and the Lesbian Sisterhood at UCLA, the GPU at Stanford, and the GSU and Lesbian Union at UC Berkeley—offered peer counseling.[109] UCLA's GSU had a "counseling program coordinator" whose responsibilities included maintaining a list of counselors, publicizing the availability of counseling, and providing referrals, training, and facilities. GSU members valued these peer counseling services.[110]

Hotlines or switchboards served students on individual campuses and reached into local communities, as was the case for the "Gay Switchboard" operated by the GPU at CSU Chico.[111] The GPU at UC Santa Barbara also sought to support its peer counseling program with a phone service.[112] And in 1975, UCLA's GSU set up a hotline that offered both referrals and counseling: "Call us if you need to talk to someone. The Gay Students of UCLA want to help or direct you to someone who can. We are non-judgmental and understanding." Scott Beardsley recalled that the students received crisis-call training from a faculty member and typically worked four-hour shifts, receiving calls redirected from a central number. By the fall of 1975, students from both the GSU and the Lesbian Sisterhood were staffing the lines, and campus administrators concerned about sexual encounters in bathroom stalls turned to the GSU for help. The group's solution was to post stickers that featured the hotline number and the message "SEX? Police frequently patrol this restroom because of complaints. UCLA Gay Student Union."[113]

The Stanford GPU's logbook recorded phone calls as well as visitors to the office. Callers sought resources, information about the organization and the local community, or just a chance to chat about coming out, sexuality, or anything else that was on their minds. Nonstudent callers included faculty members from other universities who were looking for guest speakers and a student from the Gay People's Alliance at Western Washington University who wanted to know how gay studies was or was not being implemented in the San Francisco Bay Area. While the line was staffed primarily by men, lesbians worked on designated "women's nights," which were important in broadening the GPU's reach.[114] Phone access enabled the organization to connect with students, interested community members, faculty, and others who were unwilling or unable to attend meetings in person or stop by an office.

When LGBT students in California began publicly organizing in the late 1960s and 1970s, they needed to create new infrastructure. Organizing homes provided spaces and resources from which to build support for their work. Beginning with existing social relationships and off-campus political work, these early attempts to institutionalize LGBT organizing used these new structures and spaces not only to make connections with each other socially but also to begin to satisfy unmet needs. But the continued existence of such organizing homes was not a given. Campus-based organizations sometimes faced uphill battles to secure official recognition, and these struggles provide especially useful insights into the internal and external challenges to LGBT student organizing.

CHAPTER TWO

Navigating Struggles for Recognition

In February 1972, journalist Leo Laurence suggested that the "gay student movement" was facing pushback on campuses across the United States. Students' willingness to defend their organizing, Laurence argued, "is making some school administrators uneasy" and "frightens some campus police, but seems to be proving that school no longer need be lonely for homosexuals."[1] But public organizing sparked different forms of "reactionary resistance" from those seeking to limit LGBT student visibility.[2]

On most campuses, LGBT students faced numerous everyday forms of such resistance, among them hostile letters to the editors of campus newspapers, torn or defaced meeting flyers, harassment by campus law enforcement, and complaints from angry alumni and community members.[3] One flyer posted by the Gay Student Union (GSU) at Los Angeles City College had the word Gay crossed out and replaced by fag and the phrase is bullshit added after the group's name.

On some campuses, reactionary resistance took physical form. At UC Santa Barbara, vandals repeatedly attacked the Gay People's Union (GPU) office, spray-painting antigay graffiti, throwing eggs, and smashing windows.[4] In 1979, the GPU office had its windows broken not once but three times—in January and twice in October. In the first incident, a rock was "carefully aimed to enter the office through" an anti–Briggs Initiative bumper sticker as a reminder to "all of us gay and non-gay, that attitudes on our university campus are not really all that enlightened."[5] The October attacks occurred just a few weeks before the GPU was slated to participate in a local rally corresponding with the first National March for Lesbian and Gay Rights in Washington, D.C. One of those incidents, condemned by the editors of the campus newspaper as insensitive and intolerant, included "Kill the Fags" and "Fuck You" spray-painted on the office walls.[6]

LGBT students encountered one especially significant type of reactionary resistance—denying recognition to campus-based student organizations. Formal recognition brought real material benefits—funding opportunities, access to campus spaces, and resources to support programming goals. Denial of recognition could thus complicate or even quash such organizing. On some campuses, such as UC Berkeley and UCLA, official recognition ran into no real hurdles: administrators consulted attorneys and then quietly granted recognition.[7] But when recognition was denied, LGBT student organizations could not meet on campus but instead had to find alternate venues—private residences, cafés, or sympathetic churches.[8] The lack of formal recognition meant that although USC's Gay Liberation Forum hosted numerous events, all were held off-campus.[9] On a symbolic, level denial of recognition challenged LGBT students' sense of belonging, signaling that they were not welcome.

Appealing such denials of recognition became critical as a means of not only advocating for resources but also publicly asserting visibility, claiming the right to organize, and challenging homophobia.[10] On some campuses, pressure from LGBT students and their allies brought resolution. On others, public threats of lawsuits convinced administrators to back down. And for a smaller group of campuses, recognition came only in the wake of direct pressure from legal professionals, including filing lawsuits.[11]

According to a 1973 article by Warren Blumenfeld, director of the National Gay Student Center and a former San José State student and member of the school's Gay Liberation Front (GLF), the number of schools around the country that resisted recognizing LGBT organizations was "staggering," though the precise number is hard to gauge.[12] A 1974 survey by the National Gay Student Center found that 86 percent of the thirty-five campus-based LGBT organizations that responded to a survey had "no problems getting recognition."[13] Just a year later, Steve Werner noted that the National Gay Student Center was aware of at least fifteen cases where schools had fought against recognizing LGBT groups and that there were "undoubtedly many more of which they are not aware."[14] By 1981, the *Advocate* reported that 26 percent of four-year colleges and 80 percent of public universities had recognized gay student organizations, while only 2.7 percent had refused or banned student groups. Every legal challenge to a denial of recognition had succeeded.[15]

With its large number of postsecondary educational institutions and its extensive student organizing efforts, California saw resistance to recognition in a significant number of cases: San José State College, Sacramento State College, Cal Poly San Luis Obispo, Cal State Fullerton, College of the Sequoias, College of the Redwoods, Fullerton College, Bakersfield College, and the University of Southern California.[16] The state thus provides a unique opportunity to compare and contrast such struggles at various institutions. The type of campus, the presence of allies, and the degree to which student power was already being contested played significant roles in the outcomes.

Moreover, struggles for recognition highlight how interactions with campus administrators frequently required LGBT students to cultivate allies. Such struggles also publicized the organizing activity, provided platforms for LGBT students and faculty to share their experiences more broadly, and served as models for LGBT students on other campuses. LGBT students thus transformed reactionary resistance into an organizing tool to enhance peer and institutional support, in the process forging a sense of belonging. As Larry Bernard noted in the midst of the Gay Liberation Forum's 1972 battle to win recognition from USC, increased visibility constituted a step toward claiming space on campus.[17]

Justifying Denial of Recognition

Perhaps the most common argument administrators made when denying recognition to a campus-based LGBT organization was that doing so would be tantamount to sanctioning "illegal activity," especially before 1975, when homosexual sexual practices were decriminalized in California.[18] "I am not about to have this College in the position of being in any way legally or morally culpable," San José State president Hobert Burns wrote in a 1969 internal memo about recognizing the GLF, "if that illness in an individual should result in a homosexual crime with a victim," a position echoed by his counterparts at Sacramento State, Cal State Fullerton, and Bakersfield College.[19] Similarly, the dean of students at Cal Poly San Luis Obispo, Everett Chandler, claimed that because homosexuality was "not recognized in Title V [California's Education code] as an activity pursued in the normal channel of student activities," the GSU should not be allowed to use campus facilities.[20] These arguments allowed administrators to justify their decisions by pointing to an outside source—the law.

Some administrators explained their decisions in moralistic rather than legalistic terms. When the board of trustees of the California State College System discovered that students were trying to organize the GLF at San José State in 1969, trustee Dudley Swim argued that the board had an obligation to "build the moral character of students."[21] At the November 1969 trustees meeting, Swim waved a copy of the campus newspaper, the *Spartan Daily*, that included an article about the founding of the GLF and asked Burns and dean of students Robert Martin whether they were "running a cesspool."[22] Randy Schrader, a graduate student at USC who had been instrumental in the founding of the GLF while an undergraduate at UCLA, speculated that the USC board of trustees' decision to deny recognition to the Gay Liberation Forum was rooted in the belief that the group was a "threat to campus morality."[23] Cal Poly San Luis Obispo's Chandler contended in 1972 that recognition "publicly advertises and attempts to make homosexuality attractive"; alluding to the common stereotype of homosexual as child abuser, he declared, "It is unconceivable that any college would support behavior which may tend to jeopardize children in such manner."[24]

Fears regarding the impact of the presence of LGBT organizations on an institution's reputation led other administrators to refuse recognition. In addition to concerns about how alumni, local communities, and boards of trustees would respond, state institutions worried about elected officials' reactions. Going further, J. Lee Lehman of the National Gay Student Center argued in 1977 that denying recognition offered some administrators a way "to score points with conservative members of the legislature or the Board of Regents."[25] Cal State Fullerton president Donald Shields would not recognize a "group advocating illegal activities which are offensive to a great majority of the public who support higher education."[26] One student organizer believed that Shields wanted the case to go to court so that he "would remain in good standing with the community and the Board of Trustees" and the courts would "be the scapegoat."[27] One faculty member agreed, suggesting that Shields's decision had been influenced by a meeting at which Orange County assemblyman John Briggs had pressured the school president to clamp down on LGBT organizing as a way to "appease the conservative community which surrounds the campus."[28] Wiggsy Sivertsen of San José State's counseling faculty recalled the campus president's refusal to recognize the GLF there as partly a reflection of the fact that this was Ronald Reagan's California.[29]

Private universities were often more focused on boards of trustees and donors. When the USC administration rejected the Gay Liberation Forum as an official student organization, one faculty member suggested that the trustees were willing to take the issue to court because even if they lost, they would be able to "say to their conservative donors, 'We tried to keep out the queers.'"[30] One gay USC faculty member speculated that the decision was motivated by economics: financial supporters of the university's sports programs would not "tolerate a homosexual organization on campus."[31]

Larry Bernard, a USC student involved in the Gay Liberation Forum during these years, attended a meeting at a trustee's home "where the host remarked adamantly that there were no 'queers' at the university."[32] Some observers believed that recognizing LGBT organizations would draw an influx of homosexuals to campus.[33] When students organized the GSU in 1972 at the College of the Sequoias, a community college in Visalia, President Ivan Crookshanks became angry, telling the board of trustees, "I don't care if they want to be queer, and want to do their thing ... that organization doesn't belong on campus." He speculated that the campus would become "the central focal point for all the queers between Los Angeles and San Francisco."[34] These fears were expressed by other campus presidents, including Otto Butz of Sacramento State, who feared that recognition would "attract homosexuals to the campus, and ... expose minors to homosexual advocacy and practices."[35]

Many administrators prioritized resolving these struggles internally, with as little publicity as possible. San José State's Burns first tried to keep the GLF out of the public eye, apologizing to trustees about coverage in the student newspaper and assuring them that the organization would not be permitted on campus.[36] Burns planned to ask the GLF to "cool it, on the grounds (if no other) public opinion will not tolerate an officially-recognized gay group." Burns acknowledged that the GLF might "make application anyway, just to test the tolerance of the system and to put the College on the spot. I hope they won't, for the sake of the system and the College, but if they do, I'll deny recognition." Burns urged California State College chancellor Glenn Dumke not to "escalate the situation into a confrontation" but rather to handle the matter "informally and privately." Burns concluded by telling Dumke, "You can of course reassure any Trustee who inquires that we will not have a Gay Liberation Front here if I can help it."[37]

Despite these assurances, the formation of the GLF at San José State made news in both mainstream and alternative newspapers.[38] In response, irate Californians began writing letters to Burns. After Bertha Wirtz from San Diego heard about the GLF on a radio program, "the minister told us to write against this matter." She believed that with the GLF, San José State would "be runed [sic] as a Christian College": "Homosexual clubs shouldn't be allowed on any college campus," though "Christian clubs" were perfectly okay.[39] Orpha Strong Wright complained about the "new club (of homosexuals)" and urged that as a "graduate, tax-payer, and concerned person, please do not recognize them."[40] Kenneth Pascoe was even more irate in his letter to Burns, threatening to "spread the word of this festering stink on your campus.... What in God's name are you doing to the youth of this campus?" Recognizing the GLF would lead only to other "clubs and studies into necrophilia, sadism and sodomy.... You bastards! You bastards! You wretched bastards!" Burns sent copies of the letter to Governor Reagan and California state senator John Schmitz. Once again, Burns responded with reassurances that he would not recognize the organization.[41]

Campus Responses

Other members of college and university communities responded to denials of recognition in a variety of ways. In some cases, denials of recognition created opportunities for LGBT students to cultivate peers, faculty, staffers, and members of the local community as allies. Having such support could make a big difference in students' sense of belonging and often could ultimately help organizations gain recognition. Supporters came from many corners of campus. At San José State, Keith W. Johnsgard, director of the counseling center, expressed his staff's concerns about Burns's to deny recognition to the GLF, declaring that such organizations were crucial to "openly involv[ing] the homosexual in society," praising the GLF organizers for their "great courage and dedication," and arguing that the group would make "a significant contribution to the mental health and education of the college community."[42] In the spring of 1971, USC's faculty senate voted 79–19 to urge the board of trustees to reconsider its denial of recognition to the Gay Liberation Forum; the faculty vote was bolstered by Associated Students' support of the group.[43] As Professor Martin Rogers noted in a 1977 account of the struggle over the Society for Homosexual Freedom at Sacramento State, denial of recognition "reactivated in most group members other similar and painful incidents in their lives," but the support of other liberation groups, the campus newspaper, and the student government was "invaluable."[44]

When the GSU at Cal State Fullerton failed to gain recognition, Associated Students recognized the GSU as an official "A.S. commission," with all the benefits accorded to other clubs, and one former Associated Students senator filed an appeal of the denial.[45] At San José State, Associated Students voted unanimously to make the GLF an official student organization "with nary a whisper of protest or discussion."[46] Associated Students at Bakersfield College also supported the GSU there, with at least one officer citing a right to organize. Another officer described the GSU's travails as "despicable and disgusting," while other observers saw the denial as an attack on student rights of self-determination.[47] Such rights claims were repeated elsewhere, including at Cal Poly San Luis Obispo, where Associated Students president Pete Evans and vice president Marianne Doshi argued that the Gay Student Union had "a perfect right to organize on campus."[48]

Some peers were less supportive. At Cal Poly San Luis Obispo, some students criticized the GSU requirement that voting members be "either homosexual or bisexual"—a key phrase that was the subject of a lawsuit—as discriminatory.[49] Other students objected to the organization on religious grounds. Farm management student Jim Hull claimed that the GSU represented how men "had abandoned the natural function of women and committed ungodly acts." Hull nevertheless "asked God to forgive all people for their sins, and that includes the gays."[50]

Such debates played out in campus newspapers as well. Ken Boegert wrote to Cal Poly San Luis Obispo's *Mustang Daily* that acceptance of homosexuality was "an abomination to God," "the lowest state of sin" and a sickness.[51] Mike Ruskovich objected to recognizing an organization that supported "such private activity as personal sexual behavior," citing a hypothetical "Dirty Old Men's Union" in declaring the idea of the GSU "ridiculous."[52] Gerald Jones responded by criticizing Ruskovich for mischaracterizing homosexuals as "interested in sex only, to the exclusion of everything else": according to Jones, the GSU had "never included the furtherance of sexual activity" as its purpose.[53] Thomas Weissbluth, in contrast, praised Ruskovich for standing "strong against the growing tide of immoral elements in society" and avowing that Cal Poly should not become a "crash pad for dirty people who do naughty, and embarrassing and unnatural acts."[54] Defenders of the GSU praised it as an organization designed to raise consciousness and criticized the mixing of religious beliefs about homosexuality with the duties of a state institution, creating a "danger of religious inquisition," in the words of Burr Hosely.[55]

At Cal State Fullerton, the editors of the *Daily Titan* argued that President Shields's denial of recognition for the GSU showed contempt "for the college's written statement of student rights and responsibilities" as well as for the U.S. Constitution and represented "an arrogant expression of power."[56] When the USC board of trustees refused to recognize the Gay Liberation Forum, the editors of the *Daily Trojan* opined that students had the right to determine their own organizations.[57] The organization's Larry Bernard made the case that recognition had been denied in part because "homosexuals are not regarded as human beings" and that such a denial of rights could not go unchallenged.[58]

LGBT organizations facing denial of recognition at times chose more direct action. In December 1969, when Dumke visited the San José State campus to dedicate a new student union building, ten members of the GLF set up informational tables and plastered the room with signs reading "Gay is Good" and "Homosexuals for Peace and Each Other."[59] At USC, members of the Gay Liberation Forum met with campus president John Hubbard to discuss the trustees' decision to deny recognition.[60] Hubbard agreed to bring the issue to the board again, though he told the *Daily Trojan* that the primary sticking point was "sections of the [Gay Liberation Forum] constitution which are in violation of California state law," though he did not elaborate.[61] Bernard did not hold out much hope: "The trustees have no intention of accepting our proposal," Bernard told the *Daily Trojan*, "because they believe our group is immoral."[62] Defying the trustees, the Gay Liberation Forum continued to meet and sponsor programs into the 1971–72 academic year.[63]

Other organizations took legal action in the face of denial of recognition. After the Society for Homosexual Freedom at Sacramento State College prevailed in lawsuit challenging the school's denial of recognition, some students saw turning to the courts to insist on constitutional rights as a promising strategy. "For once, someone must stand up to the tyrants," the Gay Liberation Forum declared when it sued USC in 1972. "Law and justice will prevail, and USC will once again join the United States, where we are governed by the Constitution and the Bill of Rights." But campus groups that chose this path faced challenges: as the National Gay Student Center's Steve Werner noted in 1975, doing so requiring marshaling all of an organization's "internal resources and as much outside support as it can." Sources of such support could be found both on-campus (student government, for example) and off-campus (national organizations such as the American Civil Liberties Union [ACLU]).[64]

At Cal State Fullerton, the ACLU stepped up to assist the GSU in the summer of 1971. Jay Murley, an ACLU board member and a regular supporter of LGBT student organizing, recalled that with the campus in conservative Orange County, the solution was both legal and political. While the ACLU provided two attorneys to represent the GSU, Murley and other ACLU members "cut a deal" with a campus administrator to convince Shields quietly to recognize the students thereby avoiding the wrath of John Briggs, who represented the area in the California Assembly, while protecting Shields's job. In late December 1971, the GSU gained formal recognition without going to court.[65]

Other groups, among them USC's Gay Liberation Forum, had difficulty obtaining legal representation. The ACLU also assisted students at Cal State Fullerton, San José State, and Fullerton College.[66] In other instances, challenges to denial of recognition relied on private attorneys: Cal Poly San Luis Obispo's student government allocated $3,000 to hire a lawyer on behalf of the school's GSU, while the organization itself held a benefit for its "Legal Defense Drive" at a local bar.[67]

Court challenges did not always succeed. The GSU at Cal Poly San Luis Obispo lost at a trial in a state superior court, with the judge ruling that the policy restricting "membership to homosexuals and bisexuals" did not garner constitutional protection. In response, the GSU claimed not only that heterosexuals were always welcome but that and the group's lawyer had said so during the trial and characterized the decision as "purely a political one."[68] Associated Students appealed the decision in the summer of 1974 but lost again in the Los Angeles District Court of Appeals.[69]

Students then vowed to take the case to the California Supreme Court. Associated Students vice president Mike Hurtado saw the case as having wider implications: "The credibility of student government [was] threatened" if students were not permitted to decide which organizations to recognize. The new president of the student government, Scott Plotkin, similarly declared, "We are asserting our authority and our responsibility to ensure the Constitutional rights of the student." When the attorney for the students failed to file the appeal in a timely manner, however, the GSU remained unrecognized. In late 1974, the group rewrote its bylaws to correct the problematic membership provision, and in April 1975, the *Mustang Daily* reported that Cal Poly San Luis Obispo's president, Robert E. Kennedy, was on the verge of approving the new bylaws. The paper suggested that the reversal had occurred as a result of the intervention of the California State University chancellor's office rather than resulting from a change of heart on Kennedy's part.[70]

Kennedy immediately denied having reached a decision on the issue, stating, "I have been busy on matters I consider more important to the university." He continued, "I don't intend to be hurried into precipitous action by pressure from anyone." Six months later, Kennedy sought the California attorney general's opinion on the matter and told the student newspaper that he continued to believe that the GSU should not be recognized because the modified bylaws represented only a "token recognition of open membership." The group "clearly" remained limited to homosexuals, and its "purpose and objectives ... have no relationship to the overall educational system of the University but are oriented to the homophile life-style." Recognizing the GSU would set a precedent that Kennedy claimed would mean recognition of the Ku Klux Klan, the American Nazi Party, the Symbionese Liberation Army (a California leftist group that had kidnapped publishing heiress Patty Hearst in February 1974 and held her until September 1975), and advocates of the "racial inferiority of Jews." If the attorney general found that Kennedy had the "legal right to deny recognition," he would do so.[71]

But when the attorney general's office condoned recognition, Kennedy officially recognized the GSU after a five-year struggle. Although GSU president Ron Pursley lamented that so much time had passed, and the group shifted its focus to "consolidation rather than recognition." The group planned to reorient itself toward meeting the needs of gay students, expanding community service opportunities, and creating a speakers' bureau. The GSU's Margo Terrill told the student newspaper that although the group remained "a controversy" in San Luis Obispo, "it's no big thing"; acceptance "will come." And when a group of students wandered into a GSU meeting and responded by laughing and running down the hall, participants just "burst into applause." Recognition brought confidence. By the following fall, the GSU was advertising its meetings in the *Mustang Daily*, and the paper printed a letter to the editor encouraging students to attend.[72]

Court challenges sometimes became opportunities to rally a variety of supporters. LGBT student organizations and others pitched in to raise funds to support the USC Gay Liberation Forum's lawsuit against the university by holding a "gay college dance" at the local Metropolitan Community Church. The May 1972 *Lesbian Tide* included a brief story about the lawsuit, noting that the Forum, like other gay groups, "fills many needs—gay self-acceptance, fellowship, education."[73] The Cal Poly San Luis Obispo GSU's challenge to its denial of recognition garnered coverage in the gay press: about two hundred supporters then rallied behind the students, taking over Aethelred's bar in San Luis Obispo (which had no gay bar).[74] The Reverend Ray Broshears, a San Francisco–based activist and the leader of the Lavender Panthers, attended the event and urged the students to "open lines of communication" with police, sheriffs, and local health groups and to form coalitions with straight students.[75] Even the San Luis Obispo County Young Republicans endorsed the GSU's right to organize on campus.[76]

These struggles for recognition were significant both symbolically and materially, in part because they generated publicity. The formation of the GLF at San José State rated mention in a June 1970 issue of *Vector*, the periodical of San Francisco's Society for Individual Rights, which expressed its hope that state colleges and universities would "realize the emergency of the current struggle and reconsider their denial of official recognition on college campuses." The *Advocate* published numerous articles showcasing gay student organizing, some of them written by Leo Laurence. When he learned about the situation at Cal Poly San Luis Obispo, Laurence wrote to GSU president Robert Christensen to find out more about "what's happening with the GSU." Laurence's interest had great meaning for Christensen: "How can we begin to thank you for the hope that you have given us. We have feared that our pursuit of campus recognition here at Cal Poly would be ended in a stalemate, with the threat of a court case stopping us. You have offered us hope and that is all we need to continue."[77]

Victory on one campus fed similar results on others. As Elizabeth Koehler argues, the successful resolution of the case at Sacramento State "made it easier for other gay organizations on California campuses to demand official recognition."[78] In the wake of Shields's decision to deny recognition to the Cal State Fullerton GSU, the school's Student Senate condemned the president's actions by a 6–5 vote and pointed out that the Sacramento decision might require the group's recognition.[79] Murley found the ACLU's accompanying brief in the Sacramento case "awful useful" in laying out the legal arguments during meetings with students and administrators from other institutions, although he "candidly" admitted that "it was all we really had."[80] Even students at the private University of Southern California, where the questions of free speech and assembly were less clear, relied on the Sacramento State case, using the decision in pursuing an injunction to prevent the board of trustees from refusing recognition.[81]

While recognition did not end reactionary resistance, success permitted LGBT students, like those at Cal Poly San Luis Obispo, to turn their attention toward engaging the growing gay and lesbian movement both on- and off-campus and embrace education—and educational institutions—as the centerpiece of an organizing strategy.

CHAPTER THREE

Claiming a Queer Education

In 1972, Warren Blumenfeld, a San José State alum and former member of the Gay Liberation Front (GLF) as well as the first director of the National Gay Student Center in Washington D.C., described a major purpose of the center: "creat[ing] an information network" for campus-based LGBT student groups and sharing educational materials such as "books, films, speakers, consultants [and] curriculum and other educational resources."[1] The center's newsletter, *Interchange*, regularly reprinted syllabi and course outlines that "might be helpful to people planning courses on campus or in communities."[2] These resources came from institutions across the country, including many in California: Sacramento State, San Francisco State, and Cal State Long Beach.

LGBT students embraced education—both their own and institutionally—as a form of personal and political transformation. In DIY fashion, they sought to fill gaps in their knowledge of homosexuality, bisexuality, gender identity, and LGBT-themed cultural, historical and scientific studies, and related issues that were not covered in traditional educational settings.[3] Students published newsletters to share information, hosted raps to explore issues, invited experts to attend meetings and share research or information, and created libraries of materials on which peers and professors could draw. Inspired by (and sometimes interconnected with) organizing around ethnic studies and women's studies, LGBT students sought to transform both course and program curricula to include relevant issues, an effort in which student-run experimental colleges played an important role. LGBT students embraced education as a form of liberation—their contribution as members of an academic community to the wider gay and lesbian and/or feminist movements.[4]

DIY Education

In 1972, Stanford students Michael Hughes and James Mitchell suggested that two prime goals of the Gay People's Union GPU were the "instilling of Gay Pride and the destruction of inner oppression"; such "inner liberation" was needed before "societal liberation" could occur.[5] Similarly, when the UCLA Gay Student Union (GSU) surveyed members about its purpose, one person responded, "educate gays on a consciousness-raising level": "How can we fight the establishment when we don't understand the hell we're going through?"[6] While LGBT students in earlier times might have engaged in similar educational journeys on their own or in small groups, those who organized openly on campus in the late 1960s and 1970s embraced the opportunity to do so publicly, as part of wider LGBT or feminist communities. Such consciousness-raising among LGBT students, inspired in many ways by the women's liberation movement, took different forms and varied from campus to campus.[7]

Like other student and social movement organizers, LGBT students shared information through self-produced newsletters and newspapers.[8] Newsletters—described by UCLA's GSU as "informational aids" for gay students—were particularly popular because they were easy to produce and distribute if students had access to a mimeograph machine.[9] As the Stanford GPU newsletter declared in 1974, unlike "some institutions in this society," newsletters provided LGBT students "complete control": a students could "contribute [their] time, talent and money and see the newsletter respond to [them] as [they] wish."[10] The power of such a vehicle for self-education was not lost on students. Cesar Blanco, editor of the UCLA GSU newsletter in 1977, argued that the newsletter enabled students to share "information about ongoing strife in the gay community," which could be "reported by all of us."[11]

Newsletters typically included meeting schedules, event advertisements, news articles, opinion pieces, ways to get involved in the local LGBT community and/or movement, and a host of creative work—including poems, short stories, and visual art. The newsletter published by Students for Gay Power at the University of California, Berkeley, began as typed meeting notes; the transformation into a mimeographed newsletter occurred after the group became the Gay Student Union.[12] Some LGBT student organizations funded their newsletters through student government. UCLA's GSU newsletter, *The Gayzette*, was sponsored by the Student Legislative Council, though numerous issues included reminders that the opinions expressed did not represent those of the council.[13] Some organizations produced only a handful of sporadic newsletters, while other groups published regularly over several years, providing insight not only into LGBT student life but also into newsletters' role in organizing.[14]

Newsletters included articles written by students as well as pieces reprinted from other sources. The topics ranged widely—campus and local community issues, political analysis, and the relationship of homosexuality to such fields as psychology, religion, literature, and the arts. In the late spring of 1974, Stanford's GPU newsletter included information about the group's meetings—men in one room, women in another—and about a how-to workshop on communication that sought to enable members to "have a chance to voice our concerns and perhaps with help get our news out to the community."[15] Newsletters also gave readers the opportunity to connect with other communities around the campus and the state. *The Gayzette* included reports of protests against a "faggots stay out" sign at a Los Angeles bar and against the Los Angeles police chief Ed Davis's harassment of members of the LGBT community as well as a piece on the experiences of gay prisoners. These kinds of stories contributed to readers' political education, immersing LGBT students in movement issues and struggles.[16]

Guest speakers at meetings offered another avenue for DIY education. Sacramento State's SSC Gay Liberation sponsored "gay orientation" meetings where participants could "get acquainted with local Gay people and their activities."[17] Visiting speakers on various campuses discussed incarcerated lesbians, lesbian mothers and child custody disputes, alcoholism in the LGBT community, lesbians and the law, and "Being Black and Gay."[18] Morris Kight, a founder of the GLF in Los Angeles and an organizer with the Gay Community Services Center, was a regular visitor to LGBT student organization meetings across Southern California.[19] LGBT organizations also invited a diverse array of speakers, as demonstrated by the Cal State Los Angeles GSU's fall 1976 lineup: a representative from the American Civil Liberties Union on "the law and the gay community"; Dorr Legg from ONE on "civil rights"; Tony Guevara from Latinos Unidos on "Gay[s] and the Chicano Community"; Tye Ray of the California Association of Sex Educators on transvestism; and Marguerite Silicero from the GSU at Cal State Long Beach on "Women and the Gay Community."[20]

Some lesbian students found feminist spaces, including women's centers, to be particularly important venues for DIY learning opportunities. The Lesbian Sisterhood at UCLA partnered with the Women's Resource Center, an umbrella organization that supported various women-focused campus groups. Opened in Powell Library in May 1972, the center provided space where the Lesbian Sisterhood could host raps, consciousness-raising groups, regular meetings, and other events.[21] According to a 1974 article, many women were initially "too shy to ask about" the Lesbian Sisterhood, "so they are informed about it immediately at the" Women's Resource Center.[22] Similarly, the Lesbian Feminist Alliance at San José State regularly met at the Women's Center, hosting programs and raps.[23] Coordinator Jacqua Miller, a graduate student, described the alliance as a "political force" to educate others about lesbians in a way that was informed by "bottom line politics": "no woman is free until all women are free." This politics of liberation included "the poor, Third World, disabled, [and] welfare lesbian mothers."[24]

LGBT student organizers, like many other activists, recognized a great need to curate their own educational materials.[25] Aware of the limitations of their campus libraries, activists created and shared their own repositories of books, magazines, and newspapers to support academic, personal, and political work. Kathryn Wright, a student at the University of California, Santa Cruz, sought resources to help develop a class on homosexuality, citing a need for "bibliographies, list[s] of publications, leaflets, and new/old sources of reliable information" and the difficulty of locating "any educational material of any merit within the realm of usual resources of the university."[26] National Gay Student Center director J. Lee Lehman described this problem as a national one: university libraries had scant resources available "for the inquiring homosexual student or student of homosexuality." Challenges included "inadequate cataloging," the disappearance of gay-related books from library shelves, and holdings that treated homosexuality as deviant or in a "negative light." Although Lehman suggested "gay bookstores" as one resource, this option was not available to all students, highlighting the need for DIY efforts on campus.[27]

The Gay Liberation Forum at USC planned to create a "gay library" that would include books, magazines, "gay periodicals and newspapers," fiction, bibliographies, and "faculty and student research papers."[28] The GSU at CSU Long Beach raised forty dollars to "purchase materials for a library on gay art, culture and organizations" and hoped to make these materials accessible on campus.[29] A proposed budget for the GPU at Stanford included funding for books and subscriptions to the *Advocate*, *Vector*, and *Lesbian Tide* that would be available at the organization's drop-in center.[30] As USC student Sal Licata noted in 1976, the "creation of gay libraries and openly hospitable environments on campuses demonstrate[s] the growing confidence of collegiate gays."[31]

These DIY education efforts were central to LGBT student organizations' work. As treasurer Richard Thomas noted in one budget request, GPU programs were designed "to offer gay students, faculty, and staff of the Stanford community a chance to learn about themselves and each other in an atmosphere of pride and self-acceptance."[32]

Promoting Academic Courses and Programs

While DIY education might have contributed to personal liberation and in the process strengthened campus organizing, LGBT students were well aware of one important structural limitation to liberation: the curriculum. With a few exceptions, including efforts by faculty members to offer LGBT-themed courses in traditional academic departments and in emerging fields like women's studies, most LGBT students found little curricular content that aligned with their emerging identities.[33] And some students found the existing curriculum oppressive, as UCLA's Richard Gollance expressed in a 1972 *Daily Bruin* piece. The educational system "represented, perhaps, the most unavoidable medium of degradation for me": it had not only ignored his "gayness as part of his positive self" but had "actively worked against those needs." According to Gollance, gay students found themselves "discussed only in psychology classes as a sick deviant—not a person, but an oddity to be analyzed by heterosexuals who have determined themselves as standards of desirability." Claiming a similarity in the demand for courses exploring Black, Chicano, Asian, and women's studies, Gollance argued that including homosexuality in courses in new ways could aid students in developing a "social and cultural identity."[34]

LGBT students began to request such content, but their appeals were often unheeded or even dismissed. Ziesel Saunders, a history major at the University of California, Santa Cruz, remembered that when students brought up LGBT issues in class, faculty members responded, "'You know we don't want to talk about that. Why do you always have to talk about what you do in the bedroom?'—that kind of attitude."[35] Such silences and such resistance motivated many LGBT students to advocate for changes.

LGBT courses first appeared at experimental colleges, many of which were organized and/or supported by LGBT students. With roots in the 1920s, experimental colleges became popular with administrators and faculty in the 1950s and 1960s as a way to meet increasing demand and promote liberal arts education. By providing accessible, high-quality, lower-cost, and interdisciplinary programs, experimental colleges addressed what reformers saw as the "disjointed education" of the postwar university, which focused too much on specialized knowledge. Experimental colleges, in contrast, reduced the fragmentation of the undergraduate experience and in some cases enjoyed both student and faculty support until the late 1960s. But these reform efforts were typically initiated by faculty and administrators, and by the middle of the decade, students began to demand more autonomy and more control over their education, asserting their own ideas about what was relevant and at times pursuing their own alternatives.[36]

With the support of student government, students across the United States began to create their own experimental colleges (sometimes called free universities), inspired by the Mississippi Freedom Schools, the Free Speech Movement at UC Berkeley, Students for a Democratic Society, and antiwar teach-ins. Student-run experimental colleges were "fundamentally a search for power," as Paul Lauter and Florence Howe noted in 1970, challenging the approaches and practices of official university courses.[37]

A number of the earliest LGBT-themed courses were offered at California's experimental colleges, including those at UC Berkeley, UC Davis, and the California State campuses at Fullerton, Northridge, Los Angeles, and San José.[38] San Francisco State's experimental college was the first in the California State College System.[39] Described by Lauter and Howe as the "paradigm success story among the free universities," San Francisco State offered many distinctly political courses with the "goal of activating students without sacrificing 'content'" and helping students refine their "political commitments to social change."[40] The experiment at San Francisco State emerged from a surge of student activism, the desire to diversify the academic experience, and assert more control. By the fall of 1966, the experimental college served almost twelve hundred students and offered almost seventy noncredit courses, among them some of the first ethnic studies courses.[41] In the fall of 1966, the experimental college offered a Black Arts and Culture series organized by the Black Student Union, part of the wider shift toward Black Power.[42] As Martha Biondi argues, experimental colleges like those at San Francisco State provided "a means of infusing the curricula with the social tumult of the 1960s and of incorporating student energy and initiative."[43]

Less well known than the experimental colleges' role as an incubator of ethnic studies courses is how San Francisco State's experimental college became a home for student-run courses addressing homosexuality. These courses emerged around the time of the 1968 student strike for ethnic studies led by the Third World Liberation Front, a crucial moment of intersection—what Irene E. Vázquez calls intersectoral "points of contact and interactions" between and among these movements.[44] After being fired for his support of the student strike, part-time instructor Morgan Pinney called for an expansion of the curriculum to address homosexuality as more than an abnormality, connecting the struggle to create Black studies with the need for gay studies.[45] "Homosexual oppression is essential to the continuance of the system," Pinney argued, and gay liberation could come only with gay studies organized "by homosexuals themselves."[46]

Exploring New Forms of Sexual Relationships, organized by graduate student Dave Allison in the spring of 1968, was the first experimental college course at San Francisco State to mention homosexuality.[47] By the early 1970s, the offerings at what had become known as the Communiversity expanded to include additional LGBT-focused courses. In 1972, the GLF sponsored History of the Gay Movements, Gay Sexuality, Gays in History, Gay Women in American Society, Gays and the Law, Survey of Gays in the Arts, and Intersexual Communication/Sexism. Movement concerns informed these choices, as the course description for Gays and the Law illustrates: a lawyer "will talk to and with the class on sex laws in California, how to avoid getting trapped, what to do if arrested and how to try to change the laws. Know your rights!" The contact person for all these courses was Jerald Jacks, GLF president.[48]

Proposed by student Rosalio Muñoz and modeled on San Francisco State, the experimental college at UCLA also became an early home for ethnic studies courses. As Muñoz recalled, courses became "opportunities for students to explore topics that interested them," more innovative than UCLA's regular courses.⁴⁹ After a brief 1971 pause, the program began to offer LGBT-themed courses as well.⁵⁰

The first, History of Human and Civil Movements and Crisis in the U.S.A., was offered in the fall of 1972 and included a focus on gay liberation.⁵¹ After LGBT students organized the campus's first Gay Awareness Week in 1974, further LGBT-themed courses were added. In the summer of 1974, Norman Isaac Lewis advertised Beginning Gay Studies, Intermediate Gay Studies, and A Non-Gay Person's Guide to Understanding the Gay Lifestyle.⁵² Activist Jim Kepner, an early member of the Los Angeles Mattachine Society, the GLF, and the ONE Institute, offered Gays in History and World Literature: A Search for Gay Identity during the 1974 fall quarter.⁵³ In a letter to interested students, Kepner expressed hope that the courses would "help this program expand and become part of the recognized UCLA curriculum."⁵⁴

The experimental college offered five other LGBT-themed courses that quarter, including The Lesbian Experience, organized by activists Jeanne Córdova, Sharon Cornielson, and Sheila Brush.⁵⁵ Their proposal argued that a course focused on gender and sexual orientation was needed because lesbians lacked a space in higher education and pointed to similar courses at Sacramento State, Boston University, San Diego State, and San Francisco State. Supported by UCLA's Gay Sisterhood, the proposal indicated a "new level of acceptance and need for lesbian women and heterosexual people to learn about themselves and each other."⁵⁶ The thirty people who enrolled included not only UCLA students but community members, among them an audio engineer, a bibliographer, a "Xerox operator," a driver, a paralegal, a "cook and unwedded mother," an editor and typist, a special education aide, a day care director, an artist, a letter carrier, a service station manager, an electrician, and a manufacturing engineer.⁵⁷ In December 1974, the *Advocate* took note of the "growing number of seminars at UCLA that deal with various aspects of the gay community."⁵⁸

While these robust offerings suggest the importance of the experimental colleges to local activists, UCLA's GSU did not directly sponsor any courses, though one key member, graduate student Gary Steele, taught The Gay Experience in 1976.⁵⁹ The GSU promoted the courses in its newsletter but admitted that it had been "only partially successful" in cultivating ties to the gay studies courses.⁶⁰ Nevertheless, the GSU was "proud to have played a part in developing various gay studies courses" not only in the experimental college but also in women's studies and in other university departments.⁶¹ By the end of the 1970s, when the experimental college ended, LGBT-themed courses found homes elsewhere at UCLA, including with the Council on Educational Development, the school's official experimental college, which sponsored courses outside of traditional departments.⁶²

Women's studies programs became especially important for incorporating LGBT content into courses. As students gained greater exposure to feminism, Toni McNaron argues, they sought more information about lesbians.[63] Alongside health clinics, women's centers, rape crisis programs, women's bookstores, and women's political organizations, women's studies programs became an important campus organizing site for women's liberation in general and lesbian students in particular.[64] As the academic arm of the women's liberation movement, women's studies programs drew participants from both campus and community, sometimes starting informally—in living rooms, community centers, and other off-campus spaces—with students as crucial organizers.[65] And California was an especially vibrant place for women's studies.[66]

Many of these programs became new spaces where lesbian students and faculty could find each other and engage in organizing, governance, curriculum reform, and programming.[67] At Sacramento State, lesbian students Freda Smith and Barbara Bryant served on the Women's Studies Board, and Patricia Person worked in the program office.[68] According to Person, only "a small group of lesbians ... were active politically on campus—I could count them on my hand"; nevertheless, women's studies provided space for their organizing.[69]

Women's studies programs could still be challenging spaces for lesbian students and faculty. At Sacramento State, Theresa Corrigan, who was a student before teaching courses in the program, faced "a real uphill struggle, trying to make [others] understand that lesbians were women, that lesbians were as involved [in women's studies] as heterosexual women were [and that] there had to be something that met [lesbians'] needs as well."[70] In Jan Aura's view, UCLA's women's studies program was less vital to lesbian student organizing on campus in the early 1970s than was the Women's Resource Center.[71] Lisa Orta, who attended UC Berkeley in the early 1970s, recalled that she "didn't always fit in so well with sort of the academic feminist crowd" at the campus women's center, which represented an outgrowth of organizing around women's studies; "the gay part of me just went back in the shell."[72] And Sugie Goen-Salter, a UC Berkeley student in the mid-1970s, found that some women's studies faculty did not like that her cohort included "so many lesbians"; although a few straight women faculty members were strong allies, Goen-Salter generally found graduate students to be more supportive.[73] These experiences mirrored those at the national level: lesbian faculty and students were involved in the National Women's Studies Association at all levels but sometimes became, in Tucker Farley's words, "lightning rods for reaction."[74]

In some cases, women's studies programs offered LGBT- or lesbian-themed content. At San Francisco State, women's studies was started by a group of students and faculty in 1969, with courses "scattered across the university" and supported by organizers of the newly created (and Associated Students–

funded) Women's Center. Even before women's studies became an independent degree program in 1976, academic departments and the experimental college offered LGBT-themed courses.[75] Speech communications professor and lesbian activist Sally Gearhart taught Social Science 350: Homosexuality as a Social Issue as early as the spring of 1972.[76] The course became a regular offering throughout the 1970s, taught by a variety of instructors, and it appeared on a list of "permanent courses" in the 1976 proposal to create a bachelor's degree in women's studies.[77] San Francisco State's women's studies courses thus included LGBT-themed courses from the beginning, as faculty member Ruth Mahaney noted, and the department lacked the chasm between straight feminists and lesbians that was common at other institutions. As a result, the program provided structural support for an atypically LGBT-inclusive curriculum.[78]

At other schools, even when women's studies programs offered LGBT-themed courses, locating them could prove challenging. At the University of California, Santa Cruz, Rachel Harwood recalled, "lesbian courses" were not readily identifiable, with ambiguous titles such as The Woman-Identified Novel in Historical and Political Perspective: "You'd have to figure out what it really was by word of mouth."[79] Sonoma State's Woman-Identified-Woman likewise implied a lesbian subject without using the term.[80]

The organizers of Sacramento State's women's studies program planned to include lesbian content but faced hurdles when attempting to implement that plan.[81] A course on the "lesbian in society" was an early core offering, and it gained national attention as one of few gay studies courses offered in California at the time.[82] But the Women's Studies Board soon found itself mired in controversy over the course, fielding complaints about the content, debating whether to substitute a more generic name for the course or eliminate it from the core offerings, and seeking ways to sustain enrollment. In November 1972, the board discussed renaming the course even though the instructor, Shannon Hennigan, wanted to "be out front" that it was about lesbians. Board members suggested Female Homosexuality in Society before opting for Female Sexuality in May 1973.[83]

In March 1974, the women's studies curriculum committee suggested that the Sacramento State program add a course titled Lesbianism and Feminism. The proposal garnered the board's full support, and it was listed as a core course. Staffing the course proved problematic, however, as the board grappled with the question of what qualifications were required for the instructor. Renamed A Society of Women, the course was offered in the fall of 1974 with Corrigan at the helm and was described as a "look at a wide range of issues related to the Lesbian and her lifestyle." A Society of Women continued on the schedule through 1980, by which time it was the only course whose description specifically mentioned lesbian content: the class would explore "concepts and issues relevant to lesbian cultures," with topics including "lesbianism and feminism" and the "status of lesbianism in current socio-political movements."[84]

In many women's studies programs, including those at UC Santa Cruz and Sonoma State, students commonly proposed and taught LGBT-themed courses. Harwood recalled these student-directed courses as of "pretty good quality," with teachers "who were dynamic and enthusiastic about the things that they had to offer. They were fresh." In some cases, faculty responded, building courses around students' expressed interests.[85]

Some LGBT students and faculty proposed new gay studies courses and less frequently programs. When the UCLA GSU conducted a 1975 survey of its members' areas of concern, fourteen of the thirty-seven respondents were "very interested" in gay studies and six were "somewhat interested." One respondent suggested that the group's social functions "need to be complemented with a strong Gay Studies program."[86] At San Francisco State, Jim Williford, secretary and treasurer of the GLF, sought faculty support for establishing a gay studies major.[87]

Sacramento State's short-lived gay studies program was credited in the LGBT press as one of the first such programs in the United States.[88] The program had its origins with faculty who developed courses like Image of the Homosexual in Literature (taught by Charles Moore of the English department), Homosexuality (Martin Rogers of the psychology department), and The Lesbian and Society (Hennigan and One Person in women's studies). According to Moore, The Lesbian and Society was the first "Gay course on our campus taught by Gay people who were open about their gayness."[89] These courses were transformative for many students, as Rogers recalled, helping students come out, find each other, meet faculty allies, and discover activism in a variety of arenas. The courses "fueled the students" and gave "energy to the campus movement." Moreover, it was "safer to take a class than it was to go to a meeting." Students Barbara Bryant and Freda Smith described the courses in similar terms.[90]

In April 1972, Sacramento State students and faculty proposed the creation of a gay studies program, basing it on the women's studies and peace studies programs.[91] The proposal outlined a structure to be designed by "Gay students and faculty" that would promote "understanding of one of America's most oppressed minorities" and provide "a sense of cultural community which it has so long been dinied [sic]." The program would be coordinated by a "gay studies board" comprising at least three men and three women, at least one of whom would be a faculty member.[92] As in women's studies, students could design, teach, and take courses, a process specifically designed to ensure gay and lesbian students key roles. Associated Students backed the proposal and provided one thousand dollars.[93]

Once again, however, implementation proved more challenging.[94] Organizers encountered numerous roadblocks—difficulty in getting courses designated as gay studies and in obtaining approval from the faculty senate, along with problems in securing office space from which to administer the program. At the time, Rogers interpreted such resistance as "another way of keeping us in the closet, keeping us out of sight of people."[95] In hindsight, he described the process as "arduous": one administrator told him that using women's studies as a model had doomed the gay studies program, that approving it had been a mistake, and that it was "not going to happen again."[96]

Gay studies organizers and LGBT student organizations published an open letter in the student newspaper in which they decried the gay studies program's inability to obtain needed resources and accusing university officials of seeking to "keep us ineffective, because they are intimidated by our presence here on campus." The letter concluded, "We cannot, and will not, put up with this wall of defiance."[97] While gay studies persisted as a series of courses offered in various academic departments and continued to attract significant numbers of students, the small number of faculty sponsors grew tired and found themselves overcommitted. At least in a formal sense, the program fizzled by the mid-1970s.[98]

In November 1972, the executive board of the Gay Students Council of Southern California, an alliance of LGBT student organizations, issued a public statement: "Our unique contribution to the gay 'movement' and to our society will be twofold: First, we will undoubtedly affect our colleagues and peers at our schools, some of the major educational institutions in the state. Second, from our varied locations, for which we seek the necessary education, we will continue to affect the future course of society." These words suggest the degree to which LGBT students saw themselves as key players in "the struggle for gay liberation and human liberation," as USC student and cochair of the Gay Students Council Larry Bernard put it.[99] Like other college students, LGBT students connected their experiences on campus with wider social movements and took it upon themselves to reach into these broader communities. They not only created bridges among activists, writers, artists, and the campus but also offered counternarratives to the prevailing homophobic discourses. In so doing, they increased the connections between education and campus organizing efforts.

CHAPTER FOUR

Opening Up People's Eyes

"In my opinion, a Gay Liberation club is about as ridiculous as a heterosexual club," wrote Muriel Bunton, a student editor of the campus newspaper at Los Angeles City College, in December 1974. "Can you imagine a group of people displaying banners saying 'WE ARE STRAIGHTS?' That is about how relevant Gay Liberation is to education. Sexual attitudes are personal and should not be flaunted in public." In addition, she declared, "Homosexuality is a sickness, but society has made it acceptable way of life."[1] The response was swift. Maxwell Harris, a "Black Gay American male" student, did not need such "biased and unfounded attention" from Bunton, who was also Black, "especially from a sister who seems to know nothing insightful or valuable about her topic." Gay liberation, Harris argued, was relevant "because of the massive ignorance we must combat which Ms. Bunton furthers."[2] Jackson Smith of the college's Gay Student Union (GSU) and the group's faculty adviser, Edward McDonnell, demanded a meeting with the campus president, journalism faculty, and Bunton. The meeting took place, though the president did not attend, and the staff of the *Collegian* subsequently apologized to the GSU. For her part, Bunton said that she "didn't really mean to say all homosexuals are sick." McDonnell described Bunton's column as "a blessing in disguise" and predicted that the GSU "will get the coverage it deserves."[3] The *Collegian* also published a rebuttal in which Smith argued that "gay liberation is education. It grows each year to reach and educate more people: to inform them that we are proud and will no longer accept invisibility."[4]

In addition to DIY efforts and advocacy for curriculum reform, LGBT students promoted campus visibility through various forms of public education. Posting flyers and tabling made their organizations and LGBT issues more visible in campus spaces. Hosting shows or being interviewed on campus radio stations enabled their voices to reach new audiences. Articles and opinion pieces in campus newspapers inserted LGBT perspectives into campus life. Speakers' bureaus became opportunities to share experiences with classmates and others. And public events drew attendees from campus and local communities.

LGBT students used these forms of public education to increase visibility and awareness and contribute to movement building. As Cal State Long Beach GSU president Tony Sacco noted in 1974, public programs were "necessary and valuable to the non-Gay community in precisely the same way [as] consciousness-raising programs of other oppressed minorities such as Blacks, Chicanos, and women."[5] Judy Heckman, the acting president of the GSU at Cal State Los Angeles, suggested in 1975, public programs were one way to "open up lines of communication between gay and non-gay students."[6] As was the case for other minority communities, such public education provided counterstories that challenged the dominant—and mostly negative—assumptions about homosexuality and LGBT people.[7]

Producing and Engaging Media

By producing and engaging various kinds of media, LGBT student organizers were following advice from more seasoned activists, including Gay Activist Alliance member Bob Roth, who advised actively seeking coverage in campus newspapers.[8] In 1971, Sacramento State student Patricia Person came out in a *State Hornet* commentary published under the title, "I am a Lesbian," thereby challenging the perception "in most people's eyes" that doing so was admitting to mental illness.[9] Writing in the *Daily Bruin* in 1974, UCLA GSU leader Dave Johnson declared that "we have been ignored, laughed at, and put down" but hoped that his column would provide a "long-deserved voice of expression: to educate all people on the forms and problems of gay oppression on this campus and elsewhere."[10]

Letters to the editor offered another way to make LGBT viewpoints known and to challenge homophobia.[11] Cal State Long Beach philosophy professor William Bonis wrote a letter critical of the decision to name the GSU the school's outstanding student organization, he suggested that gay students should be prevented from meeting and "barred from the university too on good and simple legal grounds."[12] In response, several GSU members wrote letters to correct the record: "If he is asserting that homosexuals are criminals," student Jim Hansen argued, "he would be wise to study the laws of this state. Although certain sexual practices of homosexuals and heterosexuals alike are illegal, it is not against the law to be gay. On the contrary, homosexuals are protected under the same civil rights legislation that governs all other minorities."[13] A past president of the GSU, Shelly Cooper, described Bonis's letter as "merely a rehash of the usual tiring, hackneyed, misinformed, and outdated views and literature on the subject of homosexuality."[14]

When UC Berkeley GSU president Dave Cash ran for student government, he wrote to the *Daily Californian* that some people had feared being his friend and that people "must come to realize that gay people are human beings who live and love and hurt and cry just like everyone else."[15] Similarly, UCLA student Larry Rodriguez wrote to the *Daily Bruin* about tabling on Bruin Walk for the GSU: one male student approached the table and said to his friend, "Just let me at him. I'll bust his ass," while another student told Rodriguez to "repent and mend my evil ways."[16]

Campus radio stations offered another public venue for LGBT students. UC Santa Barbara's GSU hosted a four-part series on campus radio station KCSB in the spring of 1973. What It Is Like to Be Gay in America explored "gay/non-gay relationships," the "contributions that gay liberation has made to the left," and the politics of gay liberation, with GSU members, "one male and one female," taking questions. One installment included an interview with activist Morris Kight, a founder of the Gay Liberation Front (GLF) in Los Angeles.[17] The Gay People's Union (GPU) at UC Santa Barbara continued this work, with the group's Women's Caucus sponsoring a 1977 program, Her Voice, and the larger organization hosting a weekly program, Coming Out, that was "designed to meet the needs of the gay community."[18]

In addition, CSU Long Beach GSU members served as panelists on gay-themed radio program, Radio Free UCLA; the UCLA GSU contributed to the show as a way to "bridge the gap between the GSU and the campus gay population"; members of UCLA's Lesbian Sisterhood participated in a KPFK program, Lesbian Sisters, which was "directed by gay women in the Los Angeles area"; and the GPU at Chico State discussed the "Coming Out of Gays" on KCHO radio's Call-In 91.[19] Some LGBT students produced their own radio spots. The Stanford GPU created a 1974 public service announcement regarding the American Psychiatric Association's recent decision to remove homosexuality from the Diagnostic and Statistical Manual of Mental Disorders.[20] Lending their voices to the airwaves enhanced the number and kinds of audiences LGBT students could reach, in the process enabling them to claim yet another campus institutional space.

Telling Their Own Stories

Speakers' bureaus offered a particularly powerful way for LGBT students to tell their own stories and thus educate the broader public.[21] LGBT campus-based organizations across California created such bureaus as part of their organizing work at CSU Long Beach, Sacramento State, Cal State Northridge, UC Berkeley, San José State, Stanford, UCLA, USC, UC Santa Barbara, and Cal Poly San Luis Obispo.[22] Student speakers visited classes and residence halls and in some cases community venues. Panelists answered audience questions and/

or just provided human faces for LGBT issues. According to the Women's Caucus of the GPU at Stanford, speakers' bureaus were vehicles for "spreading the word about the true nature of lesbian lifestyles."[23] Some panels challenged academic fields—a chance, as Steve Cronenwalt of the UCLA GSU described, "to discuss gay history, gay oppression, or just the experience of being gay, from an experienced and accurate viewpoint."[24] The speakers' bureau organized by the GPU at CSU Northridge sought to demonstrate that gays were "not a threat to society and aren't deviants," steering clear of politics.[25] To drum up interest, LGBT student organizations distributed flyers, posted advertisements, and sent letters to professors to make them aware of the option.[26]

Participating in speakers' bureaus could be risky for students," "openly expos[ing] them to ostracism as gay individuals." According to Cooper, "Their courageous participation has not only enlightened others, but has also aided the growth of the Gay Students Union."[27] Martin Rogers, a psychology professor who helped organize Sacramento State's speakers' bureau, recalled that participants "had to deal with a lot of horrible questions, hostile questions." Nevertheless, Rogers noted, both panelists and students benefited from the interactions.[28] In 1975, UCLA's GSU newsletter described participating in the speakers' bureau as "enormously ego enhancing and valuable to the gay community."[29]

Cooper explained, "Typically, we'd come into a class bordering on hostility at the beginning," but by the end of the day, "the gays who came into the room wrecked the students' preconceived notions." Instructor Linda Shaw concurred: speakers "opened up people's eyes."[30] A comic book created by "Superdyke" for the GSU at Cal State Long Beach shows two students anticipating a class in which "the homos are going to speak," with images of an effeminate man and a cigar-smoking butch-looking woman with the phrase Mack Truck over their head. The next image depicts the impact of the visit, with students thinking, "They look like real people!"; "I don't know . . ."; and "I wish I had the guts to sit up there and say that."[31]

Some speakers' bureaus ventured beyond campus and into local churches, organizations, and high schools. The speakers' bureau run by Sacramento State's Gay Liberation emerged from a community-based conversation among students and faculty on "gay stereotyping."[32] Graduate student Barbara Bryant participated in off-campus speaking engagements at religious institutions.[33] The GPU at UC Santa Barbara also visited high school classes, challenging local efforts to prevent teachers from inviting "homosexual speakers" to visit.[34] After visiting Cubberly High School, a middle-class, predominantly white school in Palo Alto, and Ravenswood High School, a racially and economically diverse school in East Palo Alto, one participant in the Stanford GPU's speakers' bureau reflected that Ravenswood offered not only more intense initial resistance but also a more authentic dialogue. "Beyond the hostility and banter, communication was possible" at Ravenswood, whereas the "liberal bromides and middle-class politeness" at Cubberly did not feel like a "genuine interchange."[35] Striving for such authenticity was important for LGBT students who sought less overtly political ways of engaging the broader public, allowing them, in Cooper's words, to "get our point across" without "beating a drum or having gay libbers march on campus."[36]

Public Events

Public-facing educational programs constituted perhaps the most common form of campus engagement, addressing a variety of issues—health care, mental health, law, religion, the media, and gays and lesbians in the military.[37] Fresh off its 1971 recognition by Sacramento State, the Society for Homosexual Freedom (which quickly renamed itself the Gay Liberation Front) took over sponsorship of the campus's International Women's Day after the original organizers dropped out. In addition to sessions on "sexism and imperialism" and "women and the law," the event included Patricia Person speaking on "the oppression of the 'Gay Woman.'"[38] At Cal State Long Beach, the GSU brought American Civil Liberties Union (ACLU) attorney Jay Murley to campus to speak regarding "the legal aspects of gay rights."[39] And the Lesbian Sisterhood at UCLA cosponsored a 1974 panel discussion on lesbian health care as part of Women's Health Week.[40] Other events addressing health care focused particularly on counseling services and psychiatry.[41]

LGBT students also organized events that enabled local, regional, and national poets, writers, artists, dancers, musicians, and filmmakers to share their work with the campus community.[42] Some lesbian groups partnered with feminist organizers and/or women's studies programs, as was the case in 1973 when UCLA's Lesbian Sisterhood and Women's Resource Center collaborated on Women's Week, an event that included lesbian arts programs.[43] Many of the artists who participated in these events were very well known in gay liberation and/or lesbian feminist circles, linking campuses with a wider network of LGBT cultural workers and political movements.

The programming at gay and lesbian events of the period typically featured poetry. In April 1971, the students in Sacramento State's GLF and their faculty allies organized a "Gay Scene" symposium, a first for the campus. It featured a reading by Allen Ginsberg, who suggested that his appearance there was "remarkable" since it "was the first time he had been able to read homosexual poetry for that length of time to that many people."[44] The first Gay Awareness Week at UCLA took place in 1974 and included poetry readings by Rita Mae Brown, Paul Mariah, Judy Grahn, and Pat Parker.[45] Freda Smith, a lesbian student who served on Sacramento State's Women's Studies Board, did a reading alongside Mariah, whom the *State Hornet* described as "the poet laureate of the gay movement."[46] When Parker, an African American lesbian, participated in UCLA's 1976 Gay Awareness Week, one attendee noted that "frankly, I get turned off by a lot of women's poetry [but] this one was excellent," while another described it as a "brilliant" and "truly moving event" and urged that Parker be brought back to campus.[47]

The musical artists featured at LGBT-themed events included Blackberri, the Berkeley Women's Music Collective, Malvina Reynolds, Gwen Avery, Linda Tillery and Band, and Maxine Feldman.[48] For Feldman, who wrote and recorded the lesbian-themed "Angry Anthis," which became her signature song, valued playing on college campuses because it was generally safe to be out and because the schools sponsored her appearances.[49] In March 1975, lesbian musicians Margie Adams and Cris Williamson garnered favorable reviews for their Women's Week performances at San José State.[50] And in 1978, the GSU at UC Davis cosponsored a concert by Holly Near and Mary Watkins.[51]

Public film screenings served as opportunities not just for entertainment but also for education. UCLA's GLF presented a late April 1972 film series that included several experimental films by "young, gay filmmakers" and that the organization's Randy Schrader suggested would enable "straight people ... to learn something about us and about themselves."[52] Perhaps because of its proximity to the movie industry, UCLA frequently hosted film screenings that included commentary from filmmakers such as Pat Rocco and Jan Oxenberg.[53] A screening of *Some of Your Best Friends*, directed by Ken Robinson while he was a student at USC and completed in January 1970, was advertised with a flyer declaring, "All you heteros out there!! Have you ever wondered what gay people are all about?" The film was a common choice on other campuses as well.[54] At Stanford, when the GPU and the Lesbian Alliance sponsored a screening of another popular film, the 1978 documentary *Word Is Out*, directed by the Mariposa Film Group, with an accompanying discussion featuring San Francisco activist and politician Harvey Milk and filmmaker Nancy Adair.[55]

Some educational programs focused on sexuality and gender identity, including homosexuality, lesbianism, bisexuality, transsexuality, and transvestism.[56] The GSU at UC Berkeley sponsored a 1973 panel discussion on "militant effeminism" that was titled "Drag Queers Genderfuck Swish."[57] At Cal State Long Beach, the GSU organized a workshop, "Everything You Always Wanted to Know about Homosexuality," and a panel discussion focusing on lesbianism for Women's Week.[58] For speakers, students tapped into the rich networks of LGBT expertise available on campus, in the local community, and in the vibrant LGBT communities in the Los Angeles and San Francisco Bay areas. The speakers at a March 1974 panel discussion on the "Realities of Homosexuality" organized by the GPU at Stanford included Evelyn Hooker from UCLA, San Francisco–based activists Phyllis Lyon and Del Martin, and Rogers, the Sacramento State psychology professor who had helped to organize the Society for Homosexual Freedom. Three hundred people attended.[59]

Early movement organizers were an especially important resource for student organizers, offering opportunities to connect education with politics. At one GSU event at Cal State Fullerton, sessions explored the history of the gay movement, the "new gay consciousness," and the "gay women's movement."[60] LGBT students on other campuses organized similar events showcasing prominent movement folks, including Kight and his fellow Los Angeles activist Ivy Bottini.[61] In 1975, San Francisco State's Gay Academic Union, organized primarily by students with faculty collaboration, sponsored a panel discussion with local activists Jo Daly and Del Martin alongside San Francisco State professor John De Cecco and grad student Albert Bell.[62] And at Los Angeles City College, the GSU brought in Rev. Troy Perry to speak about his experiences as a member of the National Gay Task Force when it met with presidential adviser Margaret (Midge) Costanza in 1977, the first time gay and lesbian activists had been invited to the White House. Also at the meeting was George Raya, a gay lobbyist and former Sacramento State student who had helped organize the school's Society for Homosexual Freedom in 1969.[63]

LGBT student organizations also partnered with feminist organizations on events, particularly "women's weeks," and these collaborations helped transform the feminist groups into lesbian-friendly spaces. At Cal State Long Beach, the GSU provided speakers for Women's Week in 1974.[64] The Stanford GPU budgeted for participation in a 1975 "women's day fair."[65] And after the 1973 and 1974 Women's Week programs at San José State had little lesbian content, prompting complaints, the campus's Lesbian Feminist Alliance got involved in subsequent programs. Lesbian content in 1975 included a standing-room-only keynote by Rita Mae Brown and a panel discussion focused on lesbian lifestyles.[66] The following year, among the Women's Week events were a lesbian sexuality workshop, a lesbian lifestyles panel discussion, and a talk by San Francisco State professor Sally Gearhart, who explained the concept of "women loving women" to four hundred attendees.[67]

Lesbian student involvement clearly helped shape the format and content of events focused on women, as the collaboration between the Lesbian Sisterhood and the Women's Resource Center at UCLA illustrates. The center's January 1973 Women's Day included limited lesbian-themed programming, though the event was billed as highlighting issues "from abortion to gay-straight dialog." Among the participating organizations that passed out information on campus were the Sisterhood bookstore, the ACLU Women's Caucus, sororities, and the Women Law Students Union. Organizer Suz Rosen described the day as "giving women's groups with various messages and no existing forum" the chance "to get together and communicate with each other and with the people they are trying to reach." But Rosen also stressed that "the movement is not all radicals and lesbians, although they are definitely a part of it," and the day closed with a "Vice Versa" dance, where "women will be inviting men."[68]

Two months later, the Gay Sisterhood (soon renamed the Lesbian Sisterhood) formed, and after collaborating with other community-based lesbian groups on an April 1973 "West Coast Lesbian Conference," the organization worked closely with the Women's Resource Center at UCLA to organize a Women's Week. The program included more lesbian related content, including a workshop in which Botini talked about "alternative lifestyles." After Women's Week ended, the Gay Sisterhood wrote to the *Daily Bruin* to express "how much we have to be thankful for here at UCLA. The feeling of sisterhood shared by all the women involved in the Resource Center is really beautiful." In particular, the group celebrated the "solidarity and warmth shared by the gay and straight women at UCLA" and the fact that "women from diverse backgrounds have been given the opportunity to express and share their individual gifts of womanhood."[69]

Such awareness weeks, in general, allowed marginalized students to offer campus communities perspectives that had been "omitted from educational materials" in their student experience to date, as Aviva James, dean of women at El Camino College, noted in 1973.[70] In addition to women's weeks, students organized Black awareness weeks, confabs for Chicano students, and many other kinds of events to raise their campus profiles, educate their communities, and make connections with each other.[71] LGBT students also began organizing such events, thereby creating new platforms and audiences for local, regional, and national LGBT experts, artists, musicians, writers, and activists.

As early as the mid-1970s and particularly by the early part of the following decade, these efforts were increasingly billed as gay awareness days, gay awareness weeks, gay pride, or gay and lesbian awareness weeks.[72] LGBT students were the main organizers across many kinds of campuses, including Stanford and other private universities; the California State University campuses in San José, San Francisco, Long Beach, and Los Angeles; the UC campuses at Berkeley, Santa Cruz, Los Angeles, and Santa Barbara; El Camino and other community college; and Sacramento City College and Los Angeles City College.[73] Attendees included students, faculty, staff, and community members.

The GSU at CSU Fullerton characterized its Gay Awareness Week as a way to "educate the campus community on the political, social, economic, psychic, and religious oppression of gay men and lesbian women," especially for "non-gay people."[74] Similarly, CSU Long Beach GSU organizer Mark Andrea described Gay Pride Week as "designed to give recognition to campus gays and to offer education to the university community."[75] The *Advocate*'s coverage of UCLA's first Gay Awareness Week described it as an "ambitious five day event for this super straight campus" that sought to "educate the general student body about gay life, which up until recently had been only a topic of whisper."[76] As these descriptions suggest, LGBT students placed great faith in education—particularly of non-LGBT attendees—as an organizing strategy.

Awareness weeks were also opportunities to engage in political education and advocacy. Programs focusing on gay liberation, gay pride, gay rights, equal rights, and sometimes human rights were especially common. Stanford's June 1974 Gay Pride Week, dubbed "The Spirit of '76," focused on "developing full civil rights for gay men and women in time for the United States bicentennial," in the words of the *Bay Area Reporter*.[77] The 1975 Gay Pride Day at San José State included workshops on "feminism and gay lib," "legal rights," and "political action" as well as a "human rights commission."[78] Gay Awareness Week at Cal State Long Beach in 1976 featured a keynote by Mattachine Society D.C. organizer Frank Kameny on "Political Opportunities and Responsibilities for Gay People within Traditional Politics."[79] Additional speakers included the *Advocate* publisher David Goodstein, activist Nancy Briggs, and Jo Daly and Bill Johnson, who discussed sexism in the gay movement.[80] At Cal State Fullerton, GSU member Bob Gardner told the *Los Angeles Times* that such events were opportunities to "present our side" and avoid being "stomped over by the Anita Bryants and the John Briggses." The references to these antigay activists were particularly noteworthy in light of the fact that the school lay in Briggs's California Assembly district and that the student government had refused to provide funding for the event.[81]

These events could spark both enthusiasm and conflict. In the spring of 1976, the Gay Academic Union at San Francisco State hosted a "Symposium '76."[82] Professor John De Cecco had conceived the idea and collaborated with students to create a different kind of academic conference.[83] Sessions included "Lesbian/Feminist Perspectives across Disciplines," "Gay Student Power," "Gay Prisoners," "Gays in the Media," "Gay History," "Gay Politics," "Third World Gays," and "Lesbians and Music." The three-day gathering also featured caucus meetings (including a lesbian caucus), musical performances, a dance, and interest group meetings, all of which "sparked lively interchanges."[84] Attendees came from all over California and included students (many from campus-based LGBT organizations), faculty from more than a dozen colleges and universities, activists from such organizations as Bay Area Gay Liberation, as well as others.[85] Commentator George Mendenhall called it "the most amazing and ambitious celebration of homosexuality in this bicentennial year."[86] Joe Whitney, a member of the GSU at UCLA, met "leftists, rightists, coalitionists, separatists, gay spoilers, gay fairies . . . gay androgynes" and more. "Most of all," Whitney concluded, "I learned that gay people are living and loving and creating a world."[87]

However, journalist Randy Shilts suggested in the *Advocate* that the conference had an "undercurrent of protest." The Gay Students Alliance from the nearby City College of San Francisco picketed the event, distributing a flyer suggesting that organizers "offered lesbians and Third World people only 'token' participation in panels."[88] According to the City College students, the conference reflected "the de facto classism, racism and sexism of both the academic and the gay ghetto" and sought only to make the world "safe for white, male, professional gays."[89] Don Liles, a City College faculty member and adviser to the Gay Students Alliance, privately described the symposium as "remarkably successful" but "incredibly divisive in the gay community": few women participated, and some LGBT student organizations around the state refused to become involved. While Liles thought the accusations of "academic elitism" were unsubstantiated, he deplored the infighting.[90]

John S. Blackburn, a student at San Francisco State and co-organizer of the event, responded that the "undercurrent of protest that Mr. Shilts (or that his publisher) saw was the most healthy thing to come out of this entire affair." Blackburn acknowledged that most of the conference organizers were white men but contended that the City College students had known about the event from the beginning yet had failed to "get their acts together and participate." Blackburn urged that rather than "wollowing [sic] in self-pity for being oppressed because of one's sex or color," the City College student reevaluate just how "out" they wanted to be.[91]

The involvement of LGBT people of color influenced the planning of awareness weeks. GAYTHINK IV was organized in October 1978 by the GSU at California State University, Los Angeles in partnership with Latinos Unidos, a community-based organization. The program included a diverse array of professors, students, activists, and others. Musical performers included Richard Gonzales. The welcome was delivered by the director of the Educational Opportunity Program. Ivy Bottini participated in a panel discussion on "aging in the gay subculture," while other sessions focused on "being gay and handicapped" and on "racism in the gay community." Panelists included members of Lesbians of Color and of the Alliance of Black Gays. Latinos Unidos hosted a panel, "The View through a Latin Window," though all the participants apparently were male.[92]

Events organized by LGBT students provoked pushback on many campuses. Flyers and posters were destroyed or defaced, student governments refused to provide funding, and critics wrote irate letters to campus newspapers. CSU Long Beach's 1975 Gay Pride Week sparked a variety of negative reactions—two men "claiming to be Christians ran across the grass declaring with placards and loud noise that we have among us queers, fags and half-humans"; someone spit on a glass case displaying a Gay Pride Week sign; event flyers were torn down and replaced with ones that read "Gays are the scum of the earth"; and letters to the student newspaper ran "10–1 against gays and ... coverage of the event."[93] One writer argued that Associated Students should not fund such a "small minority" and that "such bias" in favor of gays violated "the spirit of a democratic campus community."[94] Another correspondent was "disgusted and repelled by this whole fiasco of Gay Pride Week."[95] And still another letter suggested that the event be renamed "Social and Psychological Aberration Week" so that "all alcoholics, junkies, schizophrenics, and Psychopaths could join in the festivities."[96]

Similarly UCLA's 1976 Gay Awareness Week was accused of normalizing support for a lifestyle one writer described as "about as low and degrading as a human being can take himself." The author suggested that another awareness week "could accomplish one thing—to wake up those who still retain decency and some sense of morality in their lives and send the homosexuals back where they belong—in the closets."[97] Another critic equated Gay Awareness Week with "Rapist Awareness Week or Murderer Awareness Week" and compared contemporary Los Angeles to Sodom and ancient Rome: "America, LA, UCLA etc. is on the beginning of this same degradation."[98]

Despite such reactions, however, these events garnered significant support and praise, indicating that organizers had indeed reached their educational goals. One nongay writer was proud to have an opportunity to support his gay friends, offering them "solidarity as I would any other emerging oppressed minority self-liberation. I hope they won't give up on us."[99] One supporter at UCLA believed that Gay Awareness Week had served "to enlighten and educate the university community as a whole, in particular the heterosexual majority, on the social and political concerns of the gay population" and vowed to "continue to support any organization whose primary aim is the destruction of sexism in our macho-male oriented society and the preservation of individual rights, human dignity and freedom."[100]

Film historian Vito Russo, a frequent speaker on college campuses in the 1970s, attended many events organized by LGBT students. In 1976, Russo told the *Advocate* that these gatherings had originally provided opportunities for "movement oriented gay people" to meet for "strategy sessions" as well as allowed "both the rad-libs and the gay person in the street come together . . . to ask each other questions." As students became more involved, however, these events became "fused with a delightful gay imagination and sensibility" and got "a hell of a lot better with increased gay student visibility," to the point that "some conference weekends are approaching the sublime. They are becoming joyous celebrations of all that has been repressed in us through countless years in the closet."[101]

At one Cal State Long Beach event, Russo recalled, "Over the campus loudspeakers from the front lawn on the quadrangle, the voice of lesbian feminist Rita Mae Brown is exhorting men to be 'reborn as feminists' and urging her sisters and brothers to begin to 'look for each other in each other's eyes.' And all around you, people are being gay." After such events, "telephone numbers are exchanged and a network is formed from city to city. Gay people from different cultures and experiences will meet again at the next conference. They'll dance a little and tell each other some more about what it's like to be gay in our America." In addition, according to Russo, "Along the way, the others are hearing too: the straight students who write in to their school newspapers supporting the gay students, the faculty advisors to the gays who display the kind of courage and sense of purpose needed, the administrators who learn about their student body in a new way, and the gay people in the closet who watch in wonder as the living proof that they are not alone gets off buses and planes to visit their school.[102]

Awareness weeks and other kinds of educational programs and projects had tremendous meaning for LGBT students as well as for the wider lesbian and gay movement. Students embraced their role in the broader movement and used it to bring increased attention to LGBT issues and concerns as well as creative and artistic expression.

CHAPTER FIVE

Fostering Queer Creativity

In December 1972, Sacramento State College's Cultural Programs, women's studies, and some "on and off campus Lesbian Feminists" sponsored a three-day "Colloquium on Lesbian Women: Myth and Reality." Like other awareness events, the colloquium included a variety of speakers and panel presentations, including San Francisco State professor Sally Gearhart, Daughters of Bilitis cofounders Del Martin and Phyllis Lyon, and activist and writer Rita Mae Brown. The programming incorporated various forms of creative expression, including a performance by local musician Joan Hand and readings by poets Pat Parker and Judy Grahn. The Sacramento State student newspaper praised the colloquium for "exploring and exploding the myths of lesbians here on our campus."[1]

Le Theatre Lesbien, founded by Sacramento State students Cherie Gordon and Matty Wallace later known as Patricia One Person, performed an original play, *The Homobrontosaurus*, with "two lesbian brontos," Hanna and Harold, garbed in vinyl costumes designed and made by Person, with purple pubic hair and multiple breasts—hand-cast latex reproductions of the performers' breasts.[2] "We're the homobrontosauruses," sang the women, "loving our clitorises, living in the forest, the homobrontosaurus, lovely lesbiotica, prehistoric erotica."[3] Based on a poem written by Person, the play was informed by theatrical traditions of farce, satire, and commedia dell'arte. The troupe embraced fantasy and play in productions that explored such serious feminist issues as rape, lesbian sexuality, and male supremacy.[4] As Person recalled, *The Homobrontosaurus* was "a silly production, it was fun, and it made a statement," especially about women's bodies and lesbian sexuality, defining both on their own terms.[5]

Gordon, Person, and other LGBT students embraced creative expression as part world-making—queering campus through culture—and part organizing strategy.[6] Bringing LGBT artists, writers, filmmakers, and musicians to campus connected organizers to vibrant cultural scenes unleased by gay liberation and lesbian feminism, linking students and others on campus to those wider movements. Yet as Le Theatre Lesbien illustrates, showcasing queer creativity also included what LGBT students themselves performed or produced: they organized numerous venues to share such creative work, allowing those students to (re)imagine themselves in new ways—as LGBT people. Their organizational newsletters highlighted student poetry, fiction, and art.[7] Writing groups provided valuable spaces in which to share work.[8] Coffeehouses, cabarets, cultural nights, talent nights, and creativity nights became public (or semipublic) spaces where students could read their poetry and perform music.[9] All of these creative endeavors enhanced the protests, speeches, speakers' bureaus, peer advocacy, and educational programming LGBT students deployed as tools to mobilize and reach new audiences.

This chapter explores three types of queer creative practice—poetry, theater, and gender transgressive drag and genderfuck—to understand how they supported students' expressive, communicative, and political goals. These creative practices featured many common LGBT themes—coming out, the meaning of liberation, and the expression of gender identity and same-sex sexuality—as well as themes that were unique to particular students, campuses, or communities. LGBT students to expressed queer voices, explored identities, and connected creative practices to their organizing.[10] While differences in age, race, ethnicity and sexuality were critical and reflected the intersectional realities of LGBT student organizers, claims of commonality regarding their experiences as LGBT people lessened the alienation many students experienced on campus by connecting them to wider worlds they had not previously imagined. These forms of creative expression became important and visible manifestations of liberation in words, performance, and gender presentation.[11]

Poetry

Poetry created and/or shared by LGBT students blended both personal expression and political analysis, making it an accessible, meaningful, and powerful tool for organizing.[12] When the Gay Student Union (GSU) at San José State hosted a "creativity night" in 1977, student-read poetry was an important part of the festivities.[13] "While the poems were being read," the campus newspaper reported, "people began to search the room for friends—present or potential. Flashing smiles, winks and head nods passing between them provided the backdrop for oratories lamenting lost loves, gay bar courtships, and one night stands. Some sat slouched in their chairs, eyes closed while the poets droned on. Others leaned forward intently, hanging on every word. Whatever the style, all were enthusiastic and each speaker received a prolonged round of applause after every poem."[14]

As Barry Laine contended in 1976, poetry's ability to capture the ambiguity of LGBT identities and experiences through words became a movement itself, even if it was "green, rude, confused and terribly quixotic."[15] Poetry became a particularly important vehicle for expressing lesbian identity, visibility, and political analysis.[16] As Paula Bennett argues, it "had become a grassroots movement" by the 1970s, with poems appearing on "posters, T-shirts, and broadsides" as "revolutionary shibboleths" of the time. For many gay and lesbian poets, political analysis was particularly militant, a "historic necessity," as Steve Abbott argues. Many LGBT students embraced the genre as well.[17]

Charles Thorp, a San Francisco State College creative writing student, regularly connected creativity with gay liberation, contending that homosexuals "must develop the tools of pride to plant the seeds of freedom"; one of those tools "must surely be our creativity, our sensitivity, our art."[18] Thorp put these ideas into action. In August 1970, on the heels of cofounding the Gay Liberation Front (GLF) at San Francisco State, he organized a series of workshops for LGBT students and included his own poetry in his opening remarks:

> We did not seek
> > the underground
> > like rabbits
> > timid from birth
> we were called passive pansies
> > now we have come to the surface
> > to redefine ourselves
> we are violent fairies
> > each of us has that hate
> > for those that Poe-like
> > fashion buried our souls alive
> we were driven
> > from the sun that
> we should never
> > see it as the light
> > of ourselves
> > that we should see
> > only in whispers
> > and that
> we should never know of
> > heroes for
> we were to be enemies of the State
> > and but half-lovers in our Community
> we need not have sympathy for our devil
> > HeShe rises to be light upon

>   all mountains
>   where never again will
>   we be hidden undersight
>   for through and with HeShe our devil-god
>   we are all of us together to be reborn.[19]

This poem features several themes recurred in LGBT students' poetry: hiding ("underground"), oppression ("buried," "driven from the sun," "whispers," never knowing one's "heroes"), shifting gender identities ("HeShe"), coming out and being part of a wider community (repetition of *we*, "coming to the surface," "we are all of us together to be reborn"). Politics was also prominent, including a wider and intensifying social movement (from "passive pansies" to "violent fairies"), as was criticism of the state as a source of oppression (as "enemies" and "half lovers").

Living with (or transcending) secrecy was a particularly popular theme. In "Not Who I Am," Harriette Frances explored having to hide in the closet at work, lamenting,

> Because my nine-to-five friends
> Insist on my meeting
> The men who will
> Think I am
> Not who I am
> I carry my hidden self
> Heavy, from nine-to-five
> And in your six-o-clock
> Arms I can
> Lay my self down.[20]

Similarly, one UCLA student wrote,

> I have too many secrets
> Crowding at the gate
> Waiting for release
> Waiting for someone
> Who can hear them
> In a true context.[21]

In some cases, poets explored the theme in metaphorical ways, including references to darkness and shadows. In "We," Shaundel Jacobs described longing for a lover as like being in a place that is "running in the shadows / the boundaries of its solitary radiance," and "clinging to the presence of life without."[22] Other poems explored hiding, loneliness, and isolation: in the words of one UCLA student,

Everywhere
A real lack of true emotion
—a "live" performance on record
—a game of
fool all the people
all the time.[23]

Other poems explored liberation and/or freedom. One 1977 poem imagines freedom as running:

IT COULD BE, YOU AND ME
RUNNING WILD, RUNNING FREE
EXPLORING NEVER DONE BEFORE
IT COULD BE YOU AND ME EVER MORE
RUNNING WILD, RUNNING FREE . . .
BABY
YOU AND ME.[24]

Freedom included coming out.[25] "Dear Mom and Dad letters" were one format. "It feels so good to release the truth, my feelings, to you / that I am a gay man," noted one 1974 example from Stanford. "that I am able to relate / emotionally, intellectually, sexually, / and spirityally with other men."[26] Other coming-out poems drew on images of dark landscapes (at night or in fog or rain) or physical states (blindness, being asleep, feeling cold), while others emphasized the interplay of darkness and light with images of melting ice, sunshine, springtime, other natural settings.[27] "BEING OPEN is contagious / Really, there's no other way," noted one. "Hiding's only for the guilty / LIBERATION is today." Similarly, a poem by Ernie Rael noted,

In darkness, I did live
Alone with my despair
Till in my soul I found
The strength to shout and dare
"Watch me as I
Live and love, and
See the feelings
'Tween man and man."
My life became open
To any who would share
My joy in being gay
Near people who're aware.[28]

The expression of same-sex sexuality—love, longing, desire, and physical connection—and gender expression were equally important themes. In one 1974 poem, Maureen Kennedy described the joy of

> cutting class to steal more time for
> each other
> then cramming like hell at finals
> and collapsing in pleasure when it was done.

Ultimately, however, "the world wasn't ready / for our love / and perhaps our love wasn't ready for the world."[29]

Some poems explored sexual attraction, expression, and rejection:

> My hands trace
> circles on your skin
> stroking circular patterns
> to thread through the
> dark forest of you
> Lotion Locomotion
> heat spreading out
> in thin streams
> to form a pool of liquid fire for me
> At last the
> sadness in the
> back of your eyes
> is drowned
> and I am free.[30]

San José State student and GSU leader Paul Boneberg explored the dance of seduction and rejection in "Diamond Hard Words":

> In the bar by the dance floor I think:
> "This bar was not made for thought
> —no the music is too loud and the stares too long to begin,"
> to understand the whys of these faces and bodies
> or the joy and anxiety which struggle therein.

The narrator catches the eye of a "sleek bodied boy," he turns away, "expression defiant and his face saying 'i didn't want you anyway.'"[31] And in "Pardon Me, Beautiful, Where Did You Buy Your Tits?" Vincent Fanucchi explored drag, describing a "Frederick's of Hollywood baby / With curves built of rubber and steel"; "friends call him Pete / But here we all know her as Katie," and she unwraps a cigar, looking for a match "in a shiny gold handbag with real rhinestone catch."[32]

FOSTERING QUEER CREATIVITY 65

Some poetry used humor to explore serious subjects. "Ye Yeare in Reviewe," by "Geoffrey Chancre," described the challenges of organizing UCLA's first Gay Awareness Week: "We muste," declared David, "son of John / Affyrm to alle wch syde we're on; / Justice comes nott to ye meeke; / We shall have a Gaye Awarenesse Weeke!" When facing the thorny decision about whether to affiliate with the Student Legislative Council, organizers pondered the idea "that theye myght consecrate / our queste for University golde / ye keyes to wch they dyd holde." But the event was a success, and "wyth weathre faire," organizers were pleased "To viewe alle who cayme to speake / at UCLA's first Gaye Awareness Weeke."[33]

Other poetry was more directly political, exploring such themes as solidarity, oppression, resistance, liberation, sexism, racism, and homophobia. In 1970, the San José State GLF printed "The Inward Monitor," by Rebecca Lynn Williamson, who challenged readers to imagine the speaker as a mirror that "can but cast back upon you/what you have shed upon me": "with your contempt to your fellow man / be his skin black, yellow, or white / and yea / this too shall be returned to you."[34] Dave Johnson of the GSU at UCLA took up the commonly deployed stereotype of gays and lesbians as child molesters, connecting the critique to the war in Southeast Asia:

> They turn and say we are child molesters—
> But theirs is the napalm
> That seared the bodies
> Of a million Cambodian children ...
> I hear the word "queer"
> Feel the sting of contempt
> From the innocent eyes
> Of a child of six ...
> I remember the morning you left,
> A playless adult ...
> They are the molesters of children,
> And the child is us all.[35]

Similarly, UCLA student Joe Whitney connected persecution of witches to gay oppression: "Let us be faggots kindling fire / Let fire burn the witches of oppression / Let us be fairies dancing on the ashes."[36] Poetry by lesbian students especially explored intersecting political themes.[37] Lesbian students at Stanford wrote poems about sisterhood that transcended sexual orientation and race, peace politics, childbirth, male supremacy and violence, mother/daughter relationships, and the daily struggle of women in society and efforts to fight back.[38]

Theater

LGBT students also embraced theater as a form of creative expression, including guerrilla or street theater as well as formal productions. In so doing, these students engaged in what Lucy Robinson calls a "counter cultural approach to performative political practice."[39] Examples of events sponsored by students include Rebecca Valrajean's *The Lavender Troubadour*, a one-woman exploration of involvement in the "gay political movement" performed at San Francisco State in 1974, and *Virgin Beach*, staged as part of Gay Pride Week at CSU Long Beach in 1975.[40] "It's about time gays allowed themselves some happy endings," noted *Virgin Beach* creator Richard Gray in the campus newspaper, which praised the production not only for its merits as a theatrical work but also for its "educational impact concerning gay lifestyles."[41]

Few plays exploring LGBT student life from this era survive. One that does not was written by UCLA English major Larry Duplechan: *Optimistic Voices* was set in the GSU office.[42] One that does survive is Mike Rosen's 1970 play, *To Live and Die in Berkeley: A Verse Play in Three Acts*, focused on Hero, a student from Cottonwood, Idaho, who meets "college drop-out" Yippie at a protest in People's Park. Stage directions describe protesters carrying such signs as "Gay Liberation Front," "Suck Cock and Beat the Draft!" "Oral Is Moral!" and "Blow for Freedom!" Hero and Yippie discover that they are both gay and break into a song: "I'm so happy I could cry! / In a world of couples, I am not alone / In a world of soul-mates, I shall have my own / I'm so happy I could cry!" The play ends with the two men getting married by a minister in the Church of the Pregnant Virgin.[43]

UC Berkeley student Konstantin Berlandt turned an exchange with Charles Thorp into a handwritten dialogue that explored the challenges straight people faced in understanding gay identity by comparing the dynamic to that of whites seeking to understand Black struggles for liberation. After the straight friend leaves, the Thorp character reflects, "He was getting uptight. I could see it. But the Blacks are not going to stay in their ghettoes. He's going to meet lots of gay people and they're going to continue to make him uptight. And, he's going to see gay people calling each other brother and sister. He'll see Gay soul and Gay love. Honkies don't understand that. Straight people don't understand that. Brotherhood, that's what the revolution is about."[44]

The Homobrontosaurus was not Le Theatre Lesbien's first production. The small informal group of lesbian students and at least two gay male students originally performed skits at the Off Key, a lesbian bar in West Sacramento. According to Person, the group "spontaneously came about through... friendships" but became more formalized through performances on college campuses and at small venues in Berkeley and San Francisco and most notably at the West Coast Lesbian Conference at UCLA in 1973.⁴⁵ Edgar Carpenter, who had been instrumental in the founding of the Society for Homosexual Freedom at Sacramento State, came along to UCLA play male roles but was not well received, and the group chose to forgo "political" types of events in the future.⁴⁶

Both Person and Gordon had had connections with the women's studies program and Sacramento State and at Sacramento City College.⁴⁷ The first productions were organic and often lacked very formal scripts; instead, group members worked out the dialogue together onstage. To kick off Sexuality Pride Week at Sacramento City College in 1973, Le Theatre Lesbien performed *Robin Screw*, a riff on Robin Hood that explored lesbian sexuality and other feminist themes. The characters included Robin Screw, who "screwed the rich and screwed the poor too"; Fairy Marian, a lesbian godmother; and Charlotte and Stephanie, who seek revenge against Robin Screw for sexual assault.⁴⁸

Gordon and Person spent two years in Australia, returning to Sacramento inspired by how Australian women organized dances, rallies, and creative outlets, including one-off "supper shows" performed in rented spaces and followed by dancing, as well as by lesbian feminist musical groups such as the Shameless Hussies.⁴⁹ One of the first productions Gordon and Person staged when they were back in Sacramento was *Dykes on Parade: A Hersterical, Herstorical Theatrical Review of Lesbian Fashions*, performed twice at Sacramento City College in 1976.⁵⁰ With a cast of mostly college students and few professional actors, the performances drew full houses, and the audience responded with "a five minute standing ovation at the final curtain."⁵¹ The sketches featured lesbians wearing period costumes from various historical settings: Sappho ("long tunic, sandals"), Radclyffe Hall ("Spanish waist coat and hat, tailored pants, frilly shirt"), Gertrude Stein ("Sloppy sweater, baggy shirt"), and "Political Dyke" ("vest, dyke cap, tennis shoes, badges, picket sign").⁵² Participant Therese Quinn later described the production as chronicling "a still-invisible lesbian herstory" that "made our lesbian-filled present and hinted at a sexually adventurous, woman-loving future, too."⁵³

The performance, along with the visibility of the Gay People's Union (GPU) at Sacramento City College, prompted a challenge from Los Rios Community College District board member Robert Lynch. Linda Sanchez had written to the board to express her "appreciation for the production of 'Dykes on Parade,'" prompting Lynch to respond that if he had his way, "we will have no more of these damn fools on any of our campus sites. I expect now the fags will ask for equal time and probably other assorted and bizarre weirdos will want to put on shows." On the "bright side," however, "we kept a lot of lesbians off the streets for two nights running." Lynch also argued that taxpayer money should not be used "to provide a meeting place for deviates." At least fifteen gay students and their allies from Sacramento City College and American River College attended the board's next meeting "to ask that Lynch be censured for making slanderous statements about gay students on district stationery," but the board refused. When GPU organizer Ka'rtiikeya Mattos expressed concern about the impact of Lynch's comments on "young gay people," Lynch said that he couldn't care less.[54]

Subsequent productions by Le Theatre Lesbien included *Homophobia*, a "short bawdy comedy" that was first performed as part of Sacramento State's 1978 Gay Awareness Week and that addressed recent attacks on gay-rights measures, among other themes. A poster for the play shows a drawing of Anita Bryant holding a large cross.[55] Le Theatre Lesbien also performed *Homophobia* during Sacramento City College's 1978 Gay Awareness Week.[56]

In 1976, the troupe moved beyond the stage, crashing a parade celebrating the U.S. Bicentennial. Costumed, sign-carrying members of the group joined the procession, chanting slogans about remembering lesbians. Dressed as the Statue of Liberty, Quinn marched behind a contingent from a Baptist church, knowing "that it meant something really powerful that we had a banner that said 'Lesbians come out after two hundred years of oppression!' I knew it was political to be in that parade."[57] Le Theatre Lesbien also marched in Sacramento's first gay pride parade in 1979, but by that point had mostly disbanded.[58]

Le Theatre Lesbien's productions illustrate the interplay between creative expression and organizing for LGBT students. As Gordon recalled, "I think we thought, and we held sacred, that humor was so important in getting our message across, that if we came out with something heavy-handed, something more dramatic, it wouldn't have the effect that we did. I think people really needed humor at this time."[59] According to Person, "We felt the arts were a really great way to politicize people, to educate people, to open people's minds." Art, Person concluded, "is more subtle, it speaks on a different" and "more personal level" from political debates, and "people take it in in a different way."[60]

Drag and Genderfuck

Students' challenges to campus gender norms took many forms, but perhaps one of the most visible—and complicated—was drag and/or genderfuck. As a form of queer creativity, drag and genderfuck became a means of exploring identity, a form of self-expression, and a part of campus organizing. Genderfuck, which Shaun Cole defines as mixing "elements of both male and female dress together in order to confuse the gender signals given by those pieces of clothing," was a very visible way students challenged gender assumptions in everyday ways, with some embracing the look to attend class or for LGBT events.[61] For some students, the embrace of drag, long a part of queer culture, was more complicated, a symbol of the "gay establishment" and an "anathema to gay liberation," as Todd Ormsbee argues.[62] Moreover, as Betty Luther Hillman documents, some feminists (including lesbians) critiqued drag as akin to whites wearing blackface.[63]

The complicated relationship between LGBT students, drag and genderfuck is evident in a 1973 program organized by the UC Santa Barbara GSU. The Gay Follies, billed as a "fashion show in drag," featured the Madcamps, a Santa Barbara group of "female impersonators." One person wrote anonymously to the student newspaper "on behalf of those gay people who feel a little misrepresented by that display of homosexual talents" and argued that the performers did "not represent, typify, characterize, depict or prefigure 'the average gay person' today." GSU cochair Richard Robbins defended the event as seeking to "simply provide an alternative form of entertainment from the stale celluloid reruns to a campy, enjoyable, live group such as the Madcamps," not all of whom were gay. Moreover, Robbins criticized the writer's refusal to reveal their name: the members of the GSU were "out of the closets, open, honest with ourselves and others, and quite proud to be gay."[64]

Many students found drag and genderfuck intentionally playful, liberatory, and political. LGBT student organizations hosted events exploring genderfuck or sponsored drag shows. Others welcomed attendees to don drag and/or genderfuck forms of dress at dances and events.[65] Individual students praised drag and/or genderfuck as liberation. James B. Harris, a student at Lone Mountain College in San Francisco, attended a Palace Theater performance by the Cockettes, a gender-bending group that embodied the "San Francisco gay counterculture" with elements of "flower power, drag, communal living and camp."[66] Describing the venue as "a beautiful place to be gay—crowded with the extraordinary, the bizarre decadents" who "created an underground renaissance in San Francisco," Harris reflected that these forms of expression took root because they "felt good." Dressing this way "was new and outrageous. It was a life style. We didn't just put it on just before the concert and take it off when we left the theater."[67]

Other California college students embraced or at least experimented with drag and genderfuck. One person attended a UCLA GLF meeting in drag, "perfect down to the last detail of his blue eye shadow."[68] When the Stanford GPU brought the Angels of Light to campus in 1974, student Robert Croonquist went to campus in drag, the only time he did so.[69] UCLA GSU member Steve Cronenwalt "skirted the boundaries of genderfuck," wearing makeup, "pink daisy-dukes and an open shirt," platform shoes, and hair styled to resemble that of Dr. Frank-N-Furter in The Rocky Horror Picture Show.[70]

For some students, drag became synonymous with exploring their own gender identities. In 1975, San Francisco State's David Cawley, a creative writing student, characterized drag not as just a "matter of sequins and falsies" but also as "the image and the attitude one chooses to project": ways of dress demonstrated that the "boundaries between the sexes are mostly artificial." Drag allowed Cawley to "become the person I want to be."[71] Moreover, some students saw drag through lenses informed by liberation politics. Mark Thompson, a San Francisco State journalism student, observed that Tede Mathews and other younger folks were challenging old-style drag with a revolutionary approach informed by feminism and attention to working-class identities. For Mathews, such drag constituted an "extreme agglomeration of sexual identities": "Right now, Gay Lib has a lot of maleness to deal with."[72]

Dances and Halloween parties offered LGBT students opportunities for experimentation. A 1970 GSU dance at UC Berkeley drew four hundred participants, mostly men, with music provided by the Purple Earthquake and Backwater Rising. Although no men attended in drag, "a few obviously had donned wigs for the occasion."[73] Similar events also took place at UC Berkeley (a 1972 "Renaissance Costume Ball" sponsored by the GSU), CSU Long Beach (a Halloween dance on the Queen Mary to cap off the 1976 Gay Awareness Week), and California State University, Los Angeles (a "Masquerade Dance" held as part of the GAYTHINK IV conference organized by the GSU and Latinos Unidos).[74]

At one dance organized by the GSU at UCLA, Duplechan wore platform shoes, bell-bottom jeans, a multicolored tube top, and "some judiciously applied eye makeup." Though he was seeking to re-create what he described as a genderfuck look modeled on that of the New York Dolls, the result was less New York punk scene and more Pointer Sisters: people saw him and thought, "Look at that cute Black lesbian." He vowed never to dress that way again: "I was mistaken for a woman quite a lot anyway" and "got hit on by lesbians all the time," but "I was just becoming a man, and I wanted to be perceived by gay men as a man." He did not want to be "gender vague."[75]

Some lesbian feminist students criticized drag. Donna Hughes-Oldenburg, who took classes at Stanford and was involved with the GPU's Women's Collective, saw drag as a "co-opting of culture."[76] When the Angels of Light performed in drag at a GLF dance at San Francisco State, "many of the gay women were extremely angered at the mimicking" and called the performance sexist.[77] LGBT student organizations' programming occasionally approached the issue directly. When the Gay Students Coalition of San Francisco (also known as the Gay Students Coalition of the San Francisco Bay Area) hosted educational programs in the fall of 1974, one session addressed "radical drag and feminism."[78]

But lesbian students also experimented with gender presentation. Doing so could be liberating, a way to challenge gender norms, often in contradictory ways.[79] Jan Aura embraced lesbian feminism while attending UCLA in the mid-1970s, dressing "in plaid shirts . . . and Frye boots" and wearing her hair short.[80] Quinn, in contrast, adopted a more genderfuck-inspired look: "found lingerie, glitter on my cheekbones, and bright colors. I always like to wear purple and green together." She perceived putting together her thrifted and vintage outfits "as a form of art." But other lesbians believed that Quinn's "artist hippy look" was not suitable for a "proper lesbian": "You didn't dress like I dressed. You didn't wear dresses.... You didn't wear makeup. You cut your hair short, and you dressed in that sort of '70s other stereotyped style"—vest, cap, boots—a "lesbian feminist academic look."[81]

Some LGBT students saw embracing drag or genderfuck on campus as intentionally political. While attending California State University, Long Beach, Lee Mentley adopted a genderfuck look inspired by the Cockettes: denim jeans with sequins, a pink baby-doll top, and a parasol, sometimes accessorized with a handbag or a "Popeye lunch pail." He adopted this style because it was "important ... for me to be different."[82] Jack Fertig, later known as Sister Boom Boom of the Sisters of Perpetual Indulgence, dressed in drag to attend classes at UC Berkeley in the early 1970s—"the only drag queen" in the GSU.[83] He saw it as a "bizarre street theater kind of thing, just fucking with people's heads," and leaving "a trail of glitter from the elevator to my room."[84]

In 1971, Freda Smith, a lesbian student activist and member of the Women's Studies board at Sacramento State, read her poem "Dear Dora / Dangerous Derek Diesel Dyke" to the California legislature. Smith, who also served as co-chair of the California Committee for Law Reform, a group working to decriminalize homosexual sex, saw the poem as way to synthesize her experience as a lesbian and activist.[85]

The poem's main character, Dora, is threatened with exposure:

> dear dora
>
> we'd fire you   if we knew
> what you knew   what you do

Dora meets (or becomes?) "dangerous derek diesel dyke," a character who claims power through clothing and attitude:

> Friday night dangerous derek diesel dyke   dyke
> clad in low down
> mean   lean   jeans
> hugging at her hips
> molding her hips   in a bold brazen
> look at me   see
> i'm real   feel

Going braless as well ("nothing artificial under there / just skin   she's in"), Dora/Derek challenges the status quo ("thumb your nose at the gun-hip-cock-cop"; "thumb your nose against the priest-men / with their mouths full of the fires of hell"). The poem mentions lobotomies, references electroshock and aversion therapies, celebrates lesbian sexuality, and ruminates on Dora/Derek's loneliness before closing with the lines

> shazam
> shazam
> goddam   shazam
> you think derek's the tragedy
> don't you america.

Smith read "Dear Dora" in public on multiple occasions, including on the Sacramento State campus in 1973 and at a retreat for ministers in the Metropolitan Community Church, where she eventually became a minister.[86]

LGBT student activists found sharing their experiences through creative expression to be a powerful organizing method.[87] This creative work exploded myths about homosexuality, planted the seeds of freedom and liberation, and confronted the status quo in vibrant and engaging ways that often included humor. And much of this work articulated a distinctly political analysis of gender, sexuality, and sexual orientation as well as a distinctly political critique of homophobia and oppression. Moreover, creative expression enabled LGBT students to flout and challenge that oppression and to incorporate new ways of being, living, loving, and creating into campus life.

CHAPTER SIX

Forging Cross-Campus Alliances

University of Southern California student Larry Bernard, co-chair of the Gay Students Council of Southern California (GSC), believed that gay and lesbian students and faculty had reached a crossroads. "Never before has there been so much acceptance of what we are saying," Bernard wrote to the group's members in September 1972, and "there are now more gay student groups gaining recognition faster than at any time previously." Bernard suggested that "those of us who have identified ourselves with the campus gay movement are the most visible gay people in our communities (especially if yours is a small town)"; though they occupied "the most vulnerable position," they also possessed a "unique opportunity to help our gay brothers and sisters the most, and to advance the society's understanding of the happy, gay person. As students and as faculty, we carry the credentials that society is most readily able to accept, and we will be listened to." "If we have faltered," Bernard noted, "perhaps it is because we are on a road that literally has never been traveled before." He urged members to "try like hell to get every last gay person on campus into your group" and to "funnel those people with interest and potential" to the GSC.[1]

The GSC was just one of several formal cross-campus alliances organized by LGBT students in California to support each other by building connections among colleges and universities as well as within and across geographic regions.[2] Through meetings, exchanging information, newsletters, peer mentoring, social events, and political organizing, LGBT student alliances lessened the isolated nature of campus-based organizing, created additional spaces for students to network and socialize, and built camaraderie among organizers. These alliances also allowed LGBT students to advocate on behalf of their collective needs, amplifying the voice of one campus-based organization with the power of many. This process encouraged participants to become more politically engaged in the wider gay and lesbian movement.[3]

This chapter takes a closer look at three such alliances: the Gay Students Council of Southern California (1972–74), the Gay Students Coalition of San Francisco (1973–75), and the California Association of Gay Student Organizations (1975–76). Despite the many challenges of organizing across campuses, these alliances broke new ground not only in California but nationally. Though short-lived, these alliances enabled participants to learn from each other how to put ideas into practice on campus, in the local community, and within the broader gay and lesbian movement.[4] Moreover, by creating formal structures, alliances gave LGBT students critical organizing experience beyond their own campuses, exposing them to benefits and challenges of building collective power and finding allies.

Opening the Door

LGBT student alliances reflected the tradition of cross-campus organizing among other student groups and movements that had brought together the Student Non-Violent Coordinating Committee (SNCC) in the African American civil rights movement as well as coalitions of students supporting free speech, opposing the war in Southeast Asia, demanding ethnic studies, and promoting women's liberation. Many if not all of these efforts intersected with off-campus activism.[5] Outside California, some LGBT student organizers formed intercampus connections, but these efforts were usually short-lived and intermittent. In the late 1960s and early 1970s, students from Columbia, Cornell, Penn State, Rutgers, New York University, and a few other campuses created the Student Homophile League, but what Columbia's Stephen Donaldson (Robert A. Martin) envisioned as a "spreading confederation" had dissipated by the mid-1970s, although the individual groups "still worked together in harmony."[6]

Campus-based LGBT student groups across the country also organized one-off gatherings or conferences of activists from several institutions. The 1971 Conference on Gay Liberation sponsored by the Rutgers Student Homophile League, for example, drew two hundred attendees for workshops and networking.[7] Regional LGBT organizations sometimes met on college or university campuses as well: a 1973 meeting of the community-based Southeastern Gay Coalition held at the University of Georgia drew one hundred attendees, including students, from seven southern states and Washington, D.C.[8] Similarly, the December 1969 West Coast Gay Liberation Conference on the UC Berkeley campus drew students from UCLA, San Diego State College, and UC Santa Barbara.[9] But these efforts did not forge sustained organizational connections.[10]

LGBT college student organizers also sought to connect nationally but again had only limited success. In 1971, after pressure from the Gay Caucus of the National Student Association, the organization created a "gay desk" to "provide assistance to Gay Liberation organizations to overcome official heterosexist harassment at member campuses."[11] Warren Blumenfeld, an alumnus of San José State and a member of the Gay Liberation Front (GLF) while a student there, served as the desk's first director.[12] Soon renamed the National Gay Student Center, it was run on a shoestring by volunteers, among them Steve Werner, Anne Hatfield and J. Lee Lehman, with the National Student Association initially providing "supplies, a telephone," and a Washington, D.C., office.[13] Primarily through a newsletter, *Interchange*, the center served "as an information clearinghouse for gay students and other gay people."[14] It was not an activist organization: it did not plan national gatherings of student organizations or participate in activist work on individual campuses. It nevertheless provided inspiration, information, and connections for students activists.

The Alliance Turn

The first effort to create a more lasting alliance of LGBT student organizers in California was the Gay Liberation Student Conference, organized by San Francisco State student Charles Thorp, a founder of the school's GLF. Held in San Francisco at the Society for Individual Rights Center (commonly known as the SIR Center) in the summer of 1970, the event was envisioned as a meeting of "gay students from all over the country discussing their problems" alongside those of "minority students and Women's Liberation."[15] Students from California, New York, Texas, Virginia, Oregon, and Nebraska attended.[16] The gathering opened with a "State of the Gay Nation" address, followed by "reports from participants evaluating their tactics and their programs." Politics was clearly on the agenda, with workshops, a planned sit-in, and picketing.[17] Attendee Dennis Altman described the conference as a manifestation of gay liberation's shift, providing a young homosexual "with a way of accepting himself that semi-private and adult oriented liberal groups cannot" as well as promoting a "new style that is disinterested in respectability and unconcerned with 'passing.'"[18] Though this collaboration among LGBT student organizations did not yield a lasting alliance, it did set a precedent for future gatherings.

Formed in 1972, the GSC was the first sustained alliance of LGBT college student organizations in California. "As far as we know," wrote one member of Long Beach State's Gay Student Union (GSU), "the Council is the first of its kind in the world. It's making history merely by its existence, but its success depends on you!"[19] Declaring that a "ray of light has finally filtered through the smog layer of southern California," the National Gay Student Center praised the GSC as "an excellent organizing tool" that "might work effectively in other areas of the country where college campuses are densely concentrated."[20]

With the goal of assisting students in forming organizations on their campuses, the GSC welcomed "the entire segment of the gay community—men, women, all age groups, all ethnic groups, all social and economic and class groups—with one common characteristic, membership in the academic community."[21]

The GSC's founding directly influenced a similar effort in Northern California. Spencer Nutting, president of the Free Gay Students Association at the City College of San Francisco, learned about the GSC from friends and began networking with the group's leaders in the summer of 1972. Seeking to create a similar alliance in Northern California, he pulled together an organizing meeting at San Francisco's Metropolitan Community Church in 1973.[22] Activists from Southern California attended, sharing their organizing strategies with student participants from UC Davis, Sacramento State, Sacramento City College, Sonoma State University, San Francisco State, San Francisco City College, Stanford University, and Hastings College of Law. The alliance that emerged from this first meeting primarily comprised students from San Francisco City College, San Francisco State, Lone Mountain College, the University of San Francisco, Stanford University, and San José State.[23] The new Gay Students Coalition of San Francisco (GSCSF) coalesced around a mix of educational programs, sharing of information, social gatherings, and political action, advertising events in local gay and lesbian community newspapers and through colorful flyers and posters distributed on area campuses.[24]

The formation of the California Association of Gay Student Organizations (CAGSO) reflected a desire to create a statewide rather than regional network. By April 1975, the GSC had begun to decline, and activists sought to reinvigorate the group with a meeting held at UCLA. Instead, the participants—forty-five people from the GSUs at fifteen Southern California schools—formed a new group, initially called the Southern California Association of Gay Student Organizations.[25] After a few follow-up meetings, students from California State University, Long Beach; UCLA; Fresno State; California State University, Los Angeles; California Polytechnic University, San Luis Obispo; Los Angeles City College; and USC formally organized CAGSO at USC in December 1975.[26]

The GSC, GSCSF, and CAGSO created networks for peer support, provided new social spaces to meet across institutional and geographical boundaries, and became a means of sharing resources and exchanging information. Moreover, such alliances gave individual students valuable leadership and organizing experience, including opportunities to become more politically involved.[27] Despite these benefits, maintaining alliances came with ongoing and persistent challenges, as their relatively short life spans demonstrate. Those challenges included sustaining momentum; ensuring racial, ethnic, and gender diversity; and balancing alliance work with on-campus organizing.

Sharing Information and Resources

Like the National Gay Student Center, alliances became vehicles for LGBT students to exchange information and resources. Member organizations hosted formal gatherings—known as confabs—where student groups from various campuses came together and participated in workshops, peer support groups, and social events. Programming addressed what organizers saw as pressing needs: a 1972 GSC confab, for example, included a workshop on "new membership" that focused specifically on the "special problems of attracting women" and first-year students.[28] When the GSC hosted its third semiannual conference at El Camino College in Torrance in April 1973, students from nineteen campuses attended "workshops, small group activities, and programs for personal growth."[29] The GSC confab at UCLA in 1975 included workshops on "Starting Out" ("attracting members, promotion campaigns, support and interaction with the community, experiences of established and establishing groups"), "Establishment" ("dealing with student governments and school administrations, obtaining official recognition, legal precedents and support, what we can do to help each other"), "Programs" ("program idea exchange, what works, what bites, i.e. now that we're established, what do we do?"), and "Sustaining Momentum" ("maintaining vitality after the initial enthusiasm wanes, re-starting leadership, dealing with schisms").[30]

Alliances also provided opportunities for LGBT students to learn about happenings on other campuses.[31] Updates provided by alliance newsletters were designed to "foster a sense of unity and improve communications," as CAGSO's newsletter, *Patchwork*, declared in January 1976, and *Patchwork* frequently publicized events from around the state.[32] The *GSC Newsmagazine* included a "Campus Happenings" section, while the *Voice of the Gay Students Coalition of the San Francisco Bay Area* had "Gay Grams," highlighting events at Stanford, San José State, and UCLA.[33] In 1976, one student reader proclaimed that such a "communications effort" had been "needed for many years."[34]

Alliance newsletters also shared regional and national news regarding court decisions, political campaigns, and legislative efforts to prevent discrimination based on sexual orientation.[35] *The Voice of the Gay Students Coalition* included stories about Bay Area Gay Liberation and other local political organizations as well as columns by community leaders such as Harvey Milk, who, according to Mark Thompson, editor and prime organizer of the *Voice*, supported the student activists and their work.[36] *Patchwork*'s editors described their publication as an "important attempt to provide communication between all gay people at colleges and high schools in California . . . a link that must be maintained and strengthened—to provide news, feelings, and moral support for all of us who are just beginning to stand up for our human rights and our human dignity." The editors argued that contributing to the newsletter was "the only way we can feel a oneness & strength with each other, since we are all fighting hard, lonely battles in our schools."[37]

Peer Mentoring and Support

For students who consistently attended confabs, alliances offered peer mentoring, an especially important resource for students attempting to form campus-based LGBT organizations. The GSC's External Affairs Committee paired established groups with students organizing on other campuses.[38] What one newsletter described as "big brotherships" allowed organizations to "share some successful ideas—as well as things to avoid—with our sisters and brothers at a nearby campus."[39] At the January 1973 meeting of the GSC's leadership arm, the Council of Representatives, participants discussed a high-priority plan to create and distribute information packets with sections such as "How to Start a GSU on Campus" and "Maintaining a Group."[40] Campuses facing recognition challenges received particular attention.[41]

Informal cross-campus peer-to-peer counseling also occurred, but alliances could attack the problem on a broader scale. In November 1972, the GSC offered its first training workshop on peer counseling, led by faculty member Ted Lindauer from UC Irvine. The January 1973 *GSC Bulletin* encouraged students to take advantage of further trainings: "GSC members already end up counseling by virtue of their visibility in the campus setting and our groups are randomly called on to provide such services," so trainings could help members develop the needed skills.[42] Alliance members also attended events on other campuses. The GSCSF participated in a "Coming Out on Campus" workshop alongside the San José and UC Berkeley GSUs as part of Stanford's 1974 Gay Pride Week.[43]

Among the GSCSF's other goals was creating "a larger pool of resources than we could have to offer if we remained single groups and duplicated one another's functions."[44] The GSC shared this aspiration, collaborating with students from the University of Southern California to maintain a library of gay-related materials for students working on research papers. The library sought to remedy an array of problems, among them a "shortage of materials on gay topics," the "misclassification of books," and a "lack of current information on gay topics in our [campus] libraries." The project also collected newspapers and periodicals, fiction, and literature and compiled a bibliography, making all of these materials available to all GSC members.[45]

Social activities such as dances and house parties enhanced the connections made by student organizations.[46] The GSC's September 1972 gathering included a "Giant Back to School Dance."[47] At one house party, "thirty-five men and twenty-five women danced their way into the night, sometimes joined by 'straight' couples returning to the coed dorm from dates. Many of the dorm neighbors were fascinated by the sight of 'real, live gay people' but their sensitivities didn't seem to suffer too much."[48] According to Thompson, these informal gatherings were like "glue," bonding people together to face the "great big scary world out there."[49] Such social gatherings fulfilled what Gregg Schiller of the GSCSF described as the "very pervasive need to mingle, the need to pick people up or to find one's true love."[50] And when combined with workshops, meetings, and discussions, social events facilitated "getting people together who want to do something that they want to do."[51] Connecting socializing, relationship building, and organizing was a common alliance framing for this collective work.

Encouraging Political Engagement

Alliances also allowed LGBT students to forge collective power with each other and with their communities through political engagement. One facet of this effort involved connecting LGBT students to political leaders and candidates for office. Speakers at the GSC's March 1973 meeting at UC Santa Barbara included Frank Fitch, an activist from San Francisco's Society for Individual Rights, and Sally Anderson, "a gay woman ... running for the L.A. Board of Education."[52] Alliances also prompted students to organize for more direct engagement. Sal Licata, a USC student and CAGSO organizer, sought to form a political caucus within the group.[53] The "non-aligned" caucus would focus on "gay and general human rights issues" in hopes of attracting women and minority participants.[54] In a position paper likely prepared for a meeting with Los Angeles mayor Tom Bradley, the caucus called for city government to hire gay men and lesbians, a ban on discrimination, and support for "gay rights at the county, state and national levels," with these demands framed as rooted in human rights.[55] Licata and UCLA's Bob Walsh represented CAGSO at the meeting, which had more than thirty-five attendees, mostly white men, "with only about seven women and five Blacks (three of whom were female!)," as Licata reported. Noting Bradley's general support, Licata urged *Patchwork* readers to write to the mayor.[56]

Student political engagement within these alliances at times took the form of action. In 1973, the GSCSF picketed a film, *The Laughing Policeman*, that presented an unflattering portrayal of San Francisco's gay community: the movie referred to its murderous villain as a "fruiter."[57] The GSCSF participated in the San Francisco Pride march, the GSC participated in marches in Los Angeles in 1972 and in San Francisco in 1973, and CAGSO marched alongside campus-based LGBT student organizations in June 1976 pride events.[58]

Alliances also shared information with political and community leaders. In November 1972, the GSC created information packets for "distribution to state and local governmental bodies, chambers of commerce, community service groups, religious bodies, [and] media" as part of "a large effort of slow, community wide consciousness raising."[59] The GSCSF hosted a panel discussion with two openly gay candidates for public office in San Francisco.[60] The GSCSF also organized "Gay Organizations Nights," one of which attracted nearly one hundred people and "brought together for the first time in the same room, without a rumble, some of the most controversial homosexual rights activists in the Bay Area." Women's organizations were not well represented, however.[61]

LGBT student alliances framed their educational work as political, particularly appealing to students interested in reform rather than radical direct action. As Schiller, education was a "long run way of arousing people so that that they mobilize more easily to defend their interests" and ultimately become "effective apologists for the gay cause."[62] As the GSCSF found its footing, meetings became spaces for speakers, panel discussions, films, and other community events.[63] In the spring of 1974, programs included discussions of lesbian feminism, visits from political candidates, and a panel at which "several Gay lawyers, legal councellors [sic] and law students will discuss various aspects to the Law such as the Civil Rights of gay people."[64] And a fall 1975 program included a session on "approaches to gay activism."[65]

Challenges and Tensions

These alliances found themselves facing a variety of challenges that contributed to their relatively short life spans—typically only two to three years. Alliance work competed with on-campus organizing for LGBT students' time and attention.[66] In addition, students had differing ideas about the purpose of forming alliances, the degree to which they should be action-oriented, and the degree to which they should (or could) represent the diversity of campuses (and students) involved.

The GSC's shift from producing programs to serving as an information clearinghouse reflected debates over the organization's purpose. "It seems to be apparent," the November 1972 *GSC Bulletin* noted, that the GSC "will never be a task oriented organization, and well it should not be." Because member organizations needed the autonomy to carry out campus projects, the alliance came to see its role as "represent[ing] the mood and thoughts of the gay academic community of southern California ... carrying out those programs that are best suited to joint action." Furthermore, "talented, hard-working persons should not be pulled away from their local group."[67]

Whether alliances should engage directly in protest and other forms of activism or take a primarily social and educational tack was another point of contention. The GSCSF addressed this dilemma by mixing social, educational, and political work, allowing individuals to participate as they wanted rather than forcing them to follow their organizations' direction. According to Schiller, most GSCSF members agreed with the general goal of eliminating oppression of LGBT people, but differences in how they framed the "nature of the problem" led to "areas of friction." In Schiller's view, the alliance illustrated a new kind of student activism, where "confrontation and demonstration" were part of a wider strategy and not just a tactic. Participation should not "require subordinating oneself to 'The Cause.' It is a leisure activity, not a missionary crusade. Its discipline is flexible in contrast to the hard line of, say, the civil rights movement. Its aim is to change custom rather than law."[68] Thompson similarly noted, "We were not Marxists; we were gay liberationists," and finding common ground was more important than any one political program or set of beliefs.[69]

Like campus-based organizations, alliances faced challenges in attracting and maintaining diversity among leaders and members, with very few women and students of color.[70] Women organizers may have had different priorities from the white gay men who tended to dominate the alliances.[71] In 1974, Carole Mathews, a founder of the GSC as well as the GSU at the Claremont Colleges, wrote to the *Lesbian Tide* regarding her experience at the 1973 West Coast Lesbian Conference at UCLA. Before attending the conference, she wrote, "I felt that gay men were trying and that we should give them all the sisterly help we could to help them learn to be fully human. Likewise, I hoped they would help us develop atrophied aspects of our natures. We were a close-knit group, and I believe we did help each other considerably." But the gathering upended her thinking about lesbians organizing together.[72]

Some white male alliance leaders later realized that organizational goals and projects influenced the level of interest expressed by women and students of color. At the time, however, white alliance leaders largely deflected responsibility for the lack of diversity back onto those who were disaffected. Schiller believed that lesbians "are nearly all Feminists and subscribe to a separatist ideology" that made them more likely to participate in women's organizations. The GSCSF "suffer[ed] from a de facto kind of boycott on the part of the women. Those women who do show up are discouraged by how few other women show up and do not come back.... The imbalance is just how things work out."[73]

Other alliances took a less fatalistic view and tried to increase women's participation and leadership, though women seemed to do most of this organizing. In August 1972, one of the first GSC cochairs, Scripps College student Leticia Bustos, called a meeting of all the group's women.[74] Bustos left the GSC a few weeks later for unknown reasons, and the leadership council left the seat vacant "until such time as a woman member of one of the groups wishes to take on the office."[75] The question of women's leadership resurfaced in the spring of 1973, when, according to GSC meeting notes, "no woman" had yet "emerged to fill this position." The notes also pointed out that "involvement of women has always been a problem." Although some campus-based organizations in the GSC had memberships that were evenly divided between men and women and some had women at the helm, "for some reason, women do not seem to become involved in leadership roles in GSC." The GSC thus asked members of its governing council to "speak to women members" of their groups and encourage them to attend GSC meetings. According to the meeting notes, "We get asked constantly, 'How many women will be at the next meeting?' And that's by the women in each individual group. If they all showed up, they would certainly outnumber men!" By May, Sandra Heims had stepped in to a cochair position.[76] How students of color perceived the alliances is less clear.

In an early issue of the CAGSO newsletter, editor Ron Norman called for more unity, arguing that divisions between women and men, gays and bisexuals, radical feminists and lesbians, and "political activists" and "bath-bar-disco gays" were "self-defeating." Because the straight world had so much power, "WE CANNOT AFFORD TO FIGHT AMONGST OURSELVES, to ignore each other, to hide away with our few friends, lovers and fantasies. Being gay should mean being aware and concerned about each other, and most of all, INVOLVED in the world-wide, college-wide fight for our basic human rights and personal freedoms. Gay must mean a feeling of unity."[77] But such views perhaps overlooked the issue of who was calling the shots and what issues student organizers prioritized.

In February 1979, a group of LGBT students from a variety of campuses, among them UCLA met at UC Berkeley for a "gay convocation," an effort to "to expand all gay student groups and to lay the groundwork [for the] formation of statewide groups." At the meeting, each GSU shared its history, including "organizational problems encountered, activities, successes, failures, and a general description of the group's focus and goals." According to the *Daily Bruin*, "The Berkeley seminar also served to establish a framework for a statewide association of gay groups which would help the groups keep in touch and provide each other with assistance." As Randy Grant, political director of the UCLA GSU, noted, such a statewide association "is important because GSU is big here and so many are willing to fight."[78] Stanford's Gay Awareness Week the following May featured a meeting of a group of students from the California Gay and Lesbian Student Coalition, Northern Caucus, with representatives present from Stanford, UC Davis, and Chico State. A contemporary observer noted that "Berkeley (who had originally begun the organization) and many others didn't even show up but we had a good time anyway. As of this writing (2/21/80) nothing more has been seen or heard of this noble organization."[79]

The history of LGBT student alliances in California is filled with high expectations, bursts of organizing, and eventual retreat. Like other kinds of alliances and coalitions in social movement contexts, LGBT student alliances were somewhat fragile and fractured.[80] Nevertheless, these alliances enhanced efforts to transform colleges and universities into crucial—albeit limited—participants in the lesbian and gay movement of the 1970s, serving as the kind of "social movement community centers" so important to other movements.[81] Around 1977, National Gay Student Center director J. Lee Lehman observed that "one of the strongest links in the [gay liberation] Movement is the network of gay student groups in the United States and Canada."[82] Those networks, which included the GSC, GSCSF, and CAGSO, helped build the wider gay and lesbian movement through education, activism, and connections.

Fig. 1. George Raya, a student cofounder of the Society for Homosexual Freedom and a member of Associated Students, *State Hornet*, May 5, 1970. Courtesy of *State Hornet* and Donald & Beverly Gerth Special Collections and University Archives, Sacramento State University.

Fig. 2. Performance by Le Theatre Lesbien of an original play, *The Homobrontosaurus*, at a Colloquium on Lesbian Women: Myth and Reality, Sacramento State College, December 1972. *State Hornet*, December 8, 1972. Photo by Doug Taggart. Courtesy of *State Hornet* and Donald & Beverly Gerth Special Collections and University Archives, Sacramento State University.

Fig. 3. Sacramento State student Freda Smith speaking at Gay Pride Day, Sacramento, June 1971. *Mother* 1, no. 2 (July 1971): 1.

Fig. 4. Lesbian Feminist Alliance members at San José State University. *Spartan Daily*, October 11, 1976. Photo by Scott Woodham. Courtesy of San José State University Special Collections and Archives.

Fig. 5. Members of the Gay Student Union, Los Angeles City College, ca. 1979. Los Angeles City College Gay and Lesbian Student Union Records, ONE National Gay and Lesbian Archives. USC Libraries, University of Southern California. Courtesy ONE National Gay and Lesbian Archives.

Fig. 6. Gay Student Union, UC Berkeley, Forum on Drag and Genderfuck flier, October 1973. Charles Thorpe Papers, Box 1, Folder 2, GLBT Historical Society, San Francisco. Courtesy of GLBT Historical Society.

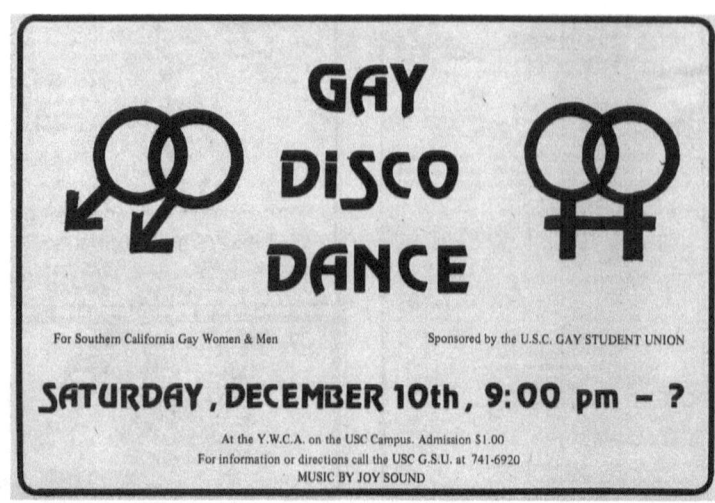

Fig. 7. Gay disco dance advertisement, Gay Student Union, University of Southern California, 1977. *Lesbian Tide*, November 1977, Periodical Collection, GLBT Historical Society. Courtesy of GLBT Historical Society.

Fig. 8. Panel from a comic, *Gay Power... Can Accomplish a Lot!*, created for the Gay Students Union at California State University, Long Beach, October 1975. Subject File: Gay Students Union—California State University Long Beach, ONE National Gay and Lesbian Archives. USC Libraries, University of Southern California. Courtesy ONE National Gay and Lesbian Archives.

Fig. 9. Panel from a comic, *Gay Power ... Can Accomplish a Lot!*, created for the Gay Students Union at California State University, Long Beach, October 1975. Subject File: Gay Students Union—California State University Long Beach, ONE National Gay and Lesbian Archives. USC Libraries, University of Southern California. Courtesy ONE National Gay and Lesbian Archives.

Fig. 10. Cover of *The Voice*, a newspaper produced by the Gay Students Coalition of the San Francisco Bay Area, May 16, 1974. Periodicals Collection, GLBT Historical Society. Courtesy of GLBT Historical Society.

Controversial Ad Not Run

Gay Libbers Accuse Daily of Censorship

By LANCE FREDERIKSEN
Daily Political Writer

A dozen supporters of Gay Liberation Front (GLF), a group endorsing homosexual activity, confronted Clyde Lawrence, Associate Professor of Advertising and Spartan Daily advertising adviser, yesterday to protest alleged censorship of an ad announcing a gay encounter group.

The ad asked for homosexuals interested in self-exploration to join a gay encounter group Monday afternoon at the Santa Clara County Mental Health Clinic, San Jose.

The group of protesters, both men and women, entered the Daily office yesterday afternoon and were referred to Lawrence. They presented him with two demands:
- Front page coverage of the incident, written and edited by the protesters, and
- An A.S. Council investigation into "de-facto censorship and bigotry" in student publications.

Frank Fertado, Spartan Daily editor, explained to the protesters, "We will not allow articles to be written and edited by persons outside the newspaper staff. We will, however, offer you space on the editorial page."

CENSORSHIP

"The elimination of the ad was censorship," claimed Zelima Williams, sophomore psychology major and member of both GLF and Women's Liberation.

Lawrence replied this was not censorship but policy. "We try to protect both the advertiser and ourselves."

"It was not the ad itself, it was the lead in the ad," said Lawrence. "The term 'self exploration' that was used would cause both the advertiser and our office a lot of crank calls. It's simply not good business."

Lawrence explained he was under the impression that Rusty Belfrage, a health clinic worker who submitted the ad, wished the ad run with the term 'exploration' included.

Miss Williams disagreed with Lawrence's explanation, stressing that the "hangups of the readers were not her fault," and that those who submitted the ad were "equipped to handle crank calls or they would not have submitted the ad."

DISCRIMINATION

The protesters complained that Daily advertising discriminated against them. "It sounds like you won't print anything that's controversial," said Miss Williams. "You allow advertising about heterosexual activities. She pointed to an advertisement for Yin Yang water beds.

"This ad said how much better sex was on a water bed, but if this had said gay sex, it would never have been run," asserted Miss Williams.

Lawrence disagreed and said the Daily would run the ad about the encounter group if the advertisers would agree to change the wording to "self-awareness." "If you'll come up with a check for $2.75, we'll run it in the classifieds tomorrow," said Lawrence.

This failed to satisfy the protesters, and they announced, "The ad is immaterial." "It's the discriminatory policy of the Daily we want to change."

"We won't give you your blood money," said Miss Williams. "You'll be hearing from us," she added.

The encounter group had a small gathering at the health clinic yesterday. It is part of a weekly program to serve the needs of persons afraid to join campus gay groups, according to Becky Williamson, GLF member.

The protesters claimed the support of GLF, Women's Liberation, San Jose Liberation Front (SJLF), Students for Community Involvement Program (SCIP), and Students for Peace and Freedom.

GAY LIBERATION—SJS Gay Liberation Front members and supporters confront Clyde Lawrence, advertising adviser (standing, far left) and Charles Pettler, Spartan Daily advertising manager (sitting at front of room) yesterday afternoon. The group was upset about Daily advertising policy.
—Daily photo by Tim Tittle

Fig. 11. San José State Gay Liberation Front members confront the *Spartan Daily*'s editors and adviser over the paper's refusal to run an advertisement for a gay encounter group. *Spartan Daily*, March 23, 1971. Courtesy of San José State University Special Collections and Archives.

Fig. 12. Members of the Stanford University Gay People's Union marching in San Francisco's Gay Freedom Day parade, ca. mid-1970s. San Francisco LGBT Groups Ephemera Collection, GLBT Historical Society. Courtesy of GLBT Historical Society.

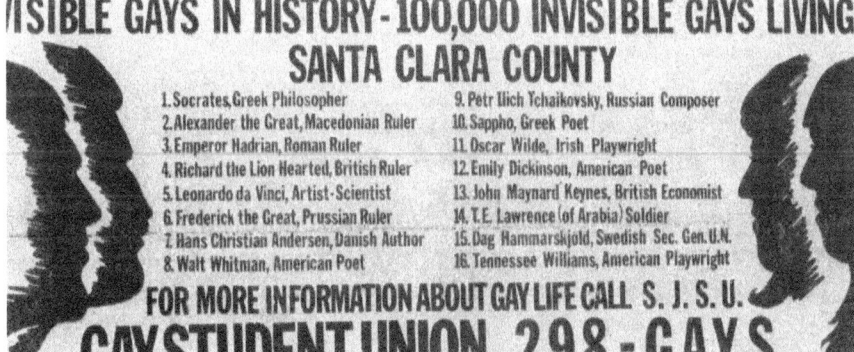

Fig. 13. Bus advertisement, "16 Visible Gays in History—100,000 Invisible Gays in Santa Clara County" from the Gay Student Union at San José State University. The city transit agency initially refused to display the advertisement, but after students complained, and with support of the Santa Clara Human Relations Commission, they prevailed. *Spartan Daily*, September 19, 1977. Courtesy of San José State University Special Collections and Archives.

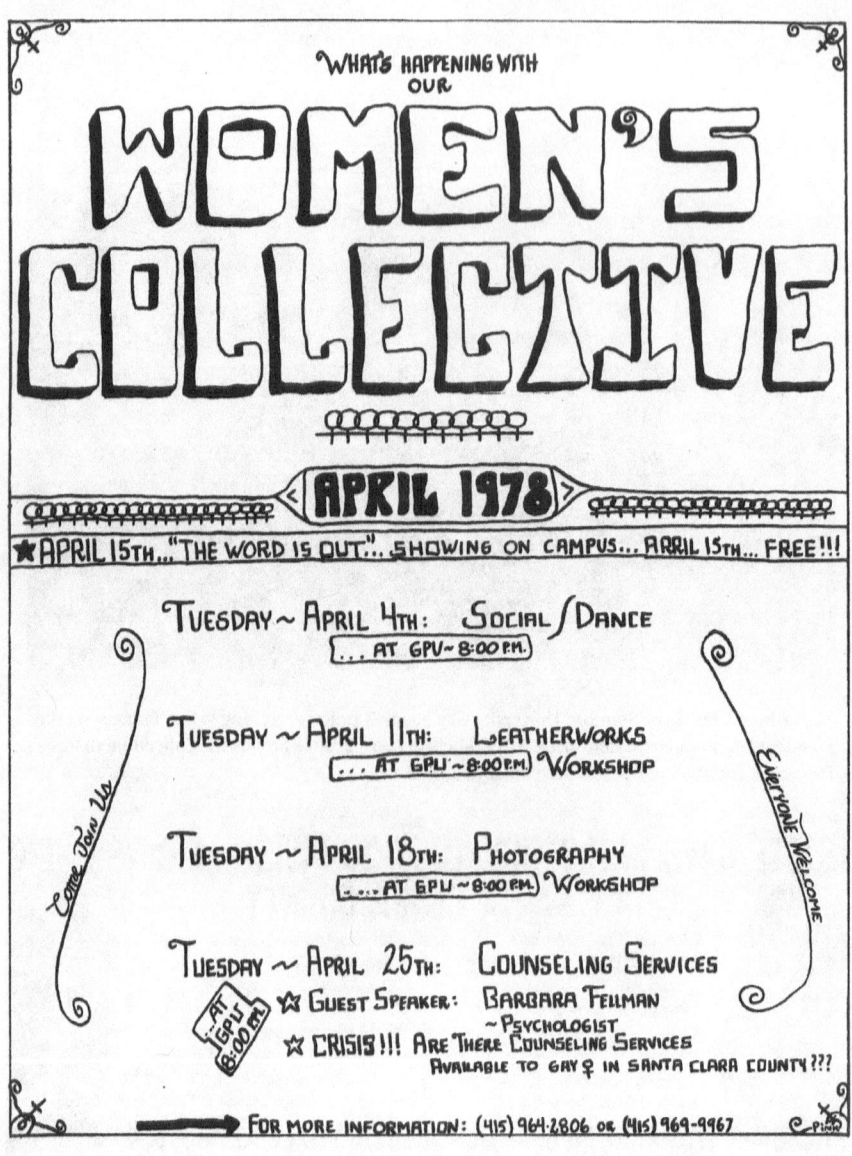

Fig. 14. Flier for the Women's Collection, Stanford University Gay People's Union, April 1978. Subject File: Stanford University, ONE National Gay and Lesbian Archives. USC Libraries, University of Southern California. Courtesy of ONE National Gay and Lesbian Archives.

CHAPTER SEVEN

Engaging Politics

In the fall of 1976, the *Advocate* published a series of articles by journalist Randy Shilts about the state of the gay student movement in the United States. Although it remained as visible and active as ever, the movement had "adopted the quiet, mild-mannered demeanor that dominates the campuses of the mid-70s. For better or worse, gay college students have traded pickets for proms and moved their campus groups straight to the center." "Light on politics and heavy on socializing and support services," campus groups reflected a shift in student preferences—more apathy, more inward-looking, "a victim of their success."[1] The editors of the Advocate concurred: "Far from being the hot-beds of radicalism gay campus groups once were, the collegiate gay movement has taken a turn toward moderation," turning away from movement-based politics and toward "services and socials," a shift editors declared a sign of success and of the "maturation of our movement and its organizations."[2]

This assessment was accurate in some respects. By the mid- to late 1970s, LGBT students began to see the fruits of their campus organizing. The battles over recognition had diminished, and students focused on providing peer services and creating new social spaces.

Yet Shilts's assessment reflects a limited view of the politics of LGBT student organizing. Informed by the feminist, gay liberation, gay and lesbian rights, and human rights movements, dances, poetry readings, Gay Awareness Weeks, advocacy for curriculum changes, DIY services, and efforts to increase LGBT visibility were just as political as the pickets Shilts celebrated. Moreover, the gay-rights gains of the early to mid-1970s provoked a backlash by the end of the decade, and California's LGBT students increasingly found themselves drawn into national struggles.

On campus, students engaged politics directly. They challenged homophobia through direct action, engaged student government as a way to seek power and resources, and sought to transform institutional policies and practices. Off campus, students became involved with local political struggles and took action in local communities, becoming critical players. Working alongside faculty and peer allies, LGBT students began to make college campuses not only into safer, more welcoming institutions but also into fluid platforms from which to engage gay and lesbian movement issues and concerns beyond those institutions.[3]

Articulating Political Consciousness

From the earliest moments of visible organizing on California's college campuses, many LGBT students connected that organizing with the wider movement frames of gay liberation and lesbian feminism. These frames provided a language to critique not only society but also college campuses. Denials of recognition taught some students hard lessons about the need for liberation politics. Working to create women's studies programs that were attentive to lesbian concerns highlighted the importance of lesbian feminism for those students.[4] And while education became a favored means to change hearts and minds—queering campus through programming and cultural events—when faced with limited resources, resistant peers, or unresponsive institutions, sometimes the only choice was to fight back. For many LGBT students, doing so meant challenging power by engaging politically.

Yet the degree to which LGBT students chose such engagement varied across campuses and time. Spurred by a campus culture of radical student protest, Students for Gay Power (SGP) emerged at UC Berkeley in association with the community-based Gay Liberation Front (GLF): membership in the two groups overlapped, and they often had joint meetings. Publicly, the SGP described itself as "primarily a non-militant group" and encouraged "those merely interested in homosexuality" to join.[5] An article in the *Daily Californian* suggested that the SGP was for "people who do not want to be as overt as the" GLF "either about their homosexuality or about their will to understand and help solve homosexuals' social problems."[6] Yet the intertwined early histories of the two organizations suggests a shared affinity for liberation politics.

By 1972, with attendance at meetings declining, the SGP shifted away from what one student described as the "radical politics and heavy off campus domination" of the SGP's early years, renaming itself the Gay Student Union (GSU) and emphasizing social events.[7] "Most gay students are not radical," GSU president Rod Gordillo concluded.[8] Five years later, however, the group again reoriented itself, becoming the Gay People's Union (GPU) and declaring its intention to become "more active politically and in the community" in hopes that Berkeley residents "would feel freer to participate in what can be a truly community-based organization."⁹ This renewed commitment to political activism raises questions about how and why such transformations occurred in such LGBT student organizations. A few factors shaped how a fluid commitment to political engagement played out in practice.

DIY educational efforts also frequently reflected political engagement, as was the case for a rap exploring the "future of lesbian feminism" organized by the Women's Collective of the Stanford GPU.¹⁰ In addition, gay and lesbian movement organizers frequently visited LGBT student organizational meetings. However, taking public political positions could jeopardize student organizations' official status—and the resources such recognition brought. After the UCLA GSU won recognition from the Student Legislative Council in 1974, GSU president Dave Johnson confirmed the organization's "commitment to remain non-political, and limit group activities to community services and education of the UCLA population."¹¹ But the GSU's definition of "community services and education" encompassed inviting local activists to meetings, organizing campus events with politics as a focus, and even the creation of a "political activities coordinator" position responsible for monitoring the "political situation for gays at UCLA."¹²

Furthermore, individual students and GSU leaders engaged with issues they deemed politically important. Some took up the pen, authoring opinion pieces for campus newspapers. Donna Hughes-Oldenberg, active in the Women's Collective of the Stanford GPU, authored a commentary on the political impact of lesbian feminism on the gay movement. "Lesbian feminists," Hughes-Oldenberg argued, "have identified and continue to develop the ideological ties that bind gay liberation to the feminist movement" even though gay male activists have "tended to be obstinately ignorant" about those ties. This "schism" between gay men and lesbians was starting to close, not only pointing the way toward a "future in which lesbians and gay men increasingly combine their political energies for the greater benefit of all gay people" but also addressing the specific issues of "Latino, black and other third world gays."¹³

LGBT student leaders who took such public positions wielded particular influence with their peers. Johnson, for example, gave speeches in Meyerhoff Park in which he urged gay students to join the GSU.¹⁴ He challenged one professor's use of queer in class and not only spoke up in a psychology class about a "behavior modification program" but lamented that he was the only person to do so because there were no other "upfront gays to respond."¹⁵ Johnson explicitly told the *Daily Bruin* that the GSU's goals were political and wrote several opinion pieces for the paper that articulated a gay liberation politics focused on building alternatives to oppressive institutions and attitudes and that demanded respect for gays and lesbians.¹⁶ When Larry Duplechan was studying at UCLA, he saw Johnson as "just one of those people who could lead and you'd follow him. He was handsome, he was articulate, and he was clear about what he would and would not take from the straight world." Johnson was Duplechan's "very first political gay man."[17] Nonpartisan thus did not equate to apolitical.

Confronting Homophobia

LGBT students translated gay and lesbian movement issues into campus political engagement by challenging homophobia, honing their political analysis in the process. San José State psychology major Zelima Williams of the GLF framed such moments as a means of asserting dignity and self-determination. Protesting the campus newspaper's refusal to publish a 1971 advertisement that included the words self-exploration in the description of a gay encounter group at the Santa Clara County Mental Health Clinic, a dozen GLF members accused the paper's advertising adviser, Professor Clyde Lawrence, and student editors of censorship and rejected their offer to run the ad without the offending phrase. The protest was empowering in and of itself: as the GLF newsletter reported, the student activists "walked in as proud human beings; the self-respect we gained through this was priceless." In the wake of the confrontation, the *Spartan Daily* published a guest column in which the GLF declared, "Gay is not only beautiful and good, gay is angry, gay is courage."[18]

In 1970, the SGP at UC Berkeley picketed Harmon Gym to protest a series of arrests of gay men by campus police for soliciting sex. Although the SGP sought change "so that guys don't have to cruise johns to find sex partners," the group nevertheless argued that the police had "no business harassing those who want to cruise."[19] The SGP pickets joined with an ongoing protest by Women's Liberation against the institution's sexist policies.[20] The groups circulated a petition demanding an end to police entrapment of homosexuals on campus and urging that any funds saved by ceasing these actions be used "to protect women from rape." Bearing signs that read, "Pigs out of Harmon" and "Love Is a Many Gendered Thing," the SGP protesters planned to consecrate one of the bathrooms as a sanctuary for gay men, with "one member of the group masquerading as a priest, complete with purple vestments," to conduct a "mock mass."[21] Several protesters were arrested, although they did not enter the building.[22] In a piece published in the *Daily Californian* a few weeks later, two SGP members connected the demonstration to larger issues, declaring U.S. sexual laws "the most regressive in the world" and arguing that in such entrapment cases, the victim was "not given the full benefit of our justice system."[23] The liberation politics evidenced in this action were likely what Shilts imagined when he remembered the radicalism of the early campus gay movement.

In 1975, UCLA's GSU connected with the Women's Resource Center to form the Coalition against the Dehumanization of Children, which objected to a "gender identity clinic" that the student newspaper described as focusing on "'evaluation and treatment' for boys between the ages of three and 12 who are thought to have 'serious difficulties in adopting normal masculine behaviors.'" The GSU's Rod Thorsen accused the program of "destroying children" and decried the "male dominance trip" as a "wrong ideal. They are trying to make one kind of man and woman."[24] Protesters demanded suspension of the program and met with the program's coordinators.[25] Thorsen attended the meeting with his head held high "through this adversity," facing the panel with "my militant, radical, 'stony,' inquiries."[26] The Coalition against the Dehumanization of Children staged a "well attended rally" that garnered attention from local media, the *Advocate*, and the *L.A. Free Press* as well as a march to the program's on-campus headquarters. Morris Kight, one of the founders of the GLF in Los Angeles, participated, and GSU members Dave Johnson and Gary Steele spoke in front of a banner that read, "Children Were Made in God's Image Not Yours."[27]

Other challenges to homophobia were more subtle but nevertheless effective. In the late 1970s, LGBT student organizations at UC Berkeley, San José State, Sacramento State, Cal Poly San Luis Obispo, Chico State, San Francisco State, and UCLA held "Denim Days" or "Gay Blue Jeans Days," asking students to wear blue jeans in support of gay rights.[28] Philip McGowen of the GPU at CSU Chico described Denim Day as claiming space on campus for "any person to be openly homosexual without fear of reprisal," challenging hostility toward gay people, and "creat[ing] an ongoing dialogue with straight people," sympathetic or not.[29] At UC Berkeley, members of the GPU described the event as an opportunity to raise awareness of the need for antidiscrimination policies and to challenge hostile reactions to increased gay visibility.[30] And UCLA's GSU declared the 1977 event a success in that it gave visibility to "what it's like to be labeled and ostracized."[31]

Gay Blue Jeans Days sometimes provoked angry reactions. At San José State in 1976, a reporter for the *Spartan Daily* interviewed denim-clad students and discovered that only a fraction of them were aware of the event. One student refused "to be intimidated by this bullshit," while another did not "give a damn."[32] At UCLA, student Chris Raymond complained that Gay Blue Jeans Day "proved nothing except [gays'] disregard for the feelings of heterosexuals" and suggested that homosexuality should remain "within the confines of one's home" and not be "propagandized on the campus of UCLA."[33] But as Vincent Fanucchi of the GSU at San José State noted in 1977, "when non-gays are caught wearing jeans they get the same odd looks and negative attitudes we're always faced with." The preceding year, a student in one of Fanucchi's classes had exclaimed to him, "Hey, you can't wear jeans. Don't you know only queers wear jeans today?" to which Fanucchi responded, "Yeah!"[34]

Engaging Student Government

LGBT students also engaged politically with student government—seeking support for organizing and recognition efforts, securing funding, asserting themselves as constituents, and running for office.[35] Associated Students named the Cal State Long Beach GSU the school's "most valuable organization of the year" in 1974.[36] On other campuses, student government joined LGBT student activists in pushing back against homophobia. When the Newman Center at Sacramento State refused to allow the Regional Conference of Gay Organizations to hold a dance on site, Associated Students voted 7–1 in favor of a resolution to support students protesting the decision.[37] And in 1977, Associated Students at San José State unanimously recognized the GSU for its efforts to promote human rights. GSU president Matthew Savoca was grateful for the support, believing that it would encourage the "approximately 2,000 gay students at SJSU" to come out.[38]

Points of contention nonetheless continued to exist, and they frequently involved funding. Some student leaders resisted LGBT student organization requests for money on the grounds that too many "nonstudents" were involved. Other individuals objected on moral or religious grounds. In one case, an Associated Students senator at Cal State Northridge voted against GSU funding "because members of the Union are gay."[39] At Cal State Fullerton in conservative Orange County, student government refused to support the West Coast Gay Academic Conference.[40] And when the GPU at UC Berkeley sought funding, one senator declared, "I can't vote for a group that is doing something that I feel is an abomination," a statement that students Kyle Counts and Brian Williams argued exemplified the use of religion as a tool to "fortify reactionary political positions." But, they concluded, gays "cannot be voted out of existence."[41]

Budget fights could connect marginalized student groups. In the spring of 1974, a UC Santa Barbara Associated Students representative questioned the expenditures of the Black Student Union, which offered a detailed response in the student newspaper and at budget meetings. GSU member Andy Rogers then wrote to the paper and explained that although he had attended a budget meeting "wondering what the [Black Student Union] could possibly do with so much money," he "left in anger that their programs must compete with insignificant other groups." Rogers thanked the group for educating him and recognized a "certain link with all oppressed minorities," suggesting that the Black Student Union and the GSU serve not just their own members but everyone. Both organizations received funding that year.[42]

Student government elections offered yet another opportunity for LGBT student organizations to assert themselves as a political force, at times forming coalitions with other marginalized student groups. At Sacramento State, the Gay Caucus (including faculty and students involved in the short-lived Gay Studies Program) joined Women's Liberation and other student organizations in an "Alternative Coalition" to run a slate of candidates in 1973. "For the first time in the history of our campus," the Gay Studies Board noted, "Gay students, women and Chicanos have joined together to fight our common oppression."[43] Candidates for student government also sought out LGBT student organization support. At UCLA in the spring of 1976, four candidates for the Student Legislative Council attended a GSU meeting, a testament to "the growing recognition of gay people on this campus as a political force," as the organization's newsletter reported.[44] Two years later, the GSU hosted a forum for student government candidates.[45] At times, LGBT student organizations campaigned for candidates.[46] According to the SGP at UC Berkeley, "close political friendships" with candidates were strategic—supporting candidates could change Associated Students at the Berkeley campus "into something more relevant to students and their needs. But for us, politics go much beyond that. It is an excellent chance for us to get out of the abnormal psychology classes where we now exist on campus" and be seen as "real human beings."[47]

LGBT students also sought office.[48] At UC Berkeley, GSU president Steve Wilford won a seat as a senator on Associated Students of the University of California as part of the Coalition for Student Action, an alliance of students who sought to challenge the status quo. As an openly gay student and a GSU leader, Wilford believed that his service in student government meant that "the GSU had an in . . . as opposed to [an] everyday run-of-the-mill faggot."[49] Dave Cash followed in Wilford's footsteps at Berkeley, winning a seat in student government in the fall of 1971 as part of a coalition. According to Cash, the campaign had included "doors slammed in my face and other negative reactions."[50] Among the other LGBT students who ran in student government elections during the 1970s were Nancy Robertson of the Lesbian Feminist Alliance at San José State, who won, and Richard Robbins at UC Santa Barbara, who lost.[51] In so doing, these activists not only promoted visibility for LGBT students and their organizations but asserted their power.

Challenging Campus Policies

LGBT students also targeted antihomosexual campus policies and procedures. At Stanford, the GPU persuaded the library to move homosexual-themed materials from locked shelves to general circulation.[52] UCLA's GSU pressed the administration to ban discrimination based on "sexual orientation or affectional preference."[53]

Elsewhere, LGBT student organizations focused on private employers and government agencies that recruited on campus. UC Berkeley's SGP and GSU sought to prohibit the campus placement center from including potential employers that discriminated based on sexual orientation.[54] In 1974, Stanford's GPU began a multiyear struggle with the Career Planning and Placement Center to require companies recruiting on campus to pledge nondiscrimination against employees based on "affectional or sexual preference." The student newspaper supported the GPU's campaign, but opponents suggested that recruiters might respond by refusing to come to campus.[55] Richard Thomas, a GPU member and graduate student in physics, was instrumental in moving this issue to the forefront: he proposed that the GPU refuse to endorse any student government candidate who did not back the idea and both publicly and privately engaged faculty and administrators, among them Stanford president Richard Lyman.[56] Thomas equated the experience of LGBT students to that of other minority groups, thereby rooting his argument in human rights. In January 1976, Thomas wrote to the chair of the Committee on Services to Students that if it chose not to implement the changes proposed by the GPU, "you must make it clear that your refusal to protect the rights of the gay student is not based on a belief that he is less worthy of that protection than those who are now protected, and you must clearly explain why you feel that you can not act to uphold his human dignity."[57] In response to Thomas's lobbying efforts the committee urged Lyman to oppose "discrimination on the basis of sexual preference," though it did not take a position on a need to "ban discriminating employers" from campus.[58]

Thomas's adoption of a human rights frame subsequently became even more pronounced.[59] In the spring of 1976, he told Stanford's dean of students, James W. Lyons, that allowing discriminatory employers on campus represented a failure to uphold "basic human rights," attaching a human rights policy from the USC Law School to the letter.[60] The GPU and other campus groups broadened the issue, calling for a new overall campus policy on human rights that would include sexual orientation. The GPU, "the Black Students Union, Hillel, the Alliance for Radical Change, the Women's Center, United Campus Ministries, the Men's Center, and United Stanford Employees" joined together to form an "ad hoc committee on Human Rights," which held a rally that drew upward of one hundred students, sixty of whom marched on the president's office. Keith Archuleta of the Black Students Union pinpointed the benefits of working together, noting that "the game of divide and conquer has been played too long.... [T]he game of divide and conquer ends here."[61]

Campus Organizing, Community Impact

Whether as individuals or as members of organizations, LGBT students participated in local protests, used university resources to produce flyers for community-based organizations, promoted the inclusion of sexual orientation in local governments' affirmative action plans, advocated for gay-rights ordinances, challenged homophobic policies in local communities, and connected themselves to wider political struggles. This participation was fluid, connecting on-campus work to community-based settings and vice versa.[62]

LGBT student organizations not only constituted a ready source of information about gay and lesbian movement politics but also encouraged involvement in protests and the writing of letters to elected officials and others. In 1970, the San José State GLF urged members to support demonstrations against recent police actions in San Francisco's Tenderloin, among them an incident in which officers forced a Mexican American gay man "into his bathtub and repeatedly sadistically beat" him while "mumbling about his sexuality."[63] When the Los Angeles GLF held a "Gay-In" at Griffith Park, the UCLA GLF extended an "open invitation to all the members of the UCLA gay community who have been interested in Gay Liberation but still don't feel safe coming to a meeting on campus."[64] The Stanford GPU newsletter shared an opportunity for members to connect with the Join Hands project, which wrote letters to gay prisoners.[65]

Some LGBT student organizations took concrete action on issues that did not directly involve gay rights, such as opposition to the Vietnam War.[66] Lesbian students played an active role in the women's liberation movement or in the creation and operation of women's centers.[67] Graduate student Barbara Bryant worked on a grant to fund the Sacramento Women's Center. The center, which sponsored programs, created a rape crisis line, and included a bookstore in the front of the building, included student staff and volunteers, many of them lesbians.[68]

LGBT students occasionally engaged local institutions directly. In October 1975, when the Palo Alto Board of Education declined to apply "specific non-discrimination protections to gay teachers," the GPU newsletter asked members to write letters to the board and to attend the board's next meeting.[69] At that session, Donna Hughes-Oldenburg of the GPU Women's Collective told board members that excluding "sexual orientation, marital status, political belief and handicap" from the protections against discrimination was "in itself discriminatory and asked that the action be reconsidered." After the board voted to "place this item on a future agenda," the GPU again rallied members to attend the next meeting.[70] "Know a gay teacher?" the November 1975 GPU newsletter asked. "We particularly need gay teachers at the Board meeting or to write/phone Board members." Don Knutson, a visiting Professor at Stanford Law School, and GPU members Richard Thomas and Arthur Corbin spoke. The Board reinstated the four areas that had been deleted from the policy by a 3–2 vote. The GPU celebrated victory in the December 1975 GPU newsletter. "The dramatic 3–2 reversal followed four weeks of concerted behind-the-scenes lobbying from GPU members, mental health professionals, clergy, and various humanist supporters in the community," the GPU newsletter noted, suggesting that the controversy had one consequence: "the strategically desirable, necessary effect of exposing various community bigots and fundamentalists."[71] In the spring, the GPU successfully worked to support the election of a favorable candidate for the school board, noting in the March 1976 newsletter that it was "our community, our schools, too."[72]

Students won successes on other campuses. For example, at San José State, the Gay Student Union sought to purchase advertising space on city busses with a list of "16 famous gays ranging from Emily Dickinson to Socrates" headlined "16 Visible Gays in History—100,000 Invisible Gays Living in Santa Clara County." The city transit agency denied the request, deeming the content "controversial and morally objectionable." The Santa Clara Human Relations Commission agreed to assist the students. After the policy was up for reconsideration in the fall of 1977, due to concerns about its constitutionality, a door opened for the GSU. The students won their battle in February 1978, and the ads began appearing on local buses.[73]

Engagement also included lobbying statewide elected officials. A good example is the struggle to pass a consenting adults law in California as a way to end the criminalization of homosexual sex.[74] When AB 489 came before the legislature in 1975, it passed the Assembly, but tied 20–20 in the California State Senate. As *The Gayzette* reported, members of the UCLA Gay Student Union took to the phones, "and began a full afternoon's work" with messages of support for an 'aye' vote to statewide officials in Los Angeles and Sacramento with other LGBT student organizations across California "joining the chorus in an impressive show of fast teamwork and coordination."[75] Lieutenant Governor Mervyn Dymally ultimately cast the tie-breaking vote, Governor Jerry Brown signed the bill, and the legislation became law in 1976.[76]

By the end of the 1970s, LGBT students on campus were increasingly drawn into statewide and national gay and lesbian movement issues, especially the struggle over Proposition 6, or the Briggs Initiative, which would have prevented gays and lesbians and their allies from teaching in public schools. As opposition to the proposition grew, so too did LGBT student involvement.[77] Whether as part of a campus LGBT organizations or on their own, students contributed to the effort, authoring articles in LGBT student organization newsletters, writing editorials for campus newspapers, sponsoring fundraisers, hosting events to raise awareness, and sponsoring rallies or conferences.[78] The CSU Northridge Gay Student Union discussed ways to fight the Briggs Initiative at meetings, a likely occurrence on many campuses.[79] The Stanford Gay People's Union vowed to create "a political version of the speakers bureau" to address, through "self-education," a plan by state senator John Briggs to bring the battle over gay rights to California through ballot initiative.[80] Students at CSU Long Beach Gay Student Union co-hosted a "Run for Rights" fundraiser.[81] USC students hosted a statewide conference to mobilize against Proposition

6 with a post-meeting disco dance at the YWCA.[82] Sonoma State students organized a "Scrap Prop. 6" poetry reading.[83] The Gay and Lesbian Alliance at UC Santa Cruz issued a press release, urging a No on 6 note.[84] The UCLA Gay Student Union hosted a "Briggs Initiative Night" in May, 1978.[85] And, the Gay Student Union of the Claremont Colleges co-sponsored a women's music concert nine days before election day in the fall of 1978 hoping to ensure good turnout.[86] In all these ways, LGBT students and allies on campus worked in creative and engaging ways to defeat Proposition 6.

College campuses also became sites where campus and community organizing converged—whether as sites where community-based organizations met or as opportunities to bring students into the campaign. The Los Angeles regional group of the California Coalition against the Briggs Initiative (CCABI) met at CSU Los Angeles. The California Conference to Defeat the Briggs Initiative held a meeting on the campus of the University of Southern California, including a special workshop for gay student organizations.[87] At a September 1978 event at San José State to raise awareness about the initiative, GSU president Paul Boneberg gave an "an emotional address" describing gays who opposed the initiative as heroes since so many were "so brutalized they can't come out of the closet."[88]

Organizations formed specifically to defeat Proposition 6 tapped students for support. The Inland Empire No on 6 Committee created a Campus Outreach Task Force.[89] A "Call for Action" issued by Lesbian Feminists of Los Angeles, Latinos Unidos (de Los Angeles), and the Coalition for Human Rights suggested that student organizations could be a source of allies.[90] The Bay Area Coalition against the Briggs Initiative gathered student addresses of students, with San Francisco State student Cleve Jones serving as the group's student outreach coordinator.[91] And a weeklong "Speak Out against Briggs" public education campaign included a "campus blitz."[92]

LGBT students and faculty also participated in off-campus organizing efforts. San Francisco State professor Sally Gearhart worked closely with the Bay Area Coalition against the Briggs Initiative alongside San Francisco supervisor Harvey Milk and many others; she also debated John Briggs on television.[93] Students from San José State's GSU and Lesbian Feminist Alliance worked to defeat Proposition 6, with Boneberg becoming involved in the Santa Clara County Human Rights Coalition and contributing stories about the coalition to the community-based Lambda News. He reported on a September 1977 rally at St. James Park that drew more than two hundred people.[94] San José State's GSU and the Women's Center collaborated on a grassroots organizing effort to educate voters not only on campus but also in the local community. And the Lesbian Feminist Alliance cosponsored a visit by openly lesbian Massachusetts state representative Elaine Noble and participated in an "education campaign against the Briggs initiative."[95] Noted Matthew Savoca of the GSU, the initiative threatened not only the gay community but "everyone. It should be frightening to everyone because if they can do it to us, they can do it to any group that's expendable."[96]

When California voters sent Proposition 6 to defeat in November 1978, students celebrated. That success capped a decade of LGBT political organizing in which college students played a significant part, both on and off campus. Rather than "trading pickets for proms," as Shilts suggested, LGBT college students in California engaged politically in many complex ways. The organizing homes these students established and sustained made possible the political engagement in which they engaged. Student struggle against Briggs represented but did not define the diversity of LGBT student political engagement throughout the 1970s, engagement that included influencing student government, taking on homophobic institutional policies, and participating in other off-campus organizing.

Conclusion

In October 1979, thousands of people gathered in Washington, D.C., for the National March on Washington for Lesbian and Gay Rights, the "first demonstration of its kind in history."[1] Organized to commemorate the tenth anniversary of the Stonewall Rebellion, the march was dedicated to the memory of Harvey Milk, who had been assassinated by former San Francisco supervisor Dan White one year earlier. Those assembled called for an "end to all social, economic, judicial and legal oppression of Lesbian & Gay people," including protecting lesbian and gay youth from discrimination and oppression in "homes, schools, jobs and social environments."[2] The event, several years in the making, propelled gay rights toward a more prominent national stage, even if the road to get there remained long and complicated.[3]

LGBT students connected to the march in varied ways. The march was endorsed by numerous LGBT student organizations from across the country, including the Gay Student Union (GSU) of Los Angeles City College.[4] The Gay People's Union at UC Santa Barbara and other California groups participated in local events aligned with the national march.[5] The cochair of the Gay and Lesbian Student Union at California State University, Los Angeles, sophomore John Dillinger, traveled to Washington to represent the group.[6] Paul Boneberg, former president of the San José State GSU and a march organizer, recalled that the informal networks cultivated in the 1970s—including LGBT student organizations—were on display there, illustrating the importance of relationships and skills on which activists would build moving into the 1980s.[7]

Nearly half a century later, many LGBTQ+ students, including those in California, still face significant challenges to their ability to thrive. Those obstacles can be particularly difficult for anyone who identifies as transgender or gender-fluid and/or who attends school in a less welcoming community.[8] Many relevant lessons may be learned from the responses of earlier generations of students. Despite various forms of reactionary resistance, these students challenged their campus communities to take a fresh look at assumptions about sexual orientation and gender identity, doing so through the visibility of themselves, their programming, and their activism. And while differences of race, ethnicity, and gender certainly shaped these students' specific experiences and at times resulted in conflict and division, as a whole, LGBT students nevertheless made strides toward creating a more welcoming climate that would allow them to find their people and their place both on campus and in the wider gay and lesbian movement.

For the most part, LGBT student organizing ebbed and flowed. Visibility varied from campus to campus and from year to year. Timing and student leadership were crucial. In the early days of gay liberation and lesbian feminist campus organizing, students rode the larger activist tide. Modeling their approach on the struggles, tactics, and successes of the African American civil rights movement, educated by antiwar organizing and angered by university and police responses, inspired by underrepresented students from racial and ethnic minorities seeking a place in the university, motivated by the gender politics of women's liberation, and directly connected to the emergence of gay liberation, LGBT students came into their own on campus as these movements percolated, sometimes drawing the students in as well. And LGBT student activism contributed to the more general student movement that sought increased autonomy and freedom from in loco parentis surveillance.

Growing visibility brought reactionary resistance to the work of some LGBT campus-based organizations, including denial of recognition. But LGBT students fought back, cultivating allies and asserting the power of self-determination. Official recognition transformed the organizations from outsiders to insiders (though sometimes uncomfortable ones) with access to the resources (meeting and office space as well as funding) that accompanied institutionalization. LGBT students and their organizations then used these resources to queer campus life through social and cultural events and provided DIY queer support where none existed, forging connections both within and across campuses. The resulting networks not only strengthened campus-specific organizing but improved the lives of LGBT students as well as the wider gay and lesbian community. By the end of the 1970s, LGBT students were more engaged and less divided and had more allies, the capstone to a decade of breaking ground and building communities.

So what do today's LGBTQ+ students need to know about their community's history? Oral histories with these former student activists reveal just how important this organizing work was at the time—and remains. Barbara Bryant believed that students must recognize how long change takes and "what so many people had lived through." Sugie Goen-Salter stressed the value of "nam[ing] my own experience on this planet in ways that were seen as intellectual, that were seen as important, that were seen as transformative, like it could change the material conditions of my neighbor." And Larry Duplechan highlighted the depth of the struggle: while some younger folks now believe that their gayness does not define them, that viewpoint reflects the battles fought and won by earlier generations. If homosexuality matters less than was previously the case, at least in some instances, or even does not matter at all in a few others, there was a day when it "really, really did." And as today's LGBTQ+ students continue to struggle, lessons from their queer ancestors sheds light on what a path forward just might look like.

ABBREVIATIONS

BAR	Bay Area Reporter
Briggs Initiative Collection	California Proposition 6 Briggs Initiative Collection, ONE National Gay and Lesbian Archives. USC Libraries, University of Southern California
Burns Records	San José State University Office of the President, Hobert W. Burns Records, University Archives, San José State University, Special Collections and Archives
CAGSO File	Subject File: California Association of Gay Student Organizations, ONE National Gay and Lesbian Archives Should end Archives. USC Libraries, University of Southern California
CSULA GSU File	Subject File: Gay Students Union—California State University, Los Angeles, ONE National Gay and Lesbian Archives. USC Libraries, University of Southern California
CSULB GSU File	Subject File: Gay Students Union—California State University, Long Beach, ONE National Gay and Lesbian Archives. USC Libraries, University of Southern California
CSUSSCUA	California State University, Sacramento, Donald & Beverly Gerth Special Collections and University Archives
DB	Daily Bruin (University of California, Los Angeles)
DC	Daily Californian (University of California, Berkeley)
DN	Daily Nexus (University of California, Santa Barbara)
DS	Daily Sundial (California State University, Northridge)
DTi	Daily Titan (California State University, Fullerton)
DTr	Daily Trojan (University of Southern California)
EC	San Francisco LGBT Groups Ephemera Collection, GLBT Historical Society
49er	Forty Niner/49er/Daily 49er (California State University, Long Beach)
GG	Gay Gazette (California State University, Long Beach)
GLBTHS	GLBT Historical Society
GLBTHS Periodicals	Periodicals Collection, GLBT Historical Society
Gordon Papers	Cherie Gordon Papers, Lavender Library

GSC File	Subject File: Gay Students Council of Southern California (GSC), ONE National Gay and Lesbian Archives. USC Libraries, University of Southern California
LT	*Lesbian Tide*
LV	*Lesbian Visions*
MD	*Mustang Daily* (California Polytechnical University, San Luis Obispo)
ONE Archives	ONE National Gay and Lesbian Archives. USC Libraries, University of Southern California
ONE Periodicals	Periodicals Collection, ONE National Gay and Lesbian Archives. USC Libraries, University of Southern California
RR	*Renegade Rip* (Bakersfield College)
Schiller GSCSF Account	Gregg Schiller [attributed], account of the formation of the Gay Students Coalition, [n.d.], Box 140, Folder 11, John De Cecco Papers, GLBT Historical Society
SFSUSCA	San Francisco State University, Special Collections and Archives
SH	*State Hornet* (Sacramento State University)
SPC	Social Protest Collection, University of California, Berkeley, Bancroft Library
SpD	*Spartan Daily* (San José State University)
Stanford QSR *Records*	Stanford University Queer Student Resources Records, Stanford University Libraries, Department of Special Collections and University Archives
StD	*Stanford Daily* (Stanford University)
SULDSC	Stanford University Libraries, Department of Special Collections and University Archives
SUPEC	Stanford University Publications and Ephemera Collection, Stanford University Libraries, Department of Special Collections and University Archives
UC Berkeley Archives	University of California, Berkeley, Bancroft Library, University Archives
UT	*University Times* (California State University, Los Angeles)
VGSC	*Voice of the Gay Students Coalition*
Wagner Papers	Sally Roesch Wagner Papers, Donald & Beverly Gerth Special Collections and University Archives, California State University, Sacramento
WSPR	Women's Studies Program Records, Donald & Beverly Gerth Special Collections and University Archives, California State University, Sacramento

NOTES

Introduction

1. George Raya to Stephen, August 26, 1974, Box 2, Raya Papers, GLBTHS

2. Orta, interview by author; "The Struggle to Be Gay," *Vector*, September 1975, 47–49; Spring, interview by author. *Vector* is available in GLBTHS Periodicals. Organization names were frequently rendered inconsistently, with *Gay Student Union*, *Gay Student's Union*, and *Gay Students Union*, for example, used interchangeably. Except in quotations, I have regularized these names as *Gay Student Union* (GSU) and *Gay People's Union* (GPU).

3. See, among others, Robert Cohen, *When the Old Left Was Young*; Biondi, *Black Revolution on Campus*; Rogers [Kendi], *Black Campus Movement*; Ferreira, "All Power to the People"; Self, *American Babylon*; Muñoz, *Youth, Identity, Power*; Evans, "Sons, Daughters, and Patriarchy."

4. Examples include Nichols and Kafka-Hozschlag, "Rutgers University Lesbian/Gay Alliance"; Rhoads, "'We're Here, We're Queer, Get Used to It,'" in *Freedom's Web* (Penn State); Beemyn, "Silence Is Broken" (Cornell); Eisenbach, *Gay Power* (Columbia); Johansen, "Out of Silence" (University of Minnesota); Staley, "Gay Liberation Comes to Appalachian State"; Faulkenbury and Hayworth, "Carolina Gay Association" (University of North Carolina); Rose-Mockry, "We're Here and We're Not Going Away" (University of Kansas); Denby, "Fighting for Inclusion" (University of Michigan).

5. For example, see James T. Sears, *Lonely Hunters*; Bailey, *Sex in the Heartland*; John Howard, *Men Like That*; Stein, *City of Sisterly and Brotherly Loves*; E. Patrick Johnson, *Sweet Tea*; Simon Hall, *American Patriotism, American Protest*. Histories of LGBT student organizing outside the United States include Marshall, "Young Gays" (Australia); Malcolm, "Curious Courage" (United Kingdom); Casey, "Radical Politics" (Ireland); Brown, "Canada's First Gay Student Activist Group."

6. See Marine, *Stonewall's Legacy*; Dilley, *Gay Liberation to Campus Assimilation*; Clawson, "Queers on Campus"; Coley, *Gay on God's Campus*; Stein, "Students, Sodomy, and the State."

7. On this historiography, see Graves, "So You Think You Have a History?"

8. Reti, *Out in the Redwoods* (UC Santa Cruz); "Gay Bears: The Hidden History of the Berkeley Campus," University Archives, University of California, Berkeley, accessed August 29, 2019, https://bancroft.berkeley.edu/collections/gaybears/; Koskovich, "Private Lives, Public Struggles" (Stanford); "Queer @ Stanford," Stanford University Libraries, accessed August 29, 2019, https://exhibits.stanford.edu/queer. See also Stein, "Teaching and Researching." Stein's bibliography includes references to other similar projects across the United States.

9. Or, as historian John D'Emilio suggests, the 1979 march represented a maturation of a movement from its decentralized and local beginnings. See D'Emilio, "1979 March's Place"; Ghaziani, *Dividends of Dissent*.

10. Bailey and Farber, introduction to *America in the Seventies*, 2. Examples of scholarship focusing on this shift outside of the United States include Porion, "Reassessing a Turbulent Decade"; Arrow, *Seventies*.

11. Schulman, "Islands in Time."

12. Schulman, *Seventies*; Bailey and Farber, *America in the Seventies*; Simon Hall, *American Patriotism, American Protest*; Simon Hall, "Protest Movements in the 1970s"; Simon Hall, "Framing the American 1960s"; Foley, *Front Porch Politics*; Kutula, *After Aquarius Dawned*; Kruse and Zelizer, *Fault Lines*.

13. Susan Lee Johnson, "My Own Private Life"; Boyd, *Wide Open Town*; Faderman and Timmons, *Gay L.A.*, 9–17; Shah, *Stranger Intimacy*; James T. Sears, *Behind the Mask*; White, *Pre-Gay L.A.*; Gallo, *Different Daughters*; Armstrong, *Forging Gay Identities*; Meeker, *Contacts Desired*.

14. Boyd, *Wide Open Town*. See also Verge, "World War II."

15. Faderman and Timmons, *Gay L.A.*; Boyd, *Wide Open Town*; Armstrong, *Forging Gay Identities*; Kenney, *Mapping Gay L.A.*

16. Jonathan Ned Katz, *Invention of Heterosexuality*; D'Emilio and Freedman, *Intimate Matters*.

17. Clare Sears, *Arresting Dress*; Faderman and Timmons, *Gay L.A.*; Ullman, "Twentieth Century Way"; Ullman, *Sex Seen*; Hurewitz, *Bohemian Los Angeles*; Craig Scott, "Lust, Language, and Legislation.

18. Hurewitz, "Between Liberation and Oppression," 326.

19. Hurewitz, *Bohemian Los Angeles*; Hurewitz, "Between Liberation and Oppression"; James T. Sears, *Behind the Mask*; White, *Pre-Gay L.A.*; Gallo, *Different Daughters*; Armstrong, *Forging Gay Identities*; Meeker, *Contacts Desired*; Loftin, *Masked Voices*.

20. Boyd, *Wide Open Town*.

21. Faderman and Timmons, *Gay L.A.*; Silverman and Stryker, *Screaming Queens*; Stryker, *Transgender History*.

22. Joseph Plaster, "A (Brief) History of Vanguard," in *Vanguard Revisited*, edited by Rohrer and Plaster, 5–8. For a thoughtful assessment of the racial and class dynamics of organizing in San Francisco's Tenderloin in the 1960s, see Hanhardt, *Safe Space*, 35–80; Sides, *Erotic City*; Hobson, *Lavender and Red*; Stein, *Rethinking the Gay and Lesbian Movement*.

23. Kissack, "Freaking Fag Revolutionaries"; Duberman, *Has the Gay Movement Failed?*, xv.

24. Sides, "Sexual Revolutions and Sexual Politics."

25. Hanhardt, *Safe Space*, 85. See also Sides, *Erotic City*, 91–96.

26. Armstrong, *Forging Gay Identities*; Faderman and Timmons, *Gay L.A.*

27. Hobson, *Lavender and Red*, 8–9.

28. Hanhardt, *Safe Space*, 21.

29. Bell, introduction to *Beyond the Politics*, 8.

30. Stein, *Rethinking the Gay and Lesbian Movement*, 121–34. See also Hurewitz, "Between Liberation and Oppression." These shifts were not limited to California. See Stewart-Winter, *Queer Clout* (Chicago); Eisenbach, *Gay Power* (New York).

31. Douglass, *California Idea*; Callan, "Higher Education in California"; Boggs and Galizio, *College for All Californians*; Gerth, *People's University*; Pelfrey, *Brief History*.

32. Bell, *California Crucible*; McGirr, *Suburban Warriors*; Clayton Howard, *Closet and the Cul-de-Sac*.

33. Lassiter, "Inventing Family Values."

34. "School Employees—Homosexuality," December 5, 1977, UC Law SF Scholarship Repository, accessed July 30, 2023, https://repository.uclawsf.edu/ca_ballot_inits/351/; Ward and Freeman, "Defending Gay Rights"; Fejes, *Gay Rights and Moral Panic*.

35. On the influence of radical grassroots organizing on gay liberation in California generally, see Hobson, *Lavender and Red*; Leighton, "All of Us Are Unapprehended Felons."

36. Dong, "Third World Liberation"; Ryan, "Counter College"; Zelnik and Cohen, *Free Speech Movement*.

37. Blumenfeld, interview by author; Raya, interview by author; Bryant, interview by author.

38. Only a few scholars have focused beyond individual campus experiences. See Clawson, "Queers on Campus"; Dilley, *Gay Liberation to Campus Assimilation*.

39. For example, see Suran, "Coming Out against the War"; Lekus, "Queer and Present Dangers"; Hobson, *Lavender and Red*; Mumford, "Trouble with Gay Rights."

40. Some scholars have described that shift as one from liberation to assimilation. For example, in *Gay Liberation to Campus Assimilation*, Patrick Dilley, argues that the earliest post-Stonewall "non-heterosexual" student organizing at Midwestern colleges and universities was more militant and revolutionary. By the mid-1970s, that organizing focused less on demanding larger social and cultural change and more on demands for inclusion and services on campus, a seat at the proverbial table.

41. In *Lavender and Red*, Hobson documents the persistence of radical gay and lesbian politics beyond the early days of gay liberation, suggesting the need to pay close attention to where such organizing happens.

42. Hobson, *Lavender and Red*, esp. 90–96; Simon Hall, "Protest Movements in the 1970s"; Lassiter, "Inventing Family Values."

43. Langman, "Cycles of Contention"; Reichard, "We Can't Hide."

44. Blackwell, *Chicana Power*; Hom, "Unifying Differences"; Quin, "To Stamp Out the Oppression." At the University of North Carolina, Chapel Hill, the Carolina Gay Association was a "primarily white association"; gay Black students "usually chose to associate with the Black Student Movement," preferring a group that "confronted racism on campus to one that advocated for gay rights, a place where they also did not have to out themselves" (Faulkenbury and Hayworth, "Carolina Gay Association," 117).

45. Marine, *Stonewall's Legacy*; Dilley, *Queer Man on Campus*; Sweat, "Crossing Boundaries"; Gomez, ""*No Te Rajes*—Don't Back Down!"; Tijerina-Revilla, "Are All Raza Womyn Queer?"; Beck, "Different Kind of Activism"; Sueyoshi, "Redefining Higher Education."

46. Jonathan Ned Katz, *Love Stories*; Wilk, "What's a Crush?"; Jacqueline Dowd Hall, "To Widen the Reach"; Syrett, "Boys of Beaver Meadow"; MacKay, introduction to *Wolf Girls at Vassar*; Sahli, "Smashing."

47. Shand-Tucci, *Crimson Letter*; Wright, *Harvard's Secret Court*; Pellegrini, "Gay Purge at Harvard."

48. D'Emilio, *Making Trouble*, 68. See also Canaday, *Straight State*.

49. David K. Johnson, *Lavender Scare*. See also Dilley, *Queer Man on Campus*.

50. Loftin, *Masked Voices*; Weiler, "Case of Martha Deane"; Nash and Silverman, "Indelible Mark"; Graves, "History."

51. Prescott, "College Mental Health"; Ross and Mendelsohn, "Homosexuality in College"; Office of the Dean of Students, "Annual Report to the President, 1950–51," July 1, 1951, Records of the Office of Student Activities, UC Berkeley Archives; "Student Cleared in Deviate Case," *San Francisco Examiner*, May 3, 1956.

52. One of San Francisco's most infamous gay bar raids—that of the Tay Bush Inn in August 1961—netted the police 103 suspected "sex deviates," among them "many" students ("Big Sex Raid—Cops Arrest 103," *San Francisco Chronicle*, August 14, 1961, 3). See also Boyd, *Wide Open Town*, 213–16; D'Emilio, *Sexual Politics, Sexual Communities*, 184.

53. Toni McNaron describes her time as an untenured junior faculty member as "encased in silence," suggesting that gay and lesbian faculty members during the 1950s and 1960s "struggled with silence as we attempted to protect ourselves and to find others like us" (McNaron, "Poisoned Ivy," 13). For a discussion of the impact of the Cold War era repression of gay and lesbian teachers and college professors, see Loftin, *Masked Voices*, 121–40.

54. Loftin, *Masked Voices*, 136–38; Syrett, *Company He Keeps*, esp. chap. 6.

55. John Howard, *Men Like That*, 69; Kleinberg, *Alienated Affections*, 13; Dilley, *Queer Man on Campus*.

56. As Cynthia Secor noted in 1975, organizations like the Daughters of Bilitis and Mattachine "were never campus-based" even though they had student members ("Lesbians: The Open Door," 14). Students occasionally wrote seeking information on joining a chapter. See Don Brown to Mattachine, November 19, 1953, Box 6, Folder 10, Mattachine Society Project Collection, ONE Archives (student at UC Berkeley); Jack [Richard J. Fanning] to Hall Call, November 20, 1959, Box 6, Folder 19, Mattachine Society Project Collection, ONE Archives (intends on enrolling in UCLA: "I may be able to do some recruiting and proselytizing"); Michael McClellan to Hal Call, January 17, 1968, Box 6, Folder 34, Mattachine Society Project Collection, ONE Archives (seeking organization for "young male adults of similar tastes. Preferably men who are currently in college or men who recently graduated.")

57. "DOB Proudly Announces Blanche M. Baker Memorial Scholarship Fund," *The Ladder*, March 1961, 5; "Scholarship Announced by DOB," *Vector*, April 1965; "A Tribute to a Friend," *The Ladder*, November 1962, 14–15. *The Ladder* is available in GLBTHS Periodicals.

58. Gallo, *Different Daughters*, 84. Members of the Daughters of Bilitis periodically emphasized that these scholarships were "not limited to 'Lesbians.' They are for *women*" ("Readers Respond," *The Ladder*, February 1967, 20).

59. Charles P. Thorp, "What It's Like to Be a Teenage Homosexual," 1969, EC.

60. "More Good Words," *Vector*, November 1968, 18.

61. Rohrer and Plaster, *Vanguard Revisited*.

62. It is difficult to determine the demographics of the student body at specific institutions during the 1970s. According to a 1998 report from the National Center for Education Statistics, the number of college students enrolled in four-year institutions increased from 1.2 million in 1970 to 1.7 million in 1977, with some decline occurring by 1979. Community college enrollment increased from just shy of 700,000 in 1970 to 1 million by 1979. By 1980, women earned about half of all undergraduate degrees but only 30 percent of professional degrees. As of 1996, 49 percent of all college students in California were from minority groups, with 90 percent of all college-bound students slated to attend public universities. See Snyder and Hoffman, *State Comparisons*, 139, 145, 171, 114, 125. Where possible, I have sought to highlight the voices of students of color to shine a light on how their experiences compared to those of their white peers. In addition, I have attempted to parse out these ethnic, racial, and gender dynamics, recognizing that they varied over time even on a particular campus.

63. Hobson argues that *gay* and *lesbian* were "less stable or rigidly bounded descriptors of sexuality and gender than they have come to be assumed" (*Lavender and Red*, 10).

64. Romesburg, introduction to *Routledge History of Queer America*, 5. As Regina Kunzel notes, many historians have "found [queer] useful as both a critical and a descriptive tool," and some have adopted it for its analytical (as opposed to descriptive) possibilities ("Review Essay," 1565). See also Hanhardt, "Queer History."

65. According to Stein, using *LGBT* poses "distinct problems for historians," who seek to avoid imposing contemporary terminology on the past (*Rethinking the Gay and Lesbian Movement*, 5–9).

66. Some cisgender student organizers sought to educate themselves and others about the experiences of transsexuals, whom Susan Stryker helpfully describes as "people who move away from the gender they were assigned at birth, people who cross over (trans-) the boundaries constructed by their culture to define and contain that gender" (*Transgender History*, 1).

67. On the importance of oral history to LGBTQ history generally, see Boyd and Ramírez, *Bodies of Evidence*.

68. For example, Patrick Dilley's recent study of "non-heterosexual" student organizing in the Midwest, *Gay Liberation to Campus Assimilation*, features chapters with narratives about individual campuses rather than the thematic approach I take here. Jonathan Coley's *Gay on God's Campus*, a study of LGBT students at Christian colleges, focuses primarily on how and why students become involved in LGBT activism in those settings, comparing and contrasting four schools in Tennessee; Washington, D.C.; Indiana; and Chicago.

69. George L. Goddett, "CSUMB Gay Club Out and Wired," *The Paper*, July–August 1996, available at https://digitalcommons.csumb.edu/thepaper/12/. The first mention of All in the Family in the campus newspaper, the *Otter Realm*, occurred in its February 1997 issue. The *Otter Realm* is available at https://digitalcommons.csumb.edu/otterrealm/index.3.html.

70. The passage of Proposition 22 motivated many activists in California's LGBTQ community to turn their attention to marriage equality (Broaddus, "Commentary"; Rofes, "After California Votes to Limit Marriage").

71. All in the Family subsequently divided into two organizations, one focused on self-support (Pride) and another focused on activism (Out and About). Out and About embraced visible public programming and calling out homophobia in the classroom, in residence halls, and on campus generally through educational campaigns and direct resistance. And while Pride continued to meet for a time, Out and About became the primary face of LGBTQ student organizing on campus, sponsoring the first Drag Balls in 2003 and 2004 and organizing campus participation in the National Day of Silence. See "What's Up at CSU Monterey Bay," *Otter Realm*, March 26, 2003; *Otter Realm*, April 30, 2003; "Silencing Ignorance," *Otter Realm*, April 29, 2004.

Chapter 1. Creating Campus Organizing Homes

1. Beemyn, "Silence Is Broken"; Eisenbach, *Gay Power*. The suggestion that student homophile leagues at Stanford and Berkeley were in the works seems to have first appeared in *Tangents*, December 1, 1966, 18. *Tangents*, a newsletter published by ONE in Los Angeles, is available at https://www.jstor.org/site/reveal-digital/independent-voices. Dean's offices on both campuses apparently had no knowledge of such organizing ("Campus Society for Homosexuals," *San Francisco Chronicle*, May 4, 1967).

2. Homophile League, "Note to File," May 15, 1967, Series I, Box 23, Folder: Homosexuality/Homophile League, Lyman Papers, SULDSC. Gerard Koskovich suggests that Stephen Donaldson (born Robert Martin), one of the founders of Columbia's Student

Homophile League, had met a Stanford student who expressed interest in organizing a group there. See Gerard Koskovich, "Out on the Farm: The Gay and Lesbian Rights Movement of Stanford University, 1968–1978," May 1988, Stanford University, Series VIII, Box 3, Folder 17, Stanford QSR Records.

3. Gerard Koskovich, "Out on the Farm: The Gay and Lesbian Rights Movement of Stanford University, 1968–1978," May 1988, Stanford University, Series VIII, Box 3, Folder 17, Stanford QSR Records; "Homosexual Group Forms," *StD*, February 2, 1968; "Panel Focuses on Homosexual Life," *StD*, February 5, 1968; Bob Beyers, memo, February 8, 1968, Series I, Box 23, Folder: Homosexuality/Homophile League, Lyman Papers, SULDSC. The *Stanford Daily* is available at https://archives.stanforddaily.com/.

4. Mrs. William A. Mudgett to President's Office, February 6, 1968, F[red] G[lover] to Lyle, February 7, 1968, both in Series I, Box 23, Folder: Homosexuality/Homophile League, Lyman Papers, SULDSC.

5. Andrew W. Doty to Mrs. William A. Mudgett, March 1, 1968, Series I, Box 23, Folder: Homosexuality/Homophile League, Lyman Papers, SULDSC.

6. "Student Homophile League," *Society for Individual Rights Gold Sheet*, April 1968, 2, GLBTHS Periodicals. Stanford's Student Homophile League appeared on a list of homophile movement organizations noted in the February–March 1969 issue of a Kansas City, Missouri, publication, the *Phoenix* (https://jstor.org/stable/community.28042799). This publication is different from the San Francisco State University newspaper by the same name.

7. *Berkeley Barb*, February 28, 1969. Capron's ad read, "BRIGHT, happy, hip gay seeking three-dimensional relationship" and drew a few responses from confused people who thought he was seeking "a three-way" encounter (Capron, interview by author). The *Berkeley Barb* is available at https://www.jstor.org/site/reveal-digital/independent-voices.

8. Capron, interview by author.

9. Chica, "Toward a Sociology" (place-making as "explicit or tacit cooperation among people to create, maintain, and give meaning to places in space through bodily occupation under different constraints and access to resources" 2).

10. SGP, "Statement of Purpose," [ca. 1969], Box 1, Folder 10, Queer Resource Center Records, UC Berkeley Archives; "Gay Students at Stanford," *South Bay Chronicle* (supplement to *Bay Area Reporter*), September 15, 1977, 35; San Francisco State GLF constitution, March 16, 1970, Box: SF State Student Organizations—Gay Lib—History Student Union, Folder: Gay Lib—National Gay Students Conference, SFSUSCA; "New Movement at UCLA: Gay Liberation Movement Surfaces Here," *DB*, May 4, 1970; "Purpose of Gay Lib—Openess [sic]," *DB*, November 3, 1970; Sacramento State College Society for Homosexual Freedom Constitution, [ca. February 1970], Box: San Francisco State Student Organizations—Gay Lib—History Student Union, Folder: Gay Lib—Various Ca. State Colleges, SFSUSCA; Fred Oakman and Maud Haimson, "Why a Gay Students' Union?," *StD*, January 7, 1971; GPU constitution, 1972, Series I, Box 2, Folder: GPU Office Records—Constitution (1972), Stanford QSR Records; Glenn Erickson, "Why Gay Students Union," *Gayzette*, February 12, 1975. The *Bay Area Reporter* is available at https://cdnc.ucr.edu/ as well as at the GLBT Historical Society. The *Daily Bruin* is available at https://guides.library.ucla.edu/c.php?g=180838&p=6669925. The *Gayzette* is available in ONE Periodicals.

11. Mentley, interview by author.

12. Gary Steele, "Gays at UCLA: An Unauthorized History," *Gayzette*, October 2, 1975; Raya, interview by author; Reichard, "We Can't Hide"; Lynn McMichael, "Dr. Marty Rogers: Evolving Gay Community," *SH*, May 19, 1971; Joel Roberts, interview by Dan-

iel Bao, December 28, 1989, Oral History Collection, GLBTHS; Koskovich, "Private Lives, Public Struggles"; Michael Silverstein, "From Professional Help to Helping Ourselves," July 1, 1974,

13. Laurence, interview by author. On the Committee for Homosexual Freedom, see Sides, *Erotic City*, 90–97. Compare "Gay Lib Conference December 28," *San Francisco Free Press*, December 22, 1969–January 7, 1970; "Gay Liberation Conference Closes Five Day Conference," *Berkeley Gazette*, December 31, 1969, Subject File: Berkeley Gay Liberation, ONE Archives; "Gay Lib Conference and Symposium," *San Francisco Free Press*, January 1970 (all noting the participation of students from multiple campuses). The *San Francisco Free Press* and the *Berkeley Gazette* are available at https://www.jstor.org/site/reveal-digital/independent-voices.

14. Don Jackson, "Gays Alive Down South," *Berkeley Barb*, January 9–15, 1970; "A Mercifully Short History of GSU/UCLA," *Gayzette*, October 2, 1974. On the connection between gay liberation and campus organizing, see D'Emilio, "Campus Environment."

15. Los Angeles Gay Liberation Conference flyer, Los Angeles City College, May 11–12[, 1970], "What Is Gay Liberation?" (flyer for Los Angeles Gay Liberation), [ca. spring 1970], "Why Haven't You Heard" (flyer), all in Subject File: Gay Liberation Front, Los Angeles, ONE Archives; "GayLib Goes to City College," *Gay Lib News*, May 31, 1970, Box 1, Folder 22, Gay Liberation Front (GLF) Los Angeles Records, ONE Archives; "LACC Picketing Opens Lines of Communication," *Advocate*, July 8–21, 1970, 2; "GLF Struggles for Heterosexual Acceptance," *Collegian*, November 3, 1970. The *Advocate* is available at the San Francisco Public Library. The *Collegian* (Los Angeles City College) is available at https://lacitycollege.contentdm.oclc.org/digital/collection/LACCNP02.

16. "Candidates Voice Platforms," *Collegian*, May 18, 1973; "Review of Student Body Candidates' Proposed Measures," *Collegian*, May 22, 1973; "Gay Activist Urges LACC Organization," *Collegian*, September 25, 1973.

17. "Gay Union Maps Future Directions," *Collegian*, November 2, 1973; "Campus Club Calendar," *Collegian*, March 1, 1974; "Bake Sales Set," *Collegian*, March 8, 1974; "Campus Club Calendar," *Collegian*, March 15, 1974; "Gay Union Holds Forum," *Collegian*, May 17, 1974; "ICC Relates Condemnation Votes," *Collegian*, April 5, 1974. By the fall of 1974, the Gay Liberation Union had again become the Gay Student Union (Gay Liberation Union meeting notice, *Collegian*, November 1, 1974; Gay Student Union meeting notice, *Collegian*, November 22, 1974; "Clubs," Los Angeles City College Student Handbook 74–75, 20, Subject File: Los Angeles City College, ONE Archives). In 1979, the GSU became the Gay and Lesbian Student Union (Gay and Lesbian Student Union meeting minutes, October 31, 1979, Subject File: Los Angeles City College (LACC) GSU, ONE Archives).

18. "The Attack of the Liberated Women: Would You Want Your Brother to Marry One?," *SH*, January 16, 1969; "The Equality Movement: Women's Liberation," *Hornet Focus* (special issue of *State Hornet*), February 25, 1970; "Women's Caucus Showing Results," *SH*, September 29, 1971.

19. "Applauds Women's Caucus," *SH*, October 11, 1974; Smith, interview by author.

20. GSU advertisement, [ca. July 14, 1972], CSULA GSU File. Over the next few semesters, the new GSU organized educational events, created a newsletter, and held socials; by 1976, it was joined on campus by a lesbian student organization, Lavender Menace ("Proud Gays Speak" (clipping), *UT*, October 4, 1972, "Gay Group Finally Gets Recognition" (clipping), *College Times*, July 28, 1972, GSU flyer, Spring 1973, all in CSULA GSU File; "Gays Hope to Improve Their Image on Campus," *Los Angeles Times*, December 7, 1975; student activities calendar, November 15–21, 1976, CSULA GSU File. The *University Times* is available at https://digitalcollections.calstatela.edu/luna/servlet/CalStateLA~3~3.

21. "Gay Students Interested in a Gay Student Union" (advertisement), *DS*, Novem-

ber 21, 1972; "Gay Students Interested in Gay Students Organization" (advertisement), *DS*, September 13, 1973. The *Daily Sundial* is available at https://digital-library.csun.edu/sundial.

22. "Gay Liberation Front at SF State" (flyer), [ca. March 1970], Box: Student Organizations—Gay Lib—History Student Organizations, Folder: Gay Lib—Flyers & Posters, SFSUSCA. On the GLF, see Stein, "Teaching and Researching." Lee Mentley recalled seeking interested students by posting flyers for a new GSU at Cal State Long Beach in the early 1970s (Mentley, interview by author).

23. Reichard, "Animating Ephemera."

24. A Gay Woman, "Adjusting to Gay Life," *StD*, October 26, 1970; Steve, "Stanford Gays," *StD*, October 28, 1970.

25. "Stanford Gay Lib or GSU Rap," *StD*, November 10, 1970; Stanford GSU meeting, *StD*, November 17, 1970; "Stanford Gay Students Union," *StD*, December 1, 1970; Robert Croonquist, interview by Ina Tiangco, May 2012, Stanford University LGBT Alumni Oral History Interviews, SULDSC.

26. Jon Haughton, "Out of the Closets," *DN*, January 6, 1971. The *Daily Nexus* is available at https://www.library.ucsb.edu/special-collections/ucsb-daily-nexus-and-antecedent-Newspapers.

27. "Gay Women and Society," *DN*, October 14, 1974.

28. GPU constitution, 1972, Series I, Box 2, Folder: GPU Office Records—Constitution (1972), Stanford QSR Records.

29. Meeting agendas, July 23, 30, 1973, Series I, Box 3, Folder: GPU Misc. Materials 1973–77, Stanford QSR Records.

30. "Identity Crisis for Gays Concerns GSU Leader," *SpD*, September 16, 1977. The *Spartan Daily* is available at https://scholarworks.sjsu.edu/spartan_daily/.

31. Ferd Lewis, "'Gay Militants' Eye Recognition," *RR*, January 7, 1972; Charles Stougard, letter to the editor, *RR*, February 4, 1972; Anna, letter to the editor, *RR*, February 4, 1972; Thomas W. Moore, "A Gay Plea for Understanding," *RR*, November 3, 1972; "GSU Charter Temporarily Blocked," *RR*, December 1, 1972; Manuel Fuentes Jr., "Rules, Rules, Rules" (letter to the editor), *RR*, January 12, 1973; "Club Week," *RR*, February 6, 1978). The *Renegade Rip* (Bakersfield College) is available at https://www.bakersfieldcollege.edu/archives/renegade-rip.

32. Reese, interview by author.

33. Examples include "Gay Women's Rap Group," *DC*, November 11, 1970; "Gay Women's Open House," *DC*, November 13, 1970; "Gay Women's Rap Group," *DC*, December 2, 1970; "Gay Awareness," *Chico Wildcat*, May 16, 1974. The *Daily Californian* is available at https://digicoll.lib.berkeley.edu/search?ln=en&cc=Daily+Cal. The *Chico Wildcat* (California State University, Chico) is available at http://archives.csuchico.edu/digital/collection/p17133coll6.

34. "Year's Plans Made at Women's Center," *SpD*, September 20, 1972; "Bum Rap for Women," *SpD*, October 11, 1972.

35. "Study, Discussion Groups Planned for I.V. Feminists," *DN*, October 2, 1972; "Women's Center a Success in I.V.," *DN*, February 6, 1974; "Gay Women's Group" (advertisement), *DN*, January 26, 1976.

36. For example, the calendar in a 1974 newsletter included a lesbian rap, a lesbian mothers' group, and a women's dance (Sacramento Women's Center newsletter, November 1974 calendar, Box 2, Folder 31, WSPR. See also Sacramento Women's Center Bookstore newsletter, June 1974, Box 3, Folder 18, WSPR. The Women's Center at San José State included similar notices in its newsletter, *Up from the Basement*. See for example, *Up from the Basement*, January 1973 (lesbian rap), May 1973 ("Gay Dance," Wom-

en's Studies Student Committee meeting, Women's Weekend in San Francisco, Women's Week at San José State), both in Box 2, Folder 33, WSPR.

37. Bryant, interview by author; Sacramento Women's Center Bookstore flyer, [ca. 1970s], Box 3, Folder 18, WSPR. As a 1973 description of the center noted, it provided not only services but also "a space for women to come together" and to "become aware of our sisterhood as well as differences due to race, class and lifestyles" (*Feminist News*, February 13, 1973, Box 5, Folder 6, WSPR; Kristen Hogan, "Women's Studies in Feminist Bookstores"; Liddle, "More Than a Bookstore").

38. Mary Wells, "Lesbians, AS Dispute Women's Center's Focus," *Zenger's/Golden Gater*, December 5, 1978; "Women's Center Opens," *Zenger's*, October 10, 1973. *Zenger's/The Golden Gater* (San Francisco State University) is available at Special Collections and Archives, J. Paul Leonard Library, San Francisco State University, San Francisco.

39. Mary Wells, "Lesbians, AS Dispute Women's Center's Focus," *Zenger's/Golden Gater*, December 5, 1978. Lesbian students, particularly those who identified as separatists, continued to find an organizing home at the center into the late 1970s despite efforts by the Gay and Lesbian Campus Community student organization to bolster lesbian involvement. See Gail Joy Stewart, "Gay Campus Group Out for More Women," *Phoenix*, November 1, 1979. The *Phoenix* (San Francisco State University) is available at Special Collections and Archives, J. Paul Leonard Library, San Francisco State University, San Francisco.

40. "Women's Centers," *Sacramento Bee*, April 12, 1977.

41. Strachan, interview by author.

42. Blumenfeld, "Gays on Campus," 24; Stein, "Teaching and Researching," 13.

43. "Gay Women at CULB: Most Remain Hidden," *49er*, April 11, 1975; "Functions Outlined for Oct. Gay Pride Week," *49er*, September 12, 1975. The *Forty Niner/49er/Daily 49er* (California State University, Long Beach) is available at https://www.digifind-it.com/csulb/views/newspapers.php?id=4.

44. GPU constitution, 1972, Series I, Box 2, Folder: GPU Office Records—Constitution (1972), Stanford QSR Records; GPU Lesbian Collective flyer, [ca. 1970s], Box 1, Folder: Gay Info, Corbin Papers, GLBTHS. Joel Roberts described the earliest iteration of the GSU at Stanford as almost all men and a little elitist (Joel Roberts, interview by Daniel Bao, December 28, 1989, Oral History Collection, GLBTHS).

45. Gay Women's Collective advertisement, *DN*, October 17, 1974; "Dykes Playday" (advertisement), *DN*, January 17, 1975.

46. Reese, interview by author.

47. *GG*, April 1974, CSULB GSU File; "Gay Women at CSULB: Most Remain Hidden," *49er*, April 11, 1975; "Functions Outlined for Oct. Gay Pride Week," *49er*, September 12, 1975.

48. Person, interview by author.

49. Freda Smith, "Gay Stereotyping: Breaking Down the Barriers," *SH*, March 1, 1972, 5; Howie Plzak, "Cal State Gay People's Union Celebrates 10th Year as CSUS," *Mom... Guess What?* November 1980, 12, GLBTHS Periodicals.

50. Stein, "Teaching and Researching," 11.

51. Paula Hamilton, "Gay Avocate" [sic], *Zenger's*, November 5, 1975, 2. Another student, John Blackburn, recalled Hamilton's work to increase lesbian participation in the Gay Academic Union (Blackburn, interview by author).

52. "Gays Hope to Improve Their Image on Campus," *Los Angeles Times*, December 7, 1975.

53. Warren Blumenfeld, "School Is Not a Gay Place to Be," *Gay Sunshine*, October–November 1971, 5, GLBTHS Periodicals; Sivertsen, interview by author; Strachan, inter-

view by author; Nutting, interview by author. Women formed the Lesbian Union at UC Berkeley because gay men "dominated 'mixed' organizations" and because same-sex attraction was not enough of a basis for forming a coherent group. The lesbians who formed the union sought "to show other gay women that they're not alone, and to educate straight people to the fact that lesbians are real people, not freaks." Moreover, the Lesbian Union worked on issues relevant to "women generally," such as protesting a policy that "forc[ed] some women to enter the birth control program in order to get a pap smear" (Mark Kenchelian, "Gays Struggle for Recognition in Political Arena," *DC*, April 25, 1974). See also Registered Student Organizations, Fall 1973–Spring 1974, Box 28, Folder 29, Records of the Office of Student Activities, UC Berkeley Archives; Lesbian Union meeting notice, *WOMAN*, May 1974, 3, Box 48, Folder: University of California Berkeley Women Student Groups, Women's Resource Center Library, Bancroft Library, University of California, Berkeley.

54. "It's Political," *Advocate*, April 9, 1975.

55. "Gay Lib Now Recognized in the Cal State System," *SpD*, March 3, 1972; Sivertsen, interview by author; "Gay Women's Groups," Box 22, Folder 6, Lyon and Martin Papers, GLBTHS; "Lesbian-Feminist Alliance of Santa Clara County," *Lesbian Voices*, Fall 1976, 56, GLBTHS Periodicals; "Misunderstanding Sexuality Cited as Problem by Lesbians," *SpD*, October 11, 1976.

56. GSU meeting notice, *SpD*, September 28, 1979.

57. Aura, interview by author; *DB*, February 5, 1973; "Gay Meeting Info Sought" (letter to the editor), *DB*, March 5, 1973. A different letter writer expressed thanks: "It is great to hear from another gay woman who is interested in the gay life on campus," she noted. "It is very difficult to meet other gay women" since others are also "reserved" about making this information public. "I am looking forward to joining the lesbian organization and finally being able to be myself, if only once a week." See "Glad Gay Women Are Speaking Out," *DB*, March 8, 1973.

58. "Gay Women Organize Here," *DB*, March 8, 1973; "More Campus Events," *DB*, March 9, 1973 (listing Gay Sisterhood, Gay Liberation, and Gay Sisterhood Coffeehouse); "Gay Sisterhood at UCLA," *LT*, March 1973. The *Lesbian Tide* is available at https://www.jstor.org/site/reveal-digital/independent-voices. Meryl Friedman, a New York schoolteacher in the 1970s, reflected on the importance of such organizations for lesbian students: "Socially, lesbian students need group or club activities to provide them with the opportunity to discover and meet each other. Such encounters would help to eliminate the depression that results from living the isolated existence that many young lesbians face" (Meryl Friedman, "Lesbian as Teacher, Teacher as Lesbian," in *Our Right to Love*, ed. Vida, 157).

59. Aura, interview by author; "A Mercifully Short History of GSU/UCLA," *Gayzette*, October 2, 1974; *Patchwork*, January 22, 1976, 2, CAGSO File.

60. Sivertsen, interview by author; Duplechan, interview by author; Willie Johnson, "GSU 'Serves Gays and Educates Non-Gays,'" *DB*, October 18, 1975. As Susan Y. F. Chen recalled of her time in college, likely in the late 1980s or early 1990s, "When I first came out in college, I was the only Asian gay or lesbian person consistently present in the 'gay' community at school.... Over the years, the experiences of meeting first, Asian feminists and then Asian lesbians, were truly lifechanging [*sic*] for me" ("Slowly but Surely," 83).

61. Reichard, "We Can't Hide"; Raya, interview by author.

62. One report estimated that "minority students" made up 75 percent of the total student population in the late 1970s: nearly half of that number were Black, with in-

creasing numbers of Latinx students. See Gold, "Institutional Research," 16; Gold, *Analysis of A.A. Degrees*, 23.

63. "Gay Celebration Gets Underway," *Hollywood Independent*, June 27, 1979, clipping in Subject File: Los Angeles City College, ONE Archives.

64. Freda Marshall's candidate profile for homecoming queer included campus activities as a "Non-Gay Member of the GSU" (clipping, [*The Collegian*?], Fall 1979, Subject File: Los Angeles City College, ONE Archives). Ann Yuri Uyeda reflected that in college, she stayed in the closet for a long time "because I just didn't think there were any queer Asian Americans—while I knew gay men and lesbians, everyone was white. My fear was that I didn't know what it would be like to be an Asian lesbian" ("All at Once, All Together," 111).

65. Lesbian feminist organizers in Los Angeles created new spaces—outside of the bars—as ways to "reinforce the distinction between themselves and the gay liberation movement." These spaces included the Gay Women's Service Center, Sisters' Liberation House, and the Westside Women's Center, all founded in 1971 or 1972 (Kenney, *Mapping Gay L.A.*, 125). See also Enke, *Finding the Movement*.

66. For examples at UCLA, see "Meetings" (UCLA Gay Lib), *DB*, October 9, 1972; "Gay Liberation," *DB*, November 9, 1972; GSU advertisements, *DB*, January 9, 1974, February 12, 1975, March 4, November 11, 1976, April 28, 1977, April 5, 1978.

67. "Gay Liberation Conference Closes Five Day Symposium," *Berkeley Gazette*, December 31, 1969, Subject File: Berkeley Gay Liberation, ONE Archives; Brian Hoey, "Identity Crisis for Gays Concerns GSU Leader," *SpD*, September 16, 1977 (most GSU meetings drew fifty attendees); Stanford GPU to Gay Community Services Center, March 22, 1973, Box 1, Folder 4, Gay and Lesbian Alliance at Stanford University Records, ONE Archives; Beardsley, interview by author (between fifty and one hundred students attended UCLA GSU meetings around 1974–75).

68. Tina McWilliams, "Gay Student Union Offers Aid, Counseling, Weekly Meetings," *DB*, October 5, 1977; Brian Hoey, "Homosexuals Escape Their Harassment," *SpD*, September 27, 1977.

69. "Gay Students' Union Anticipate[s] Official A.S. Recognition for Group," *49er*, March 7, 1972; "Gays Gather Gauging Goals, Gripes," *49er*, March 15, 1972; "GSU Continues Association, Helps Gays Seek Roles, Friendships," *49er*, October 5, 1972; "GSU Lets Campus Gays Know They're Not Alone," *49er*, October 17, 1973.

70. Bryant, interview by author.

71. Paul Wysocki, interview by Ted Sahl, in Sahl, *From Closet to Community*, 119–20.

72. Beardsley, interview by author.

73. "The Struggle to Be Gay," *Vector*, September 1975, 47–49.

74. Orta, interview by author. Orta did not recall what organization had sponsored the meeting, only that the flyer described the session as *gay*.

75. Fertig, interview by author.

76. Don Spring, "Two Outrageous Years with the UCLA GSU (or) How I Learned to Stop Worrying and Burn the Closet," *Gayzette*, June 9, 1975. Spring later recalled that at the first meeting, "it took me an hour to actually get into the room; I was really nervous" (Spring, interview by author).

77. GSU advertisement, *DS*, February 25, 1976 (both on- and off-campus meetings).

78. Warren Blumenfeld, "Reflections on Pre-Stonewall GLB Life," *Massachusetts Daily Collegian*, October 10, 1995, available at https://archive.org/details/massachuse19951996univ/page/n187/mode/2up.

79. *The Bridge* (San José Gay Liberation), August 6, 1970, GLBTHS Periodicals.

80. San José GLF press release, [ca. May 1971], Subject File: San José (Calif.), ONE Archives.

81. GSU meeting, *DC*, September 29, 1972; "The Gay Lounge," *DC*, September 14, 27, 1972. Columbia University also hosted a "gay lounge" in 1971: "All those who used the lounge reiterated their simple pleasure in now having a center where they could meet and rap congenially and unselfconsciously with people from the same community with similar interests and problems" (Liebert, "Gay Student," 40).

82. Corbin, interview by author; Gerard Koskovich and Hunter Hargraves, "Creating Queer Space at Stanford: Pages from a Student Scrapbook," April–May 2004, copy in author's possession.

83. Gary Steele, "Gays at UCLA: An Unauthorized History," *Gayzette*, October 2, 1975.

84. Duplechan, interview by author. The January 20, 1971, UC Berkeley *GSU Newsletter* noted that the organization's office was important because "many people with questions about what it is to be gay are too uptight to stand out there in public and talk to us" but "might be more at ease in the (relative) privacy of the office" (Subject File: Gay Student Union, ONE Archives).

85. "Office Rearranged," *Gayzette*, April 14, 1975.

86. Duplechan, interview by author.

87. Donald Warman, "Bob and John: Two for the Revolution," *NewsWest*, January 9–22, 1976, ONE Periodicals. San Francisco State's Gay Academic Union office was a place to drop in and meet people, an especially important venue for a commuter campus (Blackburn, interview by author).

88. Entries for January 11, 18, 21, 25, February 5, 6, 27, April 11, May 4, June 22, August 20, October 29, November 13, 1973, Gay People's Union Logbook and General Information, Series I, Box 1, Stanford QSR Records.

89. Blackburn, interview by author.

90. Jim Stebinger, "Lesbians Plan Activities," *DB*, October 30, 1974; "UCLA Lesbian Sisterhood, Women's Resource Center Lose Campus Offices," *Gayzette*, May 15, 1975.

91. See *GLF Newsletter*, September 6, 1970, 2, Box 1, Folder 29, Thorpe [Thorp] Papers, GLBTHS (San Francisco State GLF party); Gay-In Picnic advertisement, *DN*, December 4, 1970; GSU meeting and social hour, *DC*, October 5, 1972; "Let's Get Together," *Proud*, October 13, 1972, CSULB GSU File; "Gay Picnic," *DC*, October 20, 1972; "Homosexual Craze Hits Campus" (party advertisement), *DB*, April 25, 1973; "Gays Dance, Dine, Discuss," *49er*, March 20, 1973. A UCLA GSU picnic included "Food, Fun and Games, Participate in Tug-of-War, Crack the Whip (non-S&M version), Blind Man's Bluff, [and] Hide and Seek" (*Gayzette*, May 1, 1975). See also lesbian potluck dinner advertisement, *DB*, August 5, 1975; GSU game night, *DS*, October 26, 1976; GPU annual pot luck notice, *SH*, March 29, 1977; Gay Union notice, *SH*, October 11, 1977 (coffeehouse, Sacramento State and UC Davis); Gay Women's Collective coffeehouse flyer, [ca. 1977–78], Series VIII, Box 3, Folder: Gay People's Union Scrapbook, Stanford QSR Records; lesbian and bisexual potluck social advertisement, *DB*, October 20, 1977.

92. *Gayzette*, February 26, 1975.

93. SGP meeting minutes, February 4, 1970, microfilm, SPC.

94. Dilley, *Gay Liberation to Campus Assimilation*. The importance of dances was evident at the time. Noted one Pennsylvania student in 1971, "We were feeling the high energy of the revolution based on love. Dancing together is a shared thing. It takes a lot of people.... It's an interpersonal thing that gay people do because we dig each other. ... We know that sisters dancing with sisters, brothers dancing with brothers, touching, kissing and balling people of the same sex is a far loving out expression of living" (quoted in Teal, *Gay Militants*, 59).

95. *Up from the Basement*, February 1973, Series I, Box 1, Folder 20, San José State University Women's Studies Program Records, University Archives, San José State University, Special Collections and Archives.

96. "Gay Party," *DC*, November 3, 1972; Brad Altman, "GSU Lets Campus Gays Know They're Not Alone," *Daily 49er*, October 17, 1973, 3; *GAPOO*, October 2, 1974, SUPEC; "Social Calendar," *Gayzette*, October 23, 1975; GSU advertisement, *DB*, October 30, 1975; "Halloween Costume Party on the Queen Mary" (flyer), October 31, 1976, CSULB GSU File.

97. Flyer, March 16 [ca. 1970s], "St. Michaels & All Angels' Day Celestial Hop" (flyer), September 29, [ca. 1970s], "Halloween Costume Party on the Queen Mary" (flyer), October 31, 1976, all in CSULB GSU File; GPU Valentine's Dance advertisement, *DN*, February 14, 1975.

98. San José GLF press release, [ca. May 1971], Subject File: San José (Calif.), ONE Archives.

99. *GSU Newsletter*, May 18, 1970, SPC; SGP meeting minutes, April 23, 1970, Reel 27, SPC; Jan D. Blais to Andrew Jameson, June 12, 1970, Jan D. Blais to Robert L. Johnson, May 14, 1970, both in Box 1, Folder 7, Queer Resource Center Records, UC Berkeley Archives.

100. UC Berkeley GSU to Ronald and Nancy Reagan, May 15, 1970, Reel 27, SPC. On Reagan's conservative supporters, including students, at some state colleges and universities, see Lieser, "Ronald Reagan's Good University."

101. "Big Success ... ," May 25, 1970, Box 21, Lyon and Martin Papers, GLBTHS; Don Burton, "People's Dance Makes It," *Berkeley Barb*, May 29, 1970; "Gay Students Hold Decorous UC Dance," *San Francisco Examiner*, May 23, 1970; *GSU Newsletter*, June 8, 1970, Subject File: Gay Student Union, ONE Archives.

102. *GSU Newsletter*, May 25, 1970, SPC.

103. GPU dance "in honor of Anita Bryant's anti-homosexual campaign" (advertisement), *DN*, April 8, 1977.

104. "Lesbian Club Reaches Out on Campus," *SpD*, October 14, 1976. A 1973 paper noted that LGBT students were virtually without support on U.S. college campuses (Jean Hasler and James Toy, "'Gay Advocacy': A Response to the Sociosexual Needs of Gay Students," paper presented at the American Educational Research Association Conference, New Orleans, February 1973, Box 2, Folder 21, Gittings and Lahusen Collection, ONE Archives).

105. GPU newsletter, April 5, 1973, Box 1, Folder 4, Gay and Lesbian Alliance at Stanford University Records, ONE Archives.

106. Lesbian rap group advertisement, *DB*, April 29, 1974. Rap topics at Stanford's GPU included "The Future of Lesbian Feminism," "Revolution," "Gay-Straight Dialogues," "Bisexuality," and "Separatism" (Series III, Box 1, Folder: Rap Topic Outlines, Stanford QSR Records).

107. S. J. Moore, "Upset with Lesbian Rap" (letter to the editor), *SH*, April 3, 1973; Chris Farley, Joan Hand, Carol Larsen, Chris Daughty, Mary Lou Prentice, Linda Atkins, and Sal, "Gay Rap Personality Conflict Should Be Solved within the Group" (letter to the editor), *SH*, April 6, 1973.

108. Closet Cracker advertisement, *DB*, March 10, 1976; "There Will Be Another GSU 'Closet Cracker' ... ," *Gayzette*, May 20, 1976; Alan Turri, "First Impressions," *Gayzette*, February 10, 1977. An announcement in the May 20, 1976, *Daily Bruin* asked, "Think You May Be GAY? For those trying to deal with problems of their sexuality ... An informal discrete [sic] dinner sponsored by three fellow UCLA students will be held this Friday evening off campus. For information contact the Gay Counseling Hotline."

109. Steve Werner, "Gay Students and College Counselors," *Interchange*, March–April 1972, 12–14, GLBTHS Periodicals; GSU brochure, [ca. 1977], Subject File: University of California, Los Angeles (UCLA), ONE Archives; Gay Community Services Center questionnaire completed by UCLA Women's Resource Center, [ca. 1974–75], University of California, Los Angeles (UCLA), ONE Archives; Jim Stebinger, "Lesbians Plan Activities," *DB*, October 30, 1974; Gay People's Union Logbook and General Information, Series I, Box 1, Stanford QSR Records; Randall H. Alfred to James Brown, April 28, 1974, Folder: Berkeley, UC, EC.

110. Charter, October 10, 1974, Subject File: University of California, Los Angeles (UCLA)—Gay Students Union, ONE Archives; "The Activities Survey: A Sampling of Suggestions on GSU's Primary Concerns," *Gayzette*, March 5, 1975.

111. "Gay Switchboard," *Chico Wildcat*, April 6, 1976.

112. "Funds Requested by 88 Groups," *DN*, May 16, 1975.

113. "Helpline, Counseling Services Reopen," *Gayzette*, May 1, 1975; MCC Dance, *Gayzette*, May 15, 1975; advertisement, *DB*, April 30, 1975; advertisement, *TOGETHER* (supplement to the *Daily Bruin*), May 1975; Beardsley, interview by author; "'T-Room Sex': What Is G.S.U.'s Position?," *Gayzette*, November 13, 1975.

114. Entries for July 2, 1973 (information on bisexual women), February 18, 1974 (information on transvestism), January 12, 1973 (someone new to area), January 12, 1973 (student coming out), January 15, 1973 (international student with questions about deportation), January 15, 1973 (whether staff member welcome at GPU), January 19, 1973 (information for high school student), February 1, 1973 (information for De Anza College student), February 16, 1973 (GPU meetings), March 5, 1973 (information about women's resources), April 6, 1973 (lesbian conference at UCLA), August 16, 1973 (GPU meetings and events), Gay People's Union Logbook and General Information, Series I, Box 1, Stanford QSR Records; May 9, 1973 (San José State professor), October 23, 1973 (speaker for women's group at Cañada College); November 5, 1973 (Western Washington University); flyer, Gay People's Union Logbook and General Information, Series I, Box 1, Stanford QSR Records. As the first page of the logbook noted, "*All* interested people (women and men, students and non-students, white and third world, etc., gay, bisexual or straight or whatever) are welcome to either come by our office and/or call. The office offers: counseling, referrals, rapping, and a place for people to come and relax, read gay literature, rap, etc." According to the logbook, between January and April 1973, ninety-three men and eleven women staffed the office, which received 225 calls.

Chapter 2. Navigating Struggles for Recognition

1. Leo Laurence, "College: It's Not So Lonely Now," *Advocate*, February 2, 1972, 1. Laurence may have been playing on the title of a widely circulated article by Warren Blumenfeld, a San José State College alumnus and founder of the National Gay Student Center in Washington, D.C. In "School Is Not a Gay Place to Be," Blumenfeld described educational institutions as "extremely oppressive, lonely, and alienating" for homosexuals (*Gay Sunshine*, October–November 1971, 5, GLBTHS Periodicals). Laurence's article was part of a series that also included "Gay Students Exploding the Myths," *Advocate*, February 16, 1972, 16; "Mom Wasn't Shocked," *Advocate*, May 10, 1972, 6; "The Uses of Recognition," *Advocate*, July 5, 1972, 17.

2. On "reactionary resistance," see Langman, "Cycles of Contention." See also Stein, *Rethinking the Gay and Lesbian Movement*.

3. For examples of letters to the editor, see "Gays" (letter to the editor), *DB*, April 14, 1972 (describing homosexuality as "a disease, a neurotic behavior" and its preva-

lence as related to the degree of "overpopulation and industrialization"); Patrick Healy, "A Comment on Gay Week...," *DB*, May 24, 1974 (Gay Week stood "at the top of the list of the most immoral projects ever staged by UCLA"); Mary B. Saunders, "Gay Pride Week?" (letter to the editor), *SpD*, March 29, 1978 (condemning "sodomites" as "abominations in the sight of God"; urging those who engaged in homosexual behavior to do so privately, "in darkness and silence," rather than publicly; and noting the author's "deep fear for the future of our once proud and great country"). For defacing of flyers, see GSU flyer, [ca. 1979], Subject File: Los Angeles City College, ONE Archives; "Gays Deplore Destroyed Signs," *UT*, November 24, 1975; Bill Saxon, "Gay Student Union Flyers Met 'Fate Worse Than Death'" (letter to the editor), *UT*, December 5, 1975. For more on such flyers, see Reichard, "Animating Ephemera." For police harassment, see "Responsible 'Gays' Don't Meet in Bathrooms" (letter to the editor), *SpD*, January 3, 1973; "GSU Growth Leads to Problems," *Gayzette*, October 16, 1975; "'T-Room Sex': What Is G.S.U.'s Position?," *Gayzette*, November 13, 1975; "GSU v. OCDA," *New University*, April 11, 1977, clipping in Subject File: Gay Students Union—University of California, Irvine, ONE Archives. This framing builds on James Scott's concept of everyday forms of resistance—recognizing the distinct difference between resistance as a challenge to hegemony on the one hand, and reactionary resistance as oppression on the other. What I am exploring is how LGBT students confronted reactionary resistance in many everyday ways through across a multitude of contexts. See James C. Scott, *Weapons of the Weak*.

    4. See R. S. Goldstein, "Gay Week a Success" (letter to the editor), *DN*, May 12, 1977, which reported that a "bold homophobe" "spray-painted our office (insulting the dykes who he ignored, and spelling faggot wrong), this forcing us to stop procrastinating on a long overdue repainting." See also "Vandals Break Windows at Gay People's Unions Trailer," *DN*, May 22, 1978.

    5. "Gay Gathering" (letter to the editor), *DN*, February 2, 1979; GPU, "Unite and Fight" (letter to the editor), *DN*, February 13, 1979; Ward and Freeman, "Defending Gay Rights."

    6. GPU Steering Committee, "Another Senseless Attack" (letter to the editor), *DN*, October 8, 1979; "Malicious Intent," *DN*, October 8, 1979; Jerome Hurowitz, "More Violence" (letter to the editor), *DN*, October 16, 1979; Kenna Himes, "Rally Supports Gay Rights, Condemns Oppression," *DN*, October 16, 1979.

    7. Interview card, entry for October 1969: "We need to obtain the opinion of the office of the General Counsel as to whether or not we can legally reg[ister] the group." On November 4, according to the card, "Letter received from Milton H. Gordon, Office of General Counsel OK to register the group" (Milton Gordon to Arleigh Williams, November 3, 1969, Box 1, Folder 7, Queer Resource Center Records, UC Berkeley Archives). SGP, founded in the fall of 1969, appeared on the list of approved student organizations that semester ("Registered Student Organizations, Fall '69," Box 27, Records of the Office of Student Activities, UC Berkeley Archives; list of SGP officers, November 4, 1969, Box 1, Folder 7, Queer Resource Center Records, UC Berkeley Archives; Donald Reidhaar to Allan Weisblott, April 24, 1970, Box 120, Folder 245.9, Office of the Chancellor, Administrative Files of Franklin D. Murphy, University Archives, University of California, Los Angeles, Special Collections; "New Movement at UCLA: Gay Liberation Movement Surfaces Here," *DB*, May 4, 1970).

    8. "Pastor Denounces Exclusion of Gays," *SoCal*, December 4, 1972, 8 (originally published in *Our Thing*, USC, Spring 1971), Subject File: University of Southern California (USC), ONE Archives (Religious Center provided "sanctuary" for GLF on campus). The USC's Gay Liberation Forum also met at the local Metropolitan Community Church. See "Gay Lib to Meet," *DTr*, April 22, 1971; *The Bridge* (San José Gay Liberation), August 6,

1970, GLBTHS Periodicals (San José State GLF meeting in coffeehouse); *GLF Newsletter*, September 6, 1970, Box 1, Folder 29, Thorpe [Thorp] Papers, GLBTHS (San José State GLF meeting at member's house); Warren Blumenfeld, "Reflections on Pre-Stonewall GLB Life," *Massachusetts Daily Collegian*, October 10, 1995, available at https://archive.org/details/massachuse19951996univ/page/n187/mode/2up (San José State GLF meeting in a "greasy spoon" café). The *Daily Trojan* is available at https://digitallibrary.usc.edu/Archive/The-Daily-Trojan—1912—2A3BF1OGAXI?Flat=1.

9. Gay Liberation Forum meeting, *DTr*, December 1, 1971 (speaker Robert Fournier at Metropolitan Community Church); "Gay Activist Featured Tonight," *DTr*, March 14, 1972 (speaker from the Los Angeles Gay Community Alliance held at a private apartment); "Gay Lib Film," *DTr*, October 12, 1972 (screening of *Some of Your Best Friends*, directed by USC graduate student Ken Robinson, at Religious Center); Gay Liberation Forum meeting, *DTr*, November 30, 1972 (meeting with Cal State LA GSU); "Gay Liberation Forum," *DTr*, April 5, 1973 (meeting at UCLA GSU). USC's LGBT students did not win official recognition until August 1975 (Addie L. Klotz to James R. Appleton, May 22, 1975, Folder 7, Ballard Papers, ONE Archives; "Gay Student Union Gets University Recognition," *DTr*, September 18, 1975).

10. Although the Gay Student Union lost its bid to gain recognition at Cal Poly San Luis Obispo in the spring of 1973, it still advertised in the student newspaper. See "G.S.U. Gay Student Union ... Still Helping, Still Here!," *MD*, July 3, 1973, 2; "Gay Students Union," *MD*, October 1, 1974, 3 (advertising availability of speakers for campus organizations, a hotline, and a post office box). The *Mustang Daily* is available at https://digitalcommons.calpoly.edu/studentnewspaper/.

11. Warren Blumenfeld, "Are You Recognized?," *Interchange*, January–February 1973, 14, copy in author's possession. While most LGBT campus-based student organizations seem to have received recognition without resorting to the courts, dozens of such cases were filed across the nation and made their way through state—and a few federal courts—in and beyond the 1970s. See, for example, *Wood v. Davison*, 351 F. Supp. 543 (N.D. Ga. 1972); *Gay Students Organization of University of New Hampshire v. Bonner*, 509 F.2d. 652 (1st Cir. 1974), affirming 367 F. Supp. 1088 (D.N.H. 1974); *Gay Lib v. University of Missouri*, 558 F.2d 848 (8th Cir. 1977), rehearing denied 558 F.2d 859 (8th Cir. 1977); cert. denied sub nom *Ratchford v. Gay Lib*, 434 U.S. 1080 (1978) (dissent by Rehnquist); *Gay Student Services v. Texas A&M University*, 737 F.2d 1317 (5th Cir. 1984); *Gay Rights Coalition of Georgetown University Law Center v. Georgetown University*, 536 A.2d 1 (D.C. 1987). In California, the first such court case was *Associated Students of Sacramento State College v. Butz*, Civil No. 200795, Superior Court, Sacramento, California, February 15, 1971 (unreported). On this case, see Reichard, "We Can't Hide." As early as 1971, such cases merited a note in a law review ("Note: Freedom of Political Association on the Campus"). For a detailed look at these cases, see Stein, "Students, Sodomy, and the State." On *Wood v. Davison*, see Timothy Reese Cain and Hevel, "Gay People Pay Activity Fees Too." For legal histories of cases involving institutional recognition of LGBT student organizations, see Stanley, "Rights of Gay Student Organizations"; Eskridge, "Challenging the Apartheid of the Closet"; Koehler, "*Healy v. James*"; Patricia A. Cain, "Litigating for Lesbian and Gay Rights"; Rivera, "Our Straight-Laced Judges"; Hunter, "Expressive Identity"; Schacter, "Sexual Orientation, Change and the Courts."

12. Warren Blumenfeld, "Are You Recognized?," *Interchange*, January–February 1973, 14, copy in author's possession.

13. Lehman, *Gays on Campus*. Five of the thirty-five responding organizations were located in California. A subsequent article in the National Gay Student Center newslet-

ter painted a slightly darker picture, focusing on several ongoing struggles across the country. See J. Lee Lehman, "Judicial Issues," *Interchange*, 1977, 1, Folder: National Gay Student Center, EC.

14. Werner, "Gay Student Group," 31. The National Gay Student Center newsletter regularly included news of these struggles. See "New Student Groups," *Interchange*, January–February 1973, 26, copy in author's possession; "Gay Students Win Court Case," "ACLU to Represent Gay Students," and "Brigham Young Locks Closet," all in *Interchange*, March–April 1974, 2, Subject File: National Gay Student Center, ONE Archives; "Bulletin Board," *Interchange*, Summer 1974, 2, Subject File: National Gay Student Center, ONE Archives (Tulane University GSU "looking for information on recognition problems at private schools" after being denied recognition in April 1974); "Gays Gain in Virginia Suit," *Interchange*, Spring 1976, 2, Subject File: National Gay Student Center, ONE Archives (Virginia Commonwealth University Gay Alliance lawsuit for recognition). On Homophiles of Penn State, see Walters, *Homophiles of Penn State*; Burton with Loveland, *Out in Central Pennsylvania*, 65–75.

15. "Recognition for Gay Students," *Advocate*, November 26, 1981.

16. Jay Murley, a longtime ACLU board member in Orange County, who was a frequent advocate and speaker related to LGBT student organizing, recalled working on thirty-three cases over the years, including one in 2008. More than half were in California. See Murley, interview by author.

17. "Gay Lib Will File Suit to 'End Suffering,'" *DTr*, March 23, 1972.

18. "Assembly Votes to Legalize Homosexuality," *San Francisco Chronicle*, March 7, 1975; Eskridge, "Challenging the Apartheid of the Closet," 849; Koehler, "*Healy v. James*," 72. When the USC GSU finally gained recognition after a five-year struggle, this change in California law, according to student Sal Licata, "had a positive effect on the board's decision" ("Gay Student Union Gets University Recognition," *DTr*, September 18, 1975, 1).

19. Hobert Burns to Robert Martin, January 22, 1970, Box 6, Folder: Gay Liberation Front, Burns Records; "SJS 'Gay Front' Stays Unliberated," *San Jose Mercury*, February 10, 1970; Reichard, "We Can't Hide" (Sacramento State president Otto Butz denied recognition because homosexual behavior was a crime); "Cal State Prexy Nixes Fullerton Gay Group," *Advocate*, July 21–August 3, 1971; "Gay Student Union May Sue: Cal State Turns Down Homosexual Group," *Los Angeles Times*, June 23, 1971, B1. After an eight-month fight, Cal State Fullerton's GSU prevailed. See "Students Recognized," *Advocate*, December 22, 1971; "GSU Charter Temporarily Blocked," *RR*, December 1, 1972. Refusing recognition based on the illegality of homosexuality occurred on a number of other campuses (Eskridge, *Gaylaw*, 106–7).

20. Steve Ruegnitz, "GSU Bylaws Rejected," *MD*, June 2, 1972. Similarly, when the USC board of trustees denied recognition to the Gay Liberation Forum, the dean of student life informed the group that it was "not entitled to use University facilities as a student organization" (Robert L. Mannes to Michael Wayne Bennett, April 29, 1971, Box 1, Folder 7, Ballard Papers, ONE Archives).

21. "College Paper Sex Item Triggers Storm," *Long Beach Independent Press Telegram*, November 25, 1969; Lance Gilmore, "Gay Front Upsets College Trustees," *San Francisco Examiner*, November 25, 1969.

22. "San Jose Cesspool," *Gay Sunshine*, August–September 1970, GLBTHS Periodicals; Jeff Kenyon, "Swim, Rafferty, Attack Spartan Daily," *SpD*, November 25, 1969; "Gay Story: College Cesspool? Rafferty Rages," *San Francisco Examiner*, November 24, 1969; "San Jose 'Gay Front' Upsets Two Trustees," *San Francisco Examiner*, November 25, 1969. Raf-

ferty later became dean of the School of Education at Troy University, and in 1977 he argued that gays should not be allowed to teach in public schools (Rafferty, "Should Gays Teach School?")

23. "Gay Lib: Up from Darkness," *DTr*, April 26, 1971. The Gay Liberation Forum originated from a fall 1970 experimental college course by that title ("College Extends Sign-Up Deadline," *DTr*, October 9, 1970).

24. Steve Ruegnitz, "GSU Bylaws Rejected," *MD*, June 2, 1972.

25. Lehman, "Judicial Issues," 1.

26. "AS Charters Gay Lib Union as Commission," *DTi*, June 30, 1971; "Cal State Prexy Nixes Fullerton Gay Group," *Advocate*, July 21–August 3, 1971. The *Daily Titan* is available at https://dailytitan.com/app/DTrarchive/.

27. "Courts Will Decide Gay Life Status at CSF," *DTi*, July 7, 1971.

28. "Cal State Prexy Nixes Fullerton Gay Group," *Advocate*, July 21–August 3, 1971. On Briggs, see Stein, *Rethinking the Gay and Lesbian Movement*, 138–42; Clayton Howard, *Closet and the Cul-de-Sac*, 283–89.

29. Sivertsen, interview by author.

30. "Student Group to Fight for Recognition at USC," *Advocate*, May 12, 1971. The group first sought recognition in December 1970 (assistant vice president of student affairs, memo to files regarding conversation with Leonard Castro, April 6, 1972, Box 1, Folder 7, Ballard Papers, ONE Archives).

31. "Gays at USC: The Unwanted Minority," *DTr*, March 19, 1973.

32. "Awareness Renewed in Land of Intolerance," *DTr*, April 13, 1983.

33. The organizers of the GSU at Bakersfield College noted that one campus administrator denied that homosexuals experienced any oppression on campus or in Bakersfield and thus saw no need for such an organization ("Bakersfield College Gay Student Union," [ca. 1973], Daniel A. Smith and Queer Blue Light Videotapes, GLBTHS). Campus president John Collins denied recognition to the GSU in late 1972 ("Gay Group Vows to Fight BC Rejection," *Bakersfield Californian*, February 2, 1973.

34. "College of Sequoias Battles 'Queers,'" *Advocate*, November 22, 1972, 10; "GSU Denied Recognition," *GSC News Magazine*, [ca. late 1972], 1, Box 15, Folder 49, L.A. Gay and Lesbian Center Records, ONE Archives.

35. Otto Butz to Stephen Whitmore, March 3, 1970, Records of the Office of the President, Box 34, Folder 9: Society for Homosexual Freedom, 1970, CSUSSCUA. Chandler made a similar argument in rejecting the bylaws for Cal Poly San Luis Obispo's GSU ("Court Decision Awaited," *MD*, October 2, 1972, 1).

36. Hobert Burns to Clifford C. Rothrock, November 28, 1969, Box 6, Folder: Gay Liberation Front, Burns Records.

37. Hobert Burns to Glenn Dumke, November 27, 1969, Box 6, Folder: Gay Liberation Front, Burns Records. According to Sivertsen, Burns denied recognition "because the Chancellor's office told him to" (Sivertsen, interview by author; Yeager, "Wiggsy Sivertsen").

38. Lance Gilmore, "Gay Front Upsets College Trustees," *San Francisco Examiner*, November 25, 1969; "SJS 'Gay Front' Stays Unliberated," *San Jose Mercury*, February 10, 1970; "Cesspool in Ronnie's Backyard," *San Francisco Free Press*, January 1970.

39. Bertha Wertz to Hobert Burns, December 11, 1969, University Archives, Box 6, Folder: Gay Liberation Front, Burns Records. Burns replied that no such club would be recognized on campus, though he corrected her misunderstanding by explaining that as a state institution, "the laws regarding separation of church and state do apply to us" (Hobert Burns to Bertha Wirtz, December 18, 1969, Box 6, Folder: Gay Liberation Front, Burns Records).

40. Orpha Strong Wright to Hobert Burns, January 24, 1970, Box 6, Folder: Gay Liberation Front, Burns Records.

41. Kenneth E. Pascoe to Hobert Burns, January 17, 1970, Hobert Burns to Kenneth E. Pascoe, February 4, 1970, both in Box 6, Folder: Gay Liberation Front, Burns Records. Burns noted in a handwritten postscript that "given your concern, which I share, with the recent trends in morality, let me suggest you stop using profanity in your letters to public officials. You could be sued for what you called me, you know."

42. Keith W. Johnsgard to Hobert W. Burns, December 10, 1969, Subject File: San José Gay Liberation, ONE Archives.

43. "Senate Backs Gay Lib Proposal," *DTr*, April 22, 1971; assistant vice president of student affairs, memo to files regarding conversation with Leonard Castro, April 6, 1972, Box 1, Folder 7, Ballard Papers, ONE Archives.

44. Martin Rogers, "Critical Incidents in the Evolution of a Gay Liberation Group," in *Gays on Campus*, edited by Lehman, 27; Rogers quoted in Warren Blumenfeld, "Are You Recognized?," *Interchange*, January–February 1973, 14, copy in author's possession. In 1977, the director of the National Gay Student Center described student government support for gay student organizations as especially consistent across U.S. colleges and universities (J. Lee Lehman, "Judicial Issues").

45. "AS Charters Gay Lib Union as Commission," *DTi*, June 30, 1971; "Appeal Aimed at Shields' GSU Decision," *DTi*, July 21, 1971. The Academic Appeals Board lacked authority to overturn the president's decision but could only make recommendations, but it unanimously supported the appeal the following week ("Academic Appeals Board Supports GSU Charter," *DTi*, July 28, 1971). Letters in support of the GSU published in the student newspaper included Rick F. Vaught, "GSU Supported," *DTi*, July 28, 1971.

46. Candy Bell, "Gay Liberation Front Granted Official Organization Status," *SpD*, December 18, 1969. Associated Students had sought advice from San José law firm Morgan, Beauzay and Hammer prior to the decision. The attorneys suggested that the right to organize the GLF was rooted not only in the student rights section of the Associated Students documents but also in First Amendment free speech and association grounds (Philip L. Hammer to James Edwards, December 17, 1969, Subject File: San José Gay Liberation, ONE Archives; Judi Schultz, "Student Council OK for SJS Gay Front," *San Jose Mercury*, December 20, 1969.

47. "GLF Voted Funds," *DTr*, April 21, 1971; "Bakersfield College Gay Student Union," [ca. 1972], Daniel A. Smith and Queer Blue Light Videotapes, GLBTHS; "GSU Charter Temporarily Blocked," *RR*, December 1, 1972.

48. "Gay Students Seek Okay from SAC and Officials," *MD*, March 2, 1972, 8; "Three Groups Seek Approval," *MD*, March 8, 1972, 1; "SAC Backs Gay Students," *MD*, March 10, 1972, 1.

49. "SAC Backs Gay Students," *MD*, March 10, 1972, 1. GSU president Robert Christensen defended this provision, arguing that the requirement was needed "to create a common bond" and that removing the provision would be "defeating the purpose of the organization." The university cited the provision as one of the bases for the rejection of the GSU's application for recognition (Steve Ruegnitz, "GSU Bylaws Rejected," *MD*, June 2, 1972).

50. Hull quoted in "SAC Backs Gay Students," *MD*, March 10, 1972, 1. Cal Poly San Luis Obispo's GSU faced a generally conservative climate, as president Bob Christensen noted at the time. When the organization was formed, someone posted a huge sign on campus that read, "Aggies Hate Gays" ("Recognition Fight Looms at Cal Poly Institute," *Advocate*, April 26, 1972, 18).

51. Ken Boegert, "Caution to SAC: Do Not Accept Homosexuality" (letter to the editor), *MD*, March 10, 1972, 2.

52. "Dirty Old Men's Union Opposes the GSU," *MD*, November 14, 1972, 2.

53. Gerald Jones, "GSU Party No More Orgy Than a High School Prom" (letter to the editor), *MD*, November 20, 1972, 2.

54. Thomas Weissbluth, "He Understands Plato" (letter to the editor), *MD*, January 11, 1973, 2. As the struggle continued into 1974, Robert Rodin, a professor in the Biological Sciences Department, authored an opinion piece in the student newspaper condemning the GSU's attempt to gain recognition on biblical grounds: "Because the gay students and their crowd have developed a public relations program to seek public approval, will we also be forced to approve clubs for incest, sodomy, adultery, and other forms of immorality?" ("Prof Cites Bible in Homosexual Group Condemnation" [letter to the editor], *MD*, January 10, 1975, 4). Steve Johnson, who noted efforts to create a Campus Crusade at another school, saw parallels between efforts to limit Christian student organizing and gay student organizing: describing Rodin's letter as "unnecessary, rude and insensitive," Johnson wrote, "I really think an apology is owed to the gay students on this campus" (*MD*, January 14, 1975, 2).

55. Burr Hosely, "GSU" (letter to the editor), *MD*, October 24, 1975, 2. For support for the GSU, see also Tatum, "Bible Ineffective Whip—Gays Part of Society" (letter to the editor), *MD*, April 3, 1972, 2.

56. "Shields Policies," *DTi*, July 14, 1971; "A Moral Question," *DTi*, October 5, 1971.

57. "Double Dealers," *DTr*, April 22, 1971.

58. Larry Bernard, "A Gay Minority," *DTr*, May 4, 1971. Bernard published several other opinion pieces, including "The Case for Gays," *DTr*, September 29, 1971, and "The Right to Be Gay," *DTr*, October 28, 1971. For similar arguments, see "Gay Lib Repression Unhelpful" (letter to the editor), *DTr*, May 14, 1971; John Jacobson, "Gays Fight for Recognition," *DTr*, September 28, 1972; "USC Suit Challenging Private College," *Advocate*, April 26, 1972.

59. Rob Brackett, "Chancellor's Visit Proves Peaceful," *SpD*, December 9, 1969. The same issue of the paper contained an editorial supporting the GLF. See "Recognize GLF," *SpD*, December 9, 1969.

60. "GLF States Complaints," *DTr*, May 5, 1971.

61. "GLF: Back to Trustees," *DTr*, May 6, 1971.

62. "GLF Says Trustees Will Reject Proposal," *DTr*, May 12, 1971. Del Whan, a language lab director at USC who had been introduced to gay liberation through a campus talk by Morris Kight, wrote an anonymous letter published in the *Daily Trojan* in which she said that she could never come out given the social consequences. Whan nonetheless started to attend meetings of the Gay Liberation Forum, noting in the summer of 1971, "We have 20 members, including students, faculty, staff and alumni." Despite the visibility her involvement brought, "nobody has tried to get me fired." See Del Whan, "Come Out!," *Everywoman*, July 9, 1971, 11, https://www.jstor.org/stable/community.28036116.

63. "Gay Lib to Defy Trustees," *DTr*, September 28, 1971; assistant vice president of student affairs, memo to files regarding conversation with Leonard Castro, April 6, 1972, Box 1, Folder 7, Ballard Papers, ONE Archives.

64. Reichard, "We Can't Hide"; "Gay Lib Suit Postponed," *DTr*, April 7, 1972; Werner, "Gay Student Group," 31. ACLU lawyers provided legal counsel in a number of cases both in California and nationally. See "Maryland Group Wins Court Case against University," *Interchange*, May–June 1972, 18, copy in author's possession; Werner, "Gay Student Group," 32.

65. "ACLU Names Attorneys to Defend Fullerton Group," *Advocate*, August 4–17, 1971; "Students Recognized," *Advocate*, December 22, 1971, 12; Murley, interview by author. Murley's initial work on the Gay Rights Committee of the ACLU in Southern California involved challenging harassment of gay bars in Los Angeles. As he noted in 1973, gays needed "non-gay allies" who "have related interests"—in Murley's case, civil liberties. See "New Legal Thrusts," *ONE Letter* 18, no. 11 (1973): 4, available at the USC Digital Library, http://digitallibrary.usc.edu.

66. "Gay Lib Suit Postponed," *DTr*, April 7, 1972; "Gay Lib Forum Suffers Setback in Fight for University Recognition," *DTr*, April 11, 1972; "USC Suit Stalled: Couldn't Get a Lawyer," *Advocate*, May 10, 1972, 6; "Gay Lib Suit to Face Trustees Next Month," *DTr*, September 28, 1972; Koehler, "*Healy v. James*," 77; "Gay Student Union Gets University Recognition," *DTr*, September 18, 1975, 1; "ACLU to Aid Gay Liberation," *San Jose News*, February 12, 1970; "SJS Gay Liberation Front Gets ACLU Backing," *San Jose Mercury News*, February 12, 1970. When the attorney originally secured to challenge the denial of recognition of the GSU at Cal Poly San Luis Obispo pulled out, the ACLU expressed interest in taking the case. Ultimately, however, the original attorney remained on the case. See "Gay Students to Receive Help in Case," *MD*, July 20, 1972, 1; "Both Sides Optimistic in Gay Students Case," *MD*, September 22, 1972, 12; Jay Murley to Joseph J. Hayes and William D. Truesdell, February 16, 1973, Box 1, Folder 1, Hayes Papers, ONE Archives; ACLU—Southern California press release, March 1973, Box 1, Folder 1, Hayes Papers, ONE Archives.

67. "GSU Bylaws Rejected—Members Fit to Be Tried," *MD*, September 28, 1972, 1; "Gay Students to Hold Benefit Saturday," *MD*, May 15, 1974, 1. The student newspaper was somewhat critical of the student government's funding of the attorney. See "Students Pay the Price but Miss the Show," *MD*, October 3, 1972, 3.

68. "Gay Students Foiled Again," *MD*, March 28, 1973, 1. The decision prompted Associated Students at Cal Poly San Luis Obispo to require all student organizations "with closed admissions standards to revise their bylaws" ("SAC Faces Ills: Budget Priority Problem Arises," *MD*, April 6, 1973, 1).

69. "GSU Decision to Be Appealed," *MD*, March 30, 1973, 1; "The Unexpected Cost of Morality," *MD*, April 4, 1973, 2; "State High Court to Rule on GSU," *Summer Mustang*, August 1, 1974, 1. The ACLU supported the appeal, as did the student newspaper, though the editors expressed concerns about the money involved.

70. "Issue of a GSU May Go Higher," *Summer Mustang*, July 25, 1974, 1; "Supreme Court Revives GSU Case," *MD*, September 26, 1974, 1; "Message from the New ASI President," *MD*, September 19, 1974, 7; "Gay Group Out on Attorney Error—Kennedy Wins," *MD*, October 3, 1974, 1; "Carsel Clarifies Litigation" (letter to the editor), *MD*, October 18, 1974, 4; "SAC Discusses GSU Litigation," *MD*, November 15, 1974, 1; "GSU Seeks Approval of Bylaws Tonight," *MD*, December 4, 1974, 1; Jim McCrumb, "SAC Thanked by Student for GSU Nod" (letter to the editor), *MD*, December 6, 1974, 3; "GSU Victor in Bylaw Battle," *MD*, April 3, 1975, 1. Kennedy at times found himself the subject of student ire because he represented an obstacle to student self-determination. In early 1975, the *Mustang Daily* ran an article referring to Kennedy as "His Majesty" and declaring that his "imperial sceptor [sic] takes care of alcoholics, gay students, uppity sociology professors and uppity Chicano department heads" and that one of his "favorite pastimes is to impose the royal morality on the subjects" (*MD*, February 5, 1975, 3).

71. "Kennedy Refutes GSU Speculation," *MD*, April 4, 1975, 1; "Attorney General to Give GSU Opinion," *MD*, October 2, 1975, 3; "The Kennedy Interview II: The President Lists the Disadvantages of His Job; Draws an Analogy between the GSU and the SLA; Clams Up on the Subject of Brad Smith's Firing," *MD*, October 21, 1975, 3. One letter to

the editor called Kennedy out on these analogies: the president's message "that the GSU is as much a threat to society" as the "noted extremist groups" "contributes to society's snub of gays and perpetuates ignorance of and pressure on the gay individual" (Dennis Hopper, "More GSU" [letter to the editor], *MD*, October 28, 1975, 2). Kennedy subsequently defended equating the groups on the grounds that whether or not the GSU was "a threat to society is a matter of individual judgement" (Robert E. Kennedy, "A Reply" [letter to the editor], *MD*, October 30, 1975, 2). Plotkin took responsibility for the erroneous newspaper report, explaining that a reporter had overheard him speculating and misunderstood ("GSU Bylaw Story, Plotkin: I'm Guilty," *MD*, April 7, 1975, 1).

72. "GSU Gains University Recognition," *MD*, January 13, 1976, 4; "Students," *Advocate*, February 11, 1986, 35; "GSU: We've Only Just Begun," *MD*, May 12, 1976, 5; "Gay Students' Union Wants Your Support. Join Us" (advertisement), *MD*, October 15, 1976, 4; T.H., letter to the editor, *MD*, November 16, 1976, 2.

73. "Gay Lib Forum Suffers Setback in Fight for University Recognition," *DTr*, April 11, 1972; "USC Suit Challenging Private College," *Advocate*, April 26, 1972; "U.S.F." [sic], *LT*, May 1972, 18.

74. "Gay Students Case Begins," *MD*, September 27, 1972; "Gay Students: Little Progress in Suit," *MD*, September 29, 1972, 1; "Court Decision Awaited," *MD*, October 2, 1972, 1; "Cal Poly GSU Suit Unresolved," *Advocate*, October 25, 1972, 14.

75. "Cal Poly Gays Come to Town," *Gay Crusader*, December–January 1973–74, GLBTHS Periodicals.

76. "Young Republicans Give Support to the GSU," *MD*, November 20, 1975, 3.

77. "Gay Lib. Takes Hold in San Jose," *Vector*, June 1970; "San Jose Cesspool," *Gay Sunshine*, August–September 1970, GLBTHS Periodicals; Robert Christensen to Leo Laurence, n.d., Subject File: Gay Students Union—California Polytechnic State University, San Luis Obispo, ONE Archives. For examples of the *Advocate*'s coverage, see "Mom Wasn't Shocked," *Advocate*, May 10, 1972, 6; "Gay Lounge: Dean Yes, President No," *Advocate*, November 8, 1972, 20; "New Hampshire Gays Called 'Filth,'" *Advocate*, February 27, 1974, 2; "Gay Students Lose in Court, Hit with Costs," *Advocate*, March 13, 1974, 6; "Student Group Wins in Court," *Advocate*, January 29, 1975, 5; "Recognition for Gay Students," *Advocate*, November 26, 1981, 10. See Robert Kroll, "Gay Liberation Conference Closes Five-Day Symposium," *Berkeley Gazette*, December 31, 1969, clipping in Subject File: Berkeley Gay Liberation, ONE Archives. A draft of an *Advocate* article criticized the GSU's exclusion of nonhomosexuals as "antithetical to what total gay lib is all about. That particular closet door at Cal Poly is hinged so that it swings only one way, whereas it should be double-hinged to swing both ways." Exclusion represented a "direct slap in the face of people who may not be homosexually oriented themselves but who may still be at least in humane sympathy with us" (Ross Calvin and Alan Whitney, untitled draft article, [ca. 1973], Subject File: Subject File: Gay Students Union—California Polytechnic State University, San Luis Obispo, ONE Archives).

78. Koehler, "*Healy v. James*," 77.

79. "Gay Student Union May Sue: Cal State Turns Down Homosexual Group," *Los Angeles Times*, June 23, 1971.

80. Murley, interview by author.

81. "Gay Lib Will File Suit to 'End Suffering,'" *DTr*, March 23, 1972.

Chapter 3. Claiming a Queer Education

1. Blumenfeld, *National Gay Student Center*, 3–4.

2. "Gay Studies," *Interchange*, January–February 1973, 25, copy in author's posses-

sion. See "Giving a Gay Course," "A Gay Feminist in Academia," and "Gay Studies Syllabi," all in *Gays on Campus*, edited by Lehman. Gary Steele, a graduate student who developed gay studies courses at UCLA in the late 1970s, saved the December 1976 issue of *Interchange* with syllabi examples (Box 1, Folder 26, Steele Papers, ONE Archives).

3. Similar DIY practices occurred in health care as part of the women's health movement and the pre-AIDS health care movement associated with gay liberation. See Nelson, *More Than Medicine*; Batza, *Before AIDS*. For DIY politics, culture, and gay liberation, see Shepard, "Play as World-Making."

4. For the efforts of LGBT faculty to promote curriculum reform, see Sueyoshi, "Redefining Higher Education." On the origins of lesbian studies, including faculty, student, and community involvement, see Freeman, "Building Lesbian Studies." For the development of the Gay Academic Union and gay studies on campus, see D'Emilio, *Making Trouble*. On lesbian faculty and graduate students in the 1990s, including integrating lesbian content into courses, see Rothblum, "Lesbians in Academia."

5. Michael Hughes and James Mitchell, "The Gay People's Union: Stanford," *Vector*, November 1972, 21.

6. *Gayzette*, March 5, 1975.

7. On consciousness-raising in the women's liberation movement, see Echols, *Daring to Be Bad*, 83–92.

8. See McMillian, *Smoking Typewriters*; Beins, *Liberation in Print*; Enszer, "Whole Naked Truth of Our Lives"; Whitt, "Labor from the Heart"; Murray, "Free for All Lesbians." On the history of the gay and lesbian press generally, see Streitmatter, *Unspeakable*; Baim, *Gay Press, Gay Power*.

9. Reichard, "Behind the Scenes"; "Wilkommen," *Gayzette*, October 2, 1974. On the importance of mimeograph machines to Students for a Democratic Society, see McMillian, "Our Founder, the Mimeograph Machine."

10. *GAPOO*, October 2, 1974, SUPEC.

11. "Dear People," *Gayzette*, January 24, 1977. See also "Proud," October 13, [probably 1972], CSULB GSU File (the masthead read "The struggle for liberation is the struggle for oneself").

12. SGP newsletters, [ca. December 1969], [ca. January 1970], April 4, 1970, all in EC; Students (and Friends) for Gay Power newsletter, April 30, 1970, EC; GSU newsletter, May 18, 25, 1970, SPC; GSU newsletter, June 1, 8, 1970, January 20, 1971, Subject File: Gay Students Union—University of California, Berkeley, ONE Archives; GSU newsletter, October 10, November 27, 1970, GLBTHS Periodicals.

13. See for example, *Gayzette*, November 13, 1974, December 4, 1975, February 10, 1977. Student government was also the source of funds for the GPU newsletter at Stanford. See transaction receipt, January 30, 1974, Series I, Box 2, Folder: GPU AS SU Student Organization Fund Account 7386, Stanford QSR Records; Richard Thomas to Frank Olivieri, February 13, 1974, Series I, Box 2, Folder: GPU Budget 1974–75, Stanford QSR Records.

14. The GPU at Stanford and the GSU at UCLA consistently produced newsletters throughout the 1970s. More limited surviving runs from other colleges and universities are scattered in various collections, primarily at the GLBT Historical Society and ONE Archives.

15. Stanford University GPU newsletter, [ca. late April 1974], GLBTHS Periodicals.

16. "Faggots Stay Out Nostalgia," *Gayzette*, December 4, 1974; "Prisoner Visits/Counseling," *Gayzette*, January 29, 1975; "Editor's Comment" and "MARCH: Ed Davis Gets Burned!," *Gayzette*, October 23, 1975. See also "March against Oppression," *Gayzette*, March 18, 1976 (on Committee to Build Stonewall '76 organization); "Coors Boycott,"

Gayzette, June 3, 1976; Hal Offen, "Gay Liberation Growing with BAGL," *VGSC*, April 18, 1975, 10, ONE Periodicals; Harvey Milk, "Gay Groupie Syndrome and the Political Bandwagon," *VGSC*, May 16, 1974, 13, GLBTHS Periodicals.

17. *SH*, October 11, 1972; "Gay Liberation Resurfaces," *SH*, February 29, 1972.

18. "Dr. Josette Mondanero, San Francisco County Women's Prison, Talk on Lesbians in Prison" (flyer), November 27 [n.d.], Reel 27, SPC; "Gay Students Union," *DC*, November 16, 1972; GSU meeting notice, *DC*, February 21, 1974; GPU meeting notice, *DC*, October 21, 1976; *DB*, February 14, 1973; Gay Liberation meeting notice, *DB*, February 15, 1973; Gay Liberation meeting notice, *DB*, February 22, 1973; GSU meeting notice, *DB*, April 5, 1973; *Gayzette*, May 1, 1975; "On Being Black and Gay" (advertisement), *DB*, May 1, 1975; GSU advertisement, *DB*, January 26, 1977; Laurie Norris to Sal Licata, January 6, 1977, Personal Papers—Licata, Box 127, Folder 10, De Cecco Papers, GLBTHS; Lesbian Sisterhood meeting notices, *DB*, February 13, May 13, 1975.

19. Morris Kight, "The Gay Movement," *UT*, October 12, 1972; "Gay Lib Founder Explains Views, Hits Psychiatrists," *DN*, January 22, 1973; "Campus Happenings," *GSC Newsmagazine*, April 1973, 5, GSC File; GSU meeting notice, *DB*, April 5, 1973; GSU meeting notice, *DS*, November 13, 1974; *Gayzette*, January 29, 1975.

20. "Gay Daze," *GSU Newsletter*, October 15 [1976], CSULA GSU File.

21. Aura, interview by author; "New Center Opens for Women," *DB*, September 25, 1972; "Gay Women Organize Here," *DB*, March 8, 1973; Lesbian rap group advertisement, *DB*, April 29, 1974; *TOGETHER* (supplement to the *Daily Bruin*), October 21, 1975.

22. Jim Stebinger, "Lesbians Plan Activities," *DB*, October 30, 1974. Advertisements for the Women's Resource Center featured the Lesbian Sisterhood (*TOGETHER* [supplement to the *Daily Bruin*], November 1974).

23. "Lesbian Club Reaches Out on Campus," *SpD*, October 14, 1976. The Women's Center at San José State also offered space for "classes and groups offered exclusively to women," including a course on "Lovers and Friends: A Personal Exploration of Lesbianism through Literature" ("Center Offers Credit," *SpD*, September 4, 1975).

24. "Lesbian Alliance a 'Political Force,'" *SpD*, October 13, 1977; "Lesbian Alliance Splits" (letter to the editor), *Plexus*, August 1978, 3, GLBTHS Periodicals; *Up from the Basement*, November 1972, January 1973, both in Box 2, Folder 33, WSPR. Lesbian raps and other programs were regular features of the Women's Center calendar as early as 1972, though the Lesbian Feminist Alliance seems to have disbanded by 1978.

25. For example, the Lesbian Mothers' National Defense Fund served as a information clearinghouse, sharing legal materials, names of expert witnesses for custody cases, and more. Other lesbian feminist communities similarly created alternative feminist institutions that included libraries of materials. See Rivers, *Radical Relations*.

26. Kathryn Wright, letter to the editor, *Interchange*, March–April 1972, 11, Newsletters Collection, GLBTHS.

27. Lee Lehman, "Gay Bookstores: An Important Resource for the Gay Student Movement," "Partial List of Gay Bookstores," *Interchange*, Fall 1974, 1, 6, Subject File: National Gay Student Center, ONE Archives. The Women's Center at San José State also maintained a library. See "Year's Plans Made at Women's Center," *SpD*, September 20, 1972.

28. "Library of Gay Information," *Sometimes Regular Newsletter of the Gay Students Council of Southern California*, [ca. Summer 1972], 2, "Introducing . . . Gay Students Council of Southern California" (flyer), [ca. 1972], both in GSC File.

29. Meeting minutes, May 6, 1973, GSC File. For San Francisco State, see "Campus 'Gay Power' Grows, Union Seeks Headquarters," *Phoenix*, September 11, 1975, 2. In the fall of 1975, Fran Kibler served as the codirector of the library. See *Gay Academic Union*

Newsletter, November 21, 1975, 2, Subject File: Gay Academic Union, San Francisco, ONE Archives; Gay Academic Union flyer, [ca. 1976], Box 12, Folder 7, De Cecco Papers, GLBTHS.

30. GPU, AS SU Budget Proposal, February 14, 1975, Series I, Box 2, Folder: GPU Budget 1974–75, Stanford QSR Records.

31. Sal Licata, "Gay Students" (letter to the editor), *Advocate*, October 6, 1976.

32. Richard Thomas to Frank Olivieri, February 13, 1974, Series I, Box 2, Folder: GPU Budget 1974–75, Stanford QSR Records.

33. Barry Dank offered a pioneering course on the Sociology of Homosexuality at California State University, Long Beach in the fall of 1970. See "Cal State Schedules Homophile Course for Fall Quarter," *Advocate*, September 16, 1970, 20; "Long Beach Homophile Course Going Well," *Advocate*, March 17, 1971, 10. Activist Barbara Gittings criticized California State University, Long Beach faculty member Barry Dank's syllabus for the Sociology of Homosexuality course for devoting only one of thirty sessions to lesbians (Barbara Gittings to Barry Dank, July 12, 1972, Box 2, Folder 25, Gittings and Lahusen Collection, ONE Archives).

34. Richard Gollance, "Gay at UCLA: The Problems Facing Gays," *DB*, May 16, 1972. Another student left a small college because a dorm director saw her lesbianism as a problem that needed a solution. See Diane Devlin, "The Plight of the Gay Student," *Off Our Backs*, May 30, 1970, 11. Compare Boxer, "Women's Studies as Women's History"; Mariscal, *Brown-Eyed Children of the Sun* (esp. chap. 6); Soldatenko, *Chicano Studies*; Blackwell, *Chicana Power* (esp. chap. 1); Acuña, *Making of Chicana/o Studies* (esp. chap. 3); Biondi, *Black Revolution on Campus*; Umemoto, "On Strike!"

35. Ziesel Saunders, interview by Alana Chazan, February 22, 2002, https://library.ucsc.edu/reg-hist/oir.exhibit/ziesel_saunders.

36. Higginson, "When Experimental Was Mainstream." On UC Berkeley, see Trow, *Habits of Mind*.

37. Paul Lauter and Florence Howe, "What Happened to the 'Free University'?," *Saturday Review*, June 20, 1970, 80–82.

38. Jim Rankin, "Proposal for Course on Homosexuality, Center for Participant Education," [ca. 1970], Folder: UC Berkeley, EC; "Gay Community," *UT*, February 1, 1972; "Women's Studies: The Gay Alternative," *California Aggie*, March 31, 1972; "Gay Life and Lib: A Study in Homosexual Lifestyles and Politics," Spring 1971, Subject File: Orange County (Calif.) I, ONE Archives; "The Gay Experience," *DS*, October 19, 1973; "Class Examines Gay Lifestyles," *SpD*, February 5, 1975. On experimental colleges and women's studies, see Bartolotto, "Early History," 15; Freeman, "Building Lesbian Studies," 232. The *California Aggie* (University of California, Davis) is available at https://cdnc.ucr.edu/?a=cl&cl=CL1&sp=UCD.

39. California State Colleges, Inglewood, Office of the Chancellor, *Experimental College Developments*. A 1978 list of experimental colleges included San Francisco State, CSU Northridge, Humboldt State, and Sacramento State (Calvert and Draves, *Free Universities and Learning Referral Centers*, 23). The number of programs dropped considerably by 1981 (Litkowski, *Free Universities and Learning Referral Centers*, 19 (only six programs listed at California's higher education institutions).

40. Paul Lauter and Florence Howe, "What Happened to the 'Free University'?," *Saturday Review*, June 20, 1970, 82. According to the 1967 catalog, San Francisco State's experimental college was organized by students to address problems they "saw in the education they were receiving" and focused on courses for "educational innovations and education for self-development" (experimental college, Summer Catalog, 1967, Box: Related Organizations, Folder: Experimental College—Catalogs, SFSUSCA). Associated

Students, the student government, provided the experimental college's budget, allocating $24,000 in 1966–67), $7,900 in 1967–68, and $15,980 in 1968–69. See "The Experimental College at S.F. State College," [ca. 1968], Box: Related Organizations, Folder: Experimental College at San Francisco State, SFSUSCA.

41. California State Colleges, Inglewood, Office of the Chancellor, *Experimental College Developments*, 3, 7; Rojas, *From Black Power to Black Studies*, 58–64.

42. Rogers [Kendi], *Black Campus Movement*; Black Student Union, "Black Studies Curriculum, Spring 1968," University Archives, J. Paul Leonard Library, San Francisco State University.

43. Biondi, *Black Revolution on Campus*, 40.

44. Dong, "Third World Liberation"; Vázquez, "Black and Brown," 71.

45. Vázquez, "Black and Brown."

46. Morgan Pinney, "Homosexuality and the Campus," [ca. 1969], 4–5, Box 1, Folder 21, Thorpe [Thorp] Papers, GLBTHS. See also Morgan Pinney, "State College from a Homosexual Perspective," *Vector*, January 1969, 5, 6, 29. Compare Wilson, "I'm Not a Man."

47. Exploring New Forms of Sexual Relationships, experimental college, Spring 1968, 14–15, Box: Related Organizations, Folder: Experimental College—Catalogs, SFSUSCA. Between fifteen and forty people attended the weekly class, and the participants "felt it was an important and illuminating experience" ("Concerning the Experimental College Course 'Exploring New Forms of Sexual Relationships,'" Box: Related Organizations, Folder: Experimental College Course Proposals, SFSUSCA).

48. GLF courses, Communiversity, Spring 1972 catalog, Box: Related Organizations, Folder: Communiversity, SFSUSCA. None of the experimental colleges on California State campuses offered courses focusing on homosexuality according to a 1969 report from the chancellor's office. See the appendixes to California State Colleges, Inglewood, Office of the Chancellor, *Experimental College Developments*. The concept of the Communiversity was rooted in Malcolm X's call for colleges and universities to work more closely with Black communities (Calvert and Draves, *Free Universities and Learning Referral Centers*; Smallwood, "Intellectual Creativity and Public Discourse"). For more on a specific proposal to create a Black Communiversity where "the campus itself would be the very sidewalks of the black community," see Killens, "Artist and the Black University," 62. In the summer of 1972, Jacks offered a series of workshops on gay liberation, further illustrating the connection between politics and the content of these courses. See "Gay Liberation Workshops," Communiversity, San Francisco State, Catalog, Summer 1972, Box: Related Organizations, Folder: Communiversity, SFSUSCA.

49. Acuña, *Making of Chicana/o Studies*; Muñoz quoted in García, *Chicano Generation*, 318. Muñoz also was elected student body president ("UCLA: Berkeley with Mothers," *West* [*Los Angeles Times* magazine], July 6, 1969). UCLA students also began offering summer courses in Asian American studies through the Asian American Experimental College, which met in private homes in 1969 (Nguyen and Gasman, "Activism, Identity and Service").

50. "Experimental College Seeks 'Old Boldness,'" *Los Angeles Times*, January 3, 1971.

51. UCLA experimental college advertisement, *DB*, October 5, 1972.

52. UCLA experimental college advertisement, 1974, *Summer Bruin*, July 5, 1974; *DB*, September 30, 1974; "Beginning Gay Studies, Norman Isaac Lewis, Instructor," Summer Session 1974, Box 9, Folder 9, Jeanne Córdova Papers, ONE Archives.

53. Jeff Miller to James Kepner, [ca. Summer 1974], Subject File: UCLA Experimental College, ONE Archives; Douglass Sarff, "Gay Studies at UCLA Expanding to 7 Courses," *Advocate*, October 9, 1974.

54. Jim Kepner to students, September 30, 1974, Box 53, Folder 6, Kepner Papers,

ONE Archives. Kepner hosted a November 1974 gathering of students at his apartment (Jim Kepner to students, November 30, 1974, Box 53, Folder 6, Kepner Papers, ONE Archives).

55. Events, *DB*, September 23, 1974 ; UCLA experimental college advertisement, *DB*, September 23, 1974; "Gay Studies: UCLA Takes Deep Plunge," *Advocate*, July 17, 1974, 21. Advanced Gay Studies, Non-Gays Guide to Understanding Gay Life Style, World Literature: Search of Gay Identity, Beginning Gay Studies, and Intermediate Gay Studies were noted in the GSU's newsletter, *Gayzette*, October 16, 1974. Kepner was the instructor for the world literature course ("Syllabus, World Literature: A Search for Gay Identity," UCLA experimental college, Fall 1974, Box 53, Folder 3, Kepner Papers, ONE Archives).

56. "The Lesbian Experience" (course proposal), [ca. 1974], Box 9, Folder 9, Jeanne Córdova Papers, ONE Archives; Rita Goldberger and Jan Field, "U.C.L.A. Lesbians Rewrite the Books," *LT*, September 1973, 9 (notes Sisterhood role in supporting a course on lesbianism). Shannon Hennigan's course at Sacramento State focused on lesbian sexuality (Freeman, "Building Lesbian Studies," 252)

57. Class roster, October 8, 1974, Box 9, Folder 9, Jeanne Córdova Papers, ONE Archives. Participants in Kepner's History of the Gay Movement and The Gay Novel also included a variety occupations: an assistant to the president, a media buyer, a hospital administrator, a financial aid counselor, an artist, a teacher, a psychologist, clerical workers, and graduate students (Registration Forms for "The Gay Movement" and "The Gay Novel," Subject File: UCLA Experimental College, ONE Archives).

58. "Exercise in Pride: Humanities Get Gay Treatment at UCLA," *Advocate*, December 18, 1974, 10. Other experimental college courses included Lesbian Sexuality and History of the Gay Movement (*Gayzette*, January 29, 1975).

59. Experimental college advertisement, *DB*, January 12, 1976; David Warrick, "Courses Offered to Public in Experimental College," *DB*, January 29, 1975. Steele's class drew thirty people to its initial session, "more than half of them persons never seen at a GSU meeting" ("Class on Gays," *Gayzette*, January 22, [1976], "Gay Experience Class a Success," *Gayzette*, January 29, 1976). In 1978, Steele taught a course, Homosexuality and Culture, through UCLA's Council on Educational Development ("Homosexuality and Culture" [course proposal], Spring 1978, Box 1, Folder 19, Steele Papers, ONE Archives). He also produced a study guide, likely for students (Gary Steele, "Homosexuality and Culture," [ca. 1980], Box 1, Folder 23, Steele Papers, ONE Archives).

60. See *Gayzette*, October 9, 16, 23, 30, November 6, 13, 20, December 4, 1974. See also "Editorial," *Gayzette*, April 14, 1975. The GSU gave Kepner a "special commendation" that in part recognized him as a "teacher of Gay Studies courses at UCLA's Experimental College" ("GSU Honors Jim Kepner," *Gayzette*, June 9, 1975).

61. "U.C.L.A. Gay Student Union" (brochure), [ca. 1976], Subject File: University of California, Los Angeles (UCLA), ONE Archives.

62. Examples include Sociology 181: Gay Women and Men in the Workforce (fall 1975), mentioned in *Gayzette*, December 4[, 1975]; Women's Studies Program courses offered, Winter Quarter 1977, *DB*, November 15, 1976; Council on Educational Development advertisement, *DB*, November 15, 1976; Luckenbill, *With Equal Pride*.

63. McNaron, "Poisoned Ivy"; Freeman, "Building Lesbian Studies."

64. Kristen Hogan, "Women's Studies in Feminist Bookstores"; Liddle, "More Than a Bookstore."

65. Christ, "Anniversary Lecture"; Mari Jo Buhle, introduction to Howe, *Politics of Women's Studies*, xv–xxvi; DuBois, "Women's Studies"; Howe, "Proper Study of Womankind."

66. "Women's Studies Programs," *Women's Studies Newsletter* 2, no. 3 (Summer 1974):

12–13. For women's studies programs in California, see Boxer, "Women's Studies as Women's History"; Salper, "San Diego State 1970"; Foulkes, "Coalitions, Collaborations, and Conflicts"; Roy, "Personal Is Historical"; Bartolotto, "Early History"; Christ, "Anniversary Lecture"; Corbett and Preston, *From the Catbird Seat*.

67. Zimmerman, "Lesbian-Feminist Journey."

68. Smith, interview by author; *Feminist News*, January 17, 1973, Box 5, Folder 6, WSPR; Women's Studies Board meeting minutes, March 6, April 23, 30, May 7, September 11, 24, October 3, 10, 17, 1973, Box 4, Folder 26, WSPR; "Women's Studies Office," *Feminist News*, October 5, 1972, Box 2, Folder 33, WSPR.

69. Person, interview by author.

70. Corrigan quoted in Astrid Olson, "Women's Studies—Then and Now," [ca. 1979], Box 4, Folder 20, Wagner Papers.

71. Aura, interview by author.

72. Orta, interview by author. Gay students at Columbia University similarly had to contend with the discomfort of their straight peers: "The campus social code is that one's sexuality is a private matter.... But in actual practice, this means that the gay students cannot engage openly in secondary affectional behavior unless it is at an explicitly 'gay' function and hidden from the view of the rest of the campus" (Liebert, "Gay Student," 39).

73. Goen-Salter, interview by author.

74. Farley, "Speaking, Silence, and Shifting Listening Space." See also Bulkin, "Heterosexism and Women's Studies"; McDaniel, "My Life."

75. "Women's Degree Wanted at SFSU," *Zenger's*, October 30, 1974; "Celebrating Sisterhood," *Zenger's*, March 5, 1975; Women's Studies Program flyer, February 5, 1976, SFSUSCA; "Women's Studies Finally Launched," *Zenger's*, September 15, 1976; "Proposal for a B.A. Degree in Women Studies," January 1976, accessed September 3, 2023, https://wgsdept.sfsu.edu/sites/default/files/documents/Spring%201977%20SFSU%20Women%20Studies%20BA%20Degree%20Program.pdf. San Francisco State had the university-run interdisciplinary New School, which offered some the campus's first women's studies courses, including a planned offering called Lesbianism. See "A Push for Women's Studies," *Phoenix*, May 3, 1973; "Women's Studies Cut," *Phoenix*, May 10, 1973; "Women's Studies Attracts Students, No Room in Classes," *Phoenix*, October 25, 1973.

76. "Something More Than Sex," *Phoenix*, March 15, 1973; "San Francisco State University Courses Relating to Women Enrollments, 1970–1978" (brochure), Spring 1972, "Women's Studies at California State University San Francisco," June 1972, "Focus on Women" (brochure), Fall 1973, Spring 1975, Spring 1976, all in Women's Studies Collection, Box 9, Folder 423, SFSUSCA. Nearly sixty students enrolled in Gearhart's "Homosexuality as a Social Issue" course, at least 75 percent of them women ("Exploding the Myth of the Homosexual," *Phoenix*, February 22, 1973, 1, 8). At least one other LGBT publication also advertised the course ("Gay Course Offered This Summer at San Francisco State College," *BAR*, June 12, 1973).

77. "Syllabus for Social Science 350: Homosexuality as a Social Issue, Spring 1976, Instructor Rochelle Gatlin," Internal Office Files, Women and Gender Studies Program, San Francisco State University; "Proposal for a B.A. Degree in Women Studies," January 1976, accessed September 3, 2023, https://wgsdept.sfsu.edu/sites/default/files/documents/Spring%201977%20SFSU%20Women%20Studies%20BA%20Degree%20Program.pdf.

78. Ruth Mahaney, interview, November 7, 1990, in Holloway Historians: Oral History Transcripts, 6–7, SFSUSCA; Orta, interview by author; "Women Studies" (poster),

[ca. early 1980s], Internal Office Files, Women and Gender Studies Program, San Francisco State University (including lesbian courses). Other LGBT-inclusive courses offered at San Francisco State included Rhetoric of Sexual Liberation (1972, 1974, 1977); Homosexuality and Literature (1971, 1972, 1973); Gays and Bisexual Literature (1976); Lesbian Lives/Lesbian Thought (1977); Homosexuality as a Social Force (1978); Gay and Lesbian Literature, Contemporary Lesbian Literature, and Lesbian History and Biography: Focus on France (all 1979) (Women's Studies brochure, Spring, Fall 1972, Spring 1973, "Focus on Women" [brochures], Spring 1978, 1979, Women's Studies Records, SFSUSCA.

79. Harwood quoted in Reti, *Out in the Redwoods*, 77. As Sharon Sievers recalled about CSU Long Beach, "every women's studies course that dealt with lesbianism in the 70s had a name like 'the study of gender' or 'seminar in gender' or something like that. We wouldn't even use the word sex anywhere"; students on campus would "know what it was, I guess." See Sharon Sievers, interview by Juliane Marie Bartolotto, November 29, 1994, California State University, Long Beach, Special Collections and University Archives.

80. Roy, "Personal Is Historical," 33.

81. A curriculum planning document suggested that an "expansion of areas within [women's studies] including older women & lesbians," while the "Women's Studies Five Year Mistress Plan" included lesbians as a "sub area" to be developed. See "Development of Program, Goal Statement: A Working Document," [ca. late 1970s], "Women's Studies Five Year Mistress Plan" and cover sheet, [ca. late 1970s], both in Box 4, Folder 26, WSPR.

82. "Women's Studies" (pamphlet), 1972, Box 19, Folder 1, Wagner Papers; National Lesbian Information Service, "Colleges and Gay Studies," May 1972, 3, Box 3, Folder 9, Wagner Papers. Another 1972 pamphlet lists Lesbians in America as the course name ("Women's Studies 1972," Box 33, Folder 13, Wagner Papers).

83. "Protection of the Core Classes and Teachers," n.d., Women's Studies Board meeting minutes, October 16, November 6, 1972, all in Box 7, Folder 1, WSPR; Women's Studies Board meeting minutes, January 22, April 23, May 29, 1973, Box 7, Folder 2, WSPR. The course drew eleven students in the fall of 1972, seven in the spring of 1973, and seventeen in the fall of 1974 ("Enrollments in Women's Studies Courses," [ca. 1974], Box 19, Folder 1, Wagner Papers). These courses were deeply connected to the broader feminist movement goal of teaching "women about their bodies and sexualities," as Susan K. Freeman argues ("Building Lesbian Studies," 232).

84. Women's Studies Board meeting minutes, March 6, 1974, attached to agenda, March 13, 1974, Box 2, Folder 34, WSPR; "Women's Studies at CSUS," [ca. 1974], Box 4, Folder 22, Wagner Papers; Women's Studies Board meeting minutes, February 26, 1975, list of Women's Studies courses, n.d., both in Box 7, Folder 4, WSPR; "Women's Studies Program, 1975–76," Box 2, Folder 34, WSPR; "Women's Studies at CSUS" (flyer), [ca. 1970s], Box 19, Folder 1, Wagner Papers; Women's Studies Board meeting minutes, February 18, 1976, Box 7, Folder 5, WSPR; "Women's Studies at CSUS," Fall 1976, Box 4, Folder 26, WSPR; "Women's Studies Program, CSU Sacramento," 1979–80, Box 19, Folder 1, Wagner Papers. The course was included on a list of "Suggestions for the Curriculum Committee for Curriculum for the Fall 1974," Box 2, Folder 35, WSPR. Minutes from the board throughout the spring of 1974 have "the lesbian class" as an agenda item with limited comment. The March 27, 1974, minutes suggested that two board members would "look into what is happening with it now" (Box 4, Folder 26, WSPR; see also agenda for April 5, 1974 [Box 4, Folder 26, WSPR]).

85. Reti, *Out in the Redwoods*, 77–78; Freeman, "Building Lesbian Studies"; Mahaney, interview by author.

86. *Gayzette*, March 5, 1975; GSU member preferences/opinion survey and result tally, 1975, Box 2, Folder 34, Steele Papers, ONE Archives. The 1973 West Coast Lesbian Conference held at UCLA had included workshops not only on women's studies but also on gay studies (agenda, [ca. April 1973], Subject File: West Coast Lesbian Conference [Los Angeles, Calif.: 1973], ONE Archives).

87. Jim Williford to San Francisco State faculty, December 2, 1971, Box 1, Folder 40, Burk Papers, GLBTHS.

88. Randy Shilts, "What's Happening with Gay Studies U.S.A.," *Advocate*, June 18, 1975, 9 (describing the program as "the most comprehensive gay studies format").

89. "Dateline: Sacramento," *Vector*, May 1972; Charles Moore, "Gay Studies Program," *Gay Sunshine*, January–February 1973, 15, GLBTHS Periodicals; "Gay Studies Courses," Box: Gay Liberation, Folder: Gay Liberation in Sacramento, EC.

90. Rogers, interview by author; Smith, interview by author; Bryant, interview by author.

91. "Gay Studies Gets Run-Around," *SH*, November 21, 1972. Moore credited anthropology professor Clark Taylor with initiating the idea. Moore also connected the desire for the program to an increasing "sense of pride in our accomplishments as Gay people," especially on the campus (Charles Moore, "Gay Studies Program," *Gay Sunshine*, January–February 1973, 15, GLBTHS Periodicals; Rogers, interview by author).

92. "Gay Studies Center at SSC," *SH*, May 12, 1972; "A Proposal for the Establishment of a Gay Studies Program at SSC," April 27, 1972, Box 34, Folder 8, Associated Students Records, CSUSSCUA; "Gay Studies Program Proposal," Box: Gay Liberation, Folder: Gay Liberation in Sacramento, EC. According to Susan K. Freeman, "Those initiating gay-themed courses were immersed in a social movement culture and their allegiance was generally strongest toward activists and newly emerging gay and lesbian communities. In some locations, gay studies was explicitly modeled on and pursued alongside the successes of ethnic, African American, Chicano, and women's studies, just as the gay liberation movement drew from liberation struggles that preceded and overlapped with them" ("Learning Alternatives").

93. Rogers, interview by author.

94. In one account, Rogers noted then that when looking for courses, "the departments were cooperative," and "there was no political repercussions even though we are in the state capital," concluding that there were "no complaints from the community." Charles Moore, also interviewed for the story, suggested few gay or lesbian faculty were willing to come forward in support—only four. See Randy Shilts, "What's Happening with Gay Studies U.S.A.," *Advocate*, June 18, 1975.

95. "Gay Studies Gets Run-Around," *SH*, November 21, 1972.

96. Rogers, interview by author.

97. "We Have a Right to Be Here," *SH*, November 29, 1972. The program listed its courses in the campus newspaper. See "Gay Studies Course Offerings," *SH*, December 12, 1972.

98. Kate Millet, a lesbian feminist writer and activist who was a distinguished visiting professor of women's studies at Sacramento State in the spring of 1973, praised the gay studies program in the student newspaper. See "Kate Millet is a 'Professed Homosexual, Revolutionary,'" *SH*, February 14, 1973; "Gay Studies Social Hour," *SH*, October 4, 1974.

99. Gay Students Council of Southern California to "Dear People," November 19, 1972, Box 15, Folder 49, L.A. Gay and Lesbian Center Records, ONE Archives; Larry Bernard, "Growing the Right Way," *Newsmagazine of the Gay Students Council of Southern California*, [ca. November 1972], 2, GSC File.

Chapter 4. Opening Up People's Eyes

1. Muriel Bunton, "Viewpoint: How Relevant Is Gay Liberation Movement in Society?," *Collegian*, December 6, 1974.

2. Maxwell Harris, "Black and Gay" (letter to the editor), *Collegian*, December 20, 1974.

3. "Campus Paper Backs Down as Gays Protest Editorial," *Advocate*, January 1, 1975, 16.

4. Jackson H. Smith, "View: The Cry Was Fire—," *Collegian*, December 13, 1974. As Michael Anderson noted in a letter to the editor, gay liberation's purpose was "to stop oppression against homosexuals. How can this be a stumbling block to education?" (*Collegian*, December 13, 1974). As Jess Clawson argues, the "gay liberation struggle was explicitly educational," designed to challenge hostile and dominant discourses ("Existing and Existing in Your Face," 143). By 1979, Los Angeles City College's renamed Gay & Lesbian Student Union continued the theme, proclaiming a motto of "Social Change through Education." "I Want *You*" (flyer for Gay & Lesbian Student Union), [ca. 1979], Subject File: Los Angeles City College, ONE Archives.

5. "GSU Non 'Self-Serving,' Says Student," *49er*, October 2, 1974.

6. "Campus Gays Want to Better Relations, Debunk Stereotypes," *UT*, November 21, 1975

7. On counterstorytelling, see Delgado, "Storytelling for Oppositionists and Others." Some scholars use the concept of counterpublics to describe how marginalized communities carve out "alternative and subversive discourses in the public sphere" (Brantley, "Shouldn't You Be Boycotting Coors?," 144); see also Warner, "Publics and Counterpublics."

8. Bob Roth, "Publicity, or Reaching the Student Body," *Interchange*, March–April 1972, 8, GLBTHS Periodicals. See also Tom Carr, "How to Get Publicity for Campus Gay Groups," in *Gays on Campus*, edited by Lehman.

9. "I Am a Lesbian," *SH*, April 27, 1971. Person's letter came on the heels of a successful symposium organized by gay and lesbian students and faculty (Gay Scene Symposium program, April 19–23, 1971, Box 54, Folder 4, AR Files, CSUSSCUA; Candy Miller, "Symposium Attempts to Dispel Myths," *SH*, April 20, 1971).

10. Dave Johnson, "The Gay Experience at UCLA," *DB*, March 6, 1974. See also GLF, "Gay Is Good," *SpD*, March 24, 1971; Lawrence Gold, "Celebration of Gay Pride," *StD*, July 12, 1974; Rod Thorson, "On the Road to Freedom," *DB*, October 31, 1974; Ray Beck, "A Disease Called Homophobia," *DB*, March 1, 1976.

11. See Gay Caucus, Gay Liberation, and Gay Students of CSUS, "We Have a Right to Be Here," *SH*, November 29, 1972 (challenging inability of a fledgling gay studies program to obtain office space); Doug Hutchinson, letter to the editor, *DB*, February 24, 1976 (promoting UCLA Gay Awareness Week); Glenn Erickson, "Gay" (letter to the editor), *DB*, May 18, 1976 (promoting a "Gay Straight Dialogue" sponsored by the GSU); Freda Smith, "Gay Activist Gets One Line," *SH*, May 21, 1974 (criticizing the paper for failing to publicize an event with Troy Perry of the Metropolitan Community Church; after the letter, the *Hornet* included Smith's article).

12. "Aware to Gay Group Protested," *49er*, September 25, 1974; "Long Beach GSU Wins School Trophy," *Advocate*, July 17, 1974, 23.

13. "Gays React to Prof's Attack," *49er*, September 27, 1974, 3.

14. "On 'Homophobia,'" *49er*, October 2, 1974. In the fall of 1975, a Cal State Long Beach student created a comic book, *Gay Power . . . Can Accomplish a Lot!*, in which the fictional Dr. Phobia engages in a debate with Dan Phelps. In the comic, the discussion

turns against the homophobic professor when a young gay man says in front of the audience, "Hi there! So your real name is Homer, huh?" He reminds the professor that they had met in the "third stall from the left" at the city park. When the young man is asked whether he is "a ghost from [Dr. Phobia's] past," the man replies, "To tell you the truth, I never saw him before in my life! I don't think he'll give you any more trouble, though!" The professor never bothers the gay men again, and "publicity for GSU membership soar[s]!" (*Gay Power . . . Can Accomplish a Lot!*, October 1975, CSULB GSU File).

15. Dave Cash, "Harassment for Gay People," *DC*, November 16, 1972.

16. Larry Rodriguez, "Reactions to Gay Lib Table" (letter to the editor), *DB*, April 19, 1971.

17. "KCSB to Air Gay Series," *DN*, February 5, 1973; "Political Aspects of Gay Lib on KCSB," *DN*, February 12, 1973; "Campus Happenings," *GSC Newsmagazine*, April 1973, 5, GSC File. Student Mark Wren's gay-themed 1977 program on KERS, Sacramento State University's radio station, included interviews with local gay and lesbian leaders, including former student and activist Freda Smith. See "KERS Slots Gay Program," *SH*, March 4, 1977. KERS's lineup included a gay-themed news program as early as 1972, when it was described as the Sacramento area's "first . . . regularly scheduled radio broadcast for gays and by gays" (KERS Schedule, [ca. 1972], Box 40, Folder 6: KERS, 1972–1973, AR Files, CSUSSCUA); KERS Gay Community News notice, *SH*, March 1, 1972; "KERS: Student Produced and Future Oriented," *SH*, April 12, 1972; "Radio KERS' Spring Schedule," *SH*, March 16, 1973.

18. "Women in the Gay People's Union" (advertisement), *DN*, April 24, 1975; *Her Voice* (advertisement), *DN*, April 18, 1977; *Coming Out* program notice, *DN*, September 27, 1979. Campus radio stations also provided platforms for gay and lesbian–themed programming at schools outside of California, including the University of Pennsylvania (WXPN) and Georgetown University (WGBT). More common were shows on public radio stations, including those affiliated with Pacifica in Berkeley, Los Angeles, New York, and Washington, D.C. See Phylis A. Johnson and Keith, *Queer Airwaves*, 27–30.

19. "Message from the Prez," *GG*, April 1974, CSULB GSU File; Monica Riordan, "Gays 'No Longer Satisfied,'" *DB*, February 14, 1974; "Gays Present Open Forum," *DB*, November 15, 1974; KCHO notice, *Chico Wildcat*, April 29, 1976.

20. "Free Speech Message," KNOR, June 17, 1974, Folder: Stanford University—Student and Faculty Groups, EC. The American Psychiatric Association's removal of homosexuality from the Diagnostic and Statistical Manual of Mental Disorders was celebrated at the time as a civil rights victory. Regina Kunzel critiques this celebration and suggests a more critical view: "Health is not just a desired state or a self-evident good but an ideology that mobilizes a set of norms, prescriptions, and hierarchies of worth"; she distances "homosexuality from gender nonconformity" ("Queer History," 316, 317).

21. On the educational focus of speakers' bureaus, see SGP meeting minutes, January 28, 1970, Folder: Students for Gay Power, EC; San José GLF press release, [ca. May 1971], Subject File: San José (Calif.), ONE Archives. See also Mayernick, "Gay Teachers Association."

22. SGP meeting minutes, February 4, 1970, SPC; San José GLF press release, [ca. May 1971], Subject File: San José (Calif.), ONE Archives ; GPU Lesbian Collective flyer, [ca. 1970s], Box 1, Folder: Gay Info, Corbin Papers, GLBTHS; "Introducing . . . Gay Students Council of Southern California" (flyer), [ca. 1972], GSC File; Rita Goldberger and Jan Field, "U.C.L.A. Lesbians Rewrite the Books," *LT*, September 1973, 10; "Notes and Announcements," *Gayzette*, December 4, 1974; "Speaking Out," *Voice of Change* [Cal Poly San Luis Obispo GSU], May 1976, copy in author's possession; "Gays to Meet," *DN*, March 7, 1973.

23. See "Speakers for Classes," *Proud*, October 13, [1972], 2, CSULB GSU File; Residence Staff Orientation Program sign-up sheet, [ca. September 1974], Series I, Box 2, Folder: Orientation 1974, Stanford QSR Records. See also "Speakers Action," *Gayzette*, February 12, 1975; GSU Speakers' Bureaus, [ca. early 1970s], Box 1, Folder 5, Hayes Papers, ONE Archives; Women's Group at the GPU flyer, [ca. October 1975], Subject File: Stanford University, ONE Archives.

24. Steve Cronenwalt to faculty, [ca. 1975], Subject File: University of California, Los Angeles (UCLA), ONE Archives.

25. Laura Fox, "Speakers Give Information on Aspects of Gay Lifestyles," *DS*, May 12, 1978.

26. See gay speakers announcement, *DB*, April 24, 1974; "Speakers Bureau Needs Suggestions for Classes," *Gayzette*, October 23, 1975; "News," *Gayzette*, November 20, 1974. The UCLA Medical School refused to place notices about the service in professors' mailboxes, prompting the GSU to ask readers of its newsletter to suggest responses (*Gayzette*, December 4, 1974).

27. "Message from the Prez," *GG*, April 1974, CSULB GSU File.

28. Rogers, interview by author.

29. "Speaking Engagement," *Gayzette*, January 29, 1975.

30. "Club of the Year: Gay Students Union," *49er*, September 17, 1974. Cooper used the pseudonym "Shirley Connor" in this article.

31. *Gay Power . . . Can Accomplish a Lot!*, October 1975, CSULB GSU File.

32. "Gay Stereotyping: Breaking Down the Barriers," *SH*, March 1, 1972; "Gay Speakers' Bureau" pamphlet, [ca. 1972–73], Box 21, Folder 6, Martin and Lyon Papers, GLBTHS; Rogers, interview by author.

33. Bryant, interview by author.

34. "Gays to Meet," *DN*, March 7, 1973; Mike Gold, "Debate on Gay Speakers," *DN*, March 9, 1973. High school students in New York and Los Angeles also visited their peers (Stephan Cohen, *Gay Liberation Youth Movement*, 62–66).

35. *GPU News*, July 30, 1975, GLBTHS Periodicals.

36. "Club of the Year: Gay Students Union," *49er*, September 17, 1974.

37. See, for example, "Lesbian Speaks on Military Gays," *SpD*, October 5, 1976; Miriam Ben-Shalom advertisement, *DC*, September 30, 1976; Larry Sterne, "Ousted Lesbian Sergeant Seeks Funds for Suit," *DC*, October 4, 1976; "Gay Rights Panel, American Civil Liberties Union," *Gayzette*, January 15, 1976.

38. Lynn McMichael, "Women's Day," *SH*, March 9, 1971.

39. "The Law and the Homosexual," *Proud*, October 13, [1972], CSULB GSU File.

40. "UCLA Women's Health Week," *DB*, April 11, 1974.

41. Gay Health Problems rap flyer, January 17, 1974, Folder: General 1970–1989, EC; "Gay Therapy" (advertisement), *DC*, April 4, 1974; "What's Happening with Our Women's Collective" (flyer), April 1978, Series VIII, Box 3, Folder: Gay People's Union Scrapbook, Stanford QSR Records. As Regina Kunzel notes, efforts to "distance homosexuality from the stigma of mental illness" were a "defining project of the emerging gay rights movement" ("Queer History," 315).

42. A 1971 Sacramento State "Gay Scene symposium" included a dance recital, folk songs, and poetry (symposium program, April 19–23, 1971, Box 54, Folder 4, AR Files, CSUSSCUA). Gay Pride Week at California State University, Long Beach in 1975 included theater, film, poetry, and music. See "A Trilogy on the Meaning of Being Gay," *49er*, October 24, 1975; "Functions Outlined for Oct. Gay Pride Week," *49er*, September 12, 1975; "Speakers, Plays, Poetry, Film Will Highlight Gay Pride Week," *49er*, October 21, 1975; "Gay Writer Talk Ends Pride Week," *49er*, October 27, 1975; "Gay Pride Week" flyer, April

18–21, [1977], CSULA GSU File (music, lesbian themed films, a slide show on lesbian art); Gay Awareness Week program, [ca. 1978], Box 41, Folder 9, Wagner Papers (art exhibit, poetry readings, theater).

43. "Women's Week to Feature Speakers, Seminars, Films," *DB*, April 2, 1973; "Films, Speeches, Panels Scheduled Today," *DB*, April 16, 1973; Women's Week calendar, *DB*, April 16, 1973.

44. Reichard, "We Can't Hide"; "Top Names Lined Up for Gay-Themed Sacramento Seminar," *Advocate*, March 17–30, 1971; Gay Scene symposium program, April 19–23, 1971, Box 54, Folder 4, AR Files, CSUSSCUA; Candy Miller, "Symposium Attempts to Dispel Myths," *SH*, April 20, 1971; Lynn McMichael, "Homosexual Symposium: Room for Competition," *SH*, April 20, 1971; Lynn McMichael, "Not a Freak Show," *SH*, April 21, 1971; Mary Hicks, "Gay Women Rap on Femininity," *SH*, April 21, 1971; Bob Warren, "Ginsberg to Do Whatever," *SH*, April 23, 1971; Nancy Jones and Vicki Sahs, "Rev. Troy Perry: Church and the Homosexual," *SH*, April 23, 1971; Nancy Jones, "Panel Examines Gay Struggle," *SH*, April 23, 1971; Nancy Skelton, "Ginsberg 'Performs' for SSC Straights," *Sacramento Bee*, April 24, 1971.

45. "Gay Artists Are Coming Out Today" (advertisement), *DB*, May 15, 1974; "Program Features Gay Artists," *DB*, May 15, 1974.

46. "Poets Bring Out Emotions of the Audience," *SH*, May 4, 1973. On Mariah, see Downs, *Stand by Me*, 146–47. Smith performed at many campus and community events throughout the 1970s. See "Gay Culture Series Planned," *SH*, November 9, 1973. For examples of poetry readings on other campuses, see "Woman Strength," *LV* [March 1975], 6, GLBTHS Periodicals; Gay Awareness Week flyer, February 1–5, 1977, Subject File: University of California, Los Angeles (UCLA), ONE Archives. In addition, between June 30 and July 3, 1972, the Bakersfield GLF sponsored the Southwest Regional Conference of the National Coalition of Gay Organizations, which included a "gay poetry reading" (conference schedule, Box 56, Folder 9, Kepner Papers, ONE Archives).

47. Pat Parker evaluation, Gay Awareness Week III (1976) Audience Evaluations, Box 1, Folder 1, UCLA Gay Awareness Week Records, ONE Archives. On Parker and lesbian poets, see Rushkin, "Pat Parker."

48. "Gay Culture Series Planned," *SH*, November 9, 1973; "Symposium Will Increase Awareness," *SH*, December 7, 1973 (musician Juanita Oribee); "Everything You Always Wanted to Know about Homosexuality" (flyer), [ca. early 1970s], CSULB GSU File (Maxine Feldman); *GPU News*, June 2, October 27, 1976, GLBTHS Periodicals (Blackberri and J. C. Maddness); Berkeley Women's Music Collective concert reservation application, November 17, 1976, Series III, Box 1, Folder: Women's Collective Weekly Meetings 1976, Stanford QSR Records; Mills Lesbian Union concert poster, [ca. late 1970s], EC (Margie Adam, Nancy Vogel and Suzanne P. Shanbaum); Linda Tillery and Band flyer, [ca. 1970s], Box 5, Folder 8, Wagner Papers; Lesbian and Gay Awareness Week poster, [ca. 1981], Poster Collection, GLBTHS (Mary Watkins Group).

49. Maxine Feldman in Morris, "In Their Own Words," 57.

50. *Gay People's Union News*, February 18, 1975, GLBTHS Periodicals; Don Weber, "Joint Effort's Women's Week Show Exceeds," *SpD*, March 11, 1975. The first time Adams sang in public was at a 1973 women's music festival at Sacramento State organized by Kate Millet, who was a visiting professor there (Morris, "In Their Own Words," 61). This event was not organized solely by lesbian students but represented a collaboration among campus feminists.

51. Holly Near and Mary Watkins concert flyer, February 10, 1978, Folder 2, Lesbian and Gay Academic Union Records, ONE Archives.

52. "Gay Liberation Sponsors Films Tonight in Haines," *DB*, April 25, 1972.

53. "GSU Meeting Agenda," *Gayzette*, November 6, 1974; "Films by and about Women" (advertisement), *DB*, February 12, 1975; "Campus Events," *DB*, April 18, 1975. In 1976, UCLA's GSU contacted in the *Lesbian Tide* seeking recommended "films and about lesbians and gay men," including "films dealing with non-white lesbians and gays." See "UCLA Wants Lesbian Films," *LT*, November–December 1976, 28.

54. "Some of Your Best Friends" (flyer), [ca. October 12, 1972], Subject File: University of Southern California (USC), ONE Archives; "USC Gay Produces Documentary Film Showing Gays as Human Beings," *Advocate*, July 18, 1973, 31–32; "Some of Your Best Friends" (advertisement), *DN*, February 7, 1973; "Some of Your Best Friends" (advertisement), *UT*, April 12, 1973. The credits for *Some of Your Best Friends* listed fifty-six gay organizations, twelve of them LGBT student organizations in California.

55. "Word Is Out" (flyer), [ca. April 15, 1978], Series VIII, Box 3, Folder: Gay People's Union Scrapbook, Stanford QSR Records; "Word Is Out" (flyer), [ca. 1978], Subject File: Sacramento (Calif.)—Gay Liberation, ONE Archives.

56. "Gay People's Union of U.C. Berkeley" (flyer), 1977, EC.

57. GSU meeting notice, *DC*, October 25, 1973; "Drag and Genderfuck" event flyer, EC.

58. "Everything You Always Wanted to Know about Homosexuality" (flyer), [ca. early 1970s], "Message from the Prez," *GG*, April 1974, both in CSULB GSU File.

59. "Realities of Homosexuality" (flyer), March 1, 1974, Series I, Box 2, Folder: GPU-3/9/74 Lecture, Stanford QSR Records; "The Realities of Homosexuality," *GPU Newsletter*, [ca. late February 1974], "Gay Lecture: The Realities of Homosexuality," *GPU Newsletter*, [ca. late March 1974], both in SUPEC; Corbin, interview by author.

60. "Perspectives on the Gay Movement" (flyer), [pre-1978], Subject File: Gay Students Union—California State University, Fullerton, ONE Archives.

61. "Strength under Oppression" (flyer), October 20, [n.d.], CSULB GSU File.

62. Meeting minutes, *Gay Academic Union Newsletter*, October 30, 1975, ONE Periodicals.

63. "Gay Reverend Urges National Leaders to Help Homosexuals," *Collegian*, April 1, 1977; Tom Pellenwessel to George Raya, October 3, 16, 1975, Box 1, Folder: Personal Correspondence, Raya Papers, GLBTHS (Raya speaking at Cal State Long Beach).

64. *GG*, [ca. April 1974], "Message from the Prez," *GG*, April 1974, both in CSULB GSU File; "The Lord Is My Shepherd . . . and He Knows I'm Gay," *49er*, April 4, 1974.

65. AS SU Budget Proposal, February 14, 1975, Series I, Box 2, Folder: GPU Budget 1974–75, Stanford QSR Records.

66. Women's Week program, April 10–15, 1972, Virginia Ellis O'Reilly to "Women's Studies People," March 25, 1974, Women's Week schedule, March 11–15, 1974, all in Series III, Box 11, Folder 542, San José State University Women's Studies Program Records, University Archives, San José State University, Special Collections and Archives; Women's Week program, May 7–11, 1973, Series I, Box 1, Folder 20, San José State University Women's Studies Program Records, University Archives, San José State University, Special Collections and Archives; "Women's Week: A Beautiful Success," *Up from the Basement*, April 1974, Series III, Box 11, Folder 550, San José State University Women's Studies Program Records, University Archives, San José State University, Special Collections and Archives; "Lesbian Urges Women to Fight Back," *SpD*, March 7, 1975; Pam Strandberg, "A Queer Lady," *LV*, [March 1975], 2, GLBTHS Periodicals.

67. Judith Schwarz Freewoman, "Women Together Day, San José State University's Women's Week," *Lesbian Voices*, Summer 1976, 19–23, GLBTHS Periodicals; Pat Callahan, "Women's Future Explored," *SpD*, March 12, 1976. See also Women's Week program, *UT*, May 20, 1974; Madeline Bickert, "Women's Week: New Image Here to Stay," *DS*, February 1, 1974.

68. "Women's Day to Feature Variety, 'Pig' Election," *DB*, January 22, 1973; "WRC Presents Women's Day," *DB*, January 26, 1973.

69. "Women's Week to Feature Speakers, Seminars, Films," *DB*, April 2, 1973; "Films, Speeches, Panels Scheduled Today," *DB*, April 16, 1973; Women's Week calendar, *DB*, April 16, 1973; Gay Sisterhood, "Gays" (letter to the editor), *DB*, June 1, 1973. The West Coast Lesbian Conference drew thousands of people and urged them "Out of the Closet and into the Movement." Keynote speakers included Robin Morgan and Kate Millet, and workshops covered such topics as lesbian activism, lesbian identity, law reform, gay mothers, gay youth, and "the lesbian and religion." The three-day event also included music, dances, and opportunities for women to network. See press release, January 1973, conference agenda, [April 1973], both in Subject File: West Coast Lesbian Conference (Los Angeles, Calif.: 1973), ONE Archives; "Lesbian Conference to Be Held," *DB*, April 13, 1973; "Personal Diary of a Mad Organizer on Her Way to First Nervous Breakdown Due [to] National Lesbian Conference UCLA, 1973, 'Birth of a Nation,'" December 12–22, 1973, Jeanne Córdova Papers, Box 2, Folder 9, ONE Archives; Rita Goldberger and Jan Field, "U.C.L.A. Lesbians Rewrite the Books," *LT*, September 1973, 9.

70. "'Weeks' Stimulate Interest in Cultural Backgrounds," *Warwoop*, March 9, 1973. The *Warwoop* (El Camino College) is available at https://elcamino.ptfs.com/knowvation/app/consolidatedSearch/#search/v=list,c=1,sm=s,l=library1_lib.

71. See, for example, "Women's Awareness Week Highlighted by Appearance of Novelist Rita Mae Brown," *The Onion*, March 12, 1975 (Chico State); "Black History Week," *RR*, February 6, 1970; "Program for Black History Week, *RR*, February 4, 1972; "Black History Week Schedule," *RR*, February 8, 1974; "Brown History Fest Opens," *RR*, May 2, 1977; "Black Day Draws Capacity Crowds," *Rampage*, December 16, 1971; "Black-In Events Set to Promote Culture Awareness," *Rampage*, May 6, 1971; "Saturday Confab Will Counsel Chicano Youth," *Rampage*, March 16, 1972; "Black Awareness Week," *Warwoop*, May 10, 1973; "AS Funds Jazz Festival, African Awareness Week," *DS*, March 3, 1977. The *Rampage* (Fresno City College) is available at https://www.therampageonline.com/archives/.

72. For the first inclusion of *lesbian* in the event's name at Cal State Long Beach, see "Come Out to the 80's" (Gay and Lesbian Awareness Week flyer), March 24–28, 1980, CSULB GSU File. San José State also held a "Lesbian and Gay Awareness Week" in 1980 ("Gay/Lesbian Awareness Weeks Set at Local Universities," *Lambda News*, April 1980, 6, San José State University, Special Collections and Archives.

73. "Gay Pride Week at Stanford University," *BAR*, June 12, 1974; Gay Freedom Day flyer, May 16, 1978, EC; Gay Awareness Week flyer, May 7–13, 1979, Series IV, Box 1, Folder: Gay Awareness Week 1979, Stanford QSR Records; *GPU News* (San José State), September 3, 1975, GLBTHS Periodicals; Gay Pride Day workshop schedule, October 3, 1975, Subject File: San José (Calif.), ONE Archives; "Functions Outlined for Oct. Gay Pride Week," *49er*, September 12, 1975; Gay Pride Day flyer, November 11, 1975, Box 1, Folder 42, Burk Papers, GLBTHS; "Gay Pride Has Its Day of Equality on Campus," *Phoenix*, November 13, 1975, 3; "UC Santa Cruz Forum Gay 'Breakthrough,'" *Advocate*, February 2, 1972; Gay Awareness Week program, April 9–13, 1973, GSC File; "Gay Union Hold Forum," *Collegian*, May 17, 1974; "Gay Day Sponsored," *Collegian*, May 27, 1977; "Gay Week Events Set," *Express*, April 21, 1977; "Play and Dance Top Off Gay Awareness Week," *Express*, April 13, 1977. The *Express* (Sacramento City College) is available at https://cdnc.ucr.edu/.

74. Gay Awareness Week, May 6–10 [n.d.], Subject File: Gay Students Union—California State University, Fullerton, ONE Archives.

75. "Speakers, Plays, Poetry, Film Will Highlight Gay Pride Week," *49er*, October 21, 1975.

76. "Straight Students at UCLA Prove They're Not So Healthy," *Advocate*, June 5, 1974.

77. "Gay Pride Week at Stanford University," *BAR*, June 12, 1974.

78. Gay Pride Day flyer, October 3, [1975]; Gay Pride Day workshop schedule, [ca. 1975], Subject File: San José (Calif.), ONE Archives. Gay Pride Day sparked a local backlash after both San José mayor Janet Hayes and the Santa Clara County Board of Supervisors declined to give the event official recognition despite a request from students ("County Says No Gay Day," *SpD*, September 12, 1975; "'Gay Pride' Day Bid Rejected," *Los Angeles Times*, September 6, 1975).

79. GayTHINK II program, October 29–31, 1976, Box 11, Folder: Gay Students Union, Daly Papers, GLBTHS.

80. "CSULB's Gay Students Union Gay Awareness Week '76" schedule, October 25–29, 1976, Box 11, Folder: Gay Students Union, Daly Papers, GLBTHS; "Gay Listeners Dispute Speaker on 'Closet,'" *49er*, October 26, 1976.

81. "Conference on Gay Life Due at Cal State: Homosexual Group Stages Event Denied Student Government Loan," *Los Angeles Times*, October 29, 1977.

82. "Campus 'Gay Power' Grows, Union Seeks Headquarters," *Phoenix*, September 11, 1975.

83. Blackburn, interview by author.

84. "Symposium 76 Draws 600, Sparked Lively Interchanges," clipping, Box 2, Folder 1/76, Burk Papers, GLBTHS; "Gay Students Hold Conference," *Phoenix*, April 22, 1976; Symposium '76 announcement and registration form, copy in author's possession.

85. Symposium '76 program and registration form, April 1976, copy in author's possession; "Gay Academic Union," *BAR*, March 4, 1976; Gay Academic Union Symposium '76 registration list, March 1976, Box 12, Folder 13, De Cecco Papers, GLBTHS.

86. George Mendenhall, "Symposium Frank Kameny 76, 3 Days to Remember," *BAR*, April 1, 1976.

87. Joe Whitney, "Symposium '76: A Fairy's Tale of How I Spent My Weekend," *Gayzette*, April 1976.

88. Randy Shilts, "An Undercurrent of Protest Dominates the California Gay Academic Union Symposium '76," *Advocate*, May 19, 1976.

89. Gay Students Alliance of City College, "We Protest Token Participation of Lesbians and Third World Gays" (flyer), [ca. April 1976], EC.

90. Don Liles to Jim and Sal Licata, March 17, 1977, Box 2, Folder 13, Steele Papers, ONE Archives.

91. John Blackburn to Randy Shilts and David B. Goodstein, May 13, 1976, copy in author's possession. De Cecco recognized the challenges of "the representation of lesbians and Third World people" but deemed the symposium a success, even if there were lessons to be learned ("Gay Academics Get It Together," *BAR*, April 29, 1976). De Cecco noted that the event "had a good representation of Third World Gays who previously found it hard to choose to identify with gays over ethnic identity" ("Gay Students Hold Conference," *Phoenix*, April 22, 1976).

92. GAYTHINK IV program, October 27–29, 1978, Box 1, Folder 7, Hayes Papers, ONE Archives; "Gay Scholars to Meet," *Coast to Coast Times*, October 11, 1978, clipping in Box 1, Folder 7, Hayes Papers, ONE Archives; Latinos Unidos, "Special Dance Edition," [ca. 1978], Box 1, Amador Papers, ONE Archives.

93. "Hate Still Lives?," *49er*, October 22, 1975; "Gay Pride Week Reaction Analyzed," *49er*, October 24, 1975.

94. "Unfair Gay Grant?," *49er*, October 20, 1975. A subsequent response rejected this claim on the grounds that funding for Gay Pride Week had "gone through all the proper channels" ("Gay Week Democratic," *49er*, October 22, 1975).

95. "Gay Pride Week Draws Storm: F-N Chastised," *49er*, October 24, 1975.

96. "Too Much Coverage," *49er*, October 24, 1975.
97. Jon Ivanoff, "Gay Awareness" (letter to the editor), *DB*, March 4, 1976.
98. Joe Phillips, "Exchanging God's Truth for a Lie," *DB*, March 5, 1976. Gay Pride Week at UC Santa Barbara in 1977 resulted in a letter highlighting the conflict between biblical teaching and homosexuality and another describing homosexuality as "morally repugnant" (Randy Evenson, letter to the editor, *DN*, May 4, 1977; Peter A. Wierenga, "Another View of Homosexuality," *DN*, May 6, 1977). For the week's events, see Gay Pride Week schedule, *DN*, May 4, 1977; Gay Pride Week calendar, *DN*, May 5, 1977.
99. "Gays Oppressed," *49er*, October 29, 1975; "Gays Threatening?," *49er*, October 29, 1975; "Close Minded to Gays," *49er*, October 31, 1975.
100. R. C. Pennie, "Awareness" (letter to the editor), *DB*, February 18, 1977.
101. Vito Russo, "Comments on Gay Conferences," *Advocate*, January 14, 1976. On Russo, see Schiavi, *Celluloid Activist*.
102. Vito Russo, "Comments on Gay Conferences," *Advocate*, January 14, 1976.

Chapter 5. Fostering Queer Creativity

1. "Lesbians Have Chosen to Fight against the Oppression of Sexist Society," *SH*, December 8, 1972. On the colloquium generally, see "Can Girls Be Gay?," *SH*, December 1, 1972; "Lesbian Women: Myth and Reality," *SH*, December 5, 1972; "How We Sabotage Ourselves," *SH*, December 6, 1972; "Colloquium on Lesbian Women: Myth and Reality" (program), December 6–8 1972, Folder: California State University, Sacramento, EC; "Lesbian Colloquium" (video recording), Sacramento State College, December 1972, Oversize Storage Box 1, F1, Gordon Papers. On the Daughters of Bilitis, see Gallo, *Different Daughters*.
2. "Lesbians Present Drama, Poetry to Close Colloquium," *SH*, December 12, 1972; Patricia (Matty) Wallace [Patricia One Person] and Cherie Gordon, *The Homobrontosaurus* (draft), [1972], Box 1, Folder 2, Gordon Papers. Members of Le Theatre Lesbien who performed that day included Cherie Gordon, Diane Bulloch, Joan Hand, and Wallace. See "Lesbian Colloquium at Sac State," 1972, Box 2, Folder 26, Gordon Papers; Gordon, interview by author; Person, interview by author.
3. Patricia (Matty) Wallace [Patricia One Person] and Cherie Gordon, "The Homobrontosaurus" (draft), [1972], 1, Box 1, Folder 2, Gordon Papers.
4. Michael Colby, "A Brief History of Le Theatre Lesbien," n.d., Gordon Papers. The Theater of the Ridiculous, a New York–based group founded by Charles Ludlam in 1967, took a similar tack: "Rather than calling for reform through protest," this type of theater reflect and satirize "contemporary life through a lens of queer identity, anti-hegemonic possibility, and the embrace of farce, danger, and the imagination" (Edgecomb, "History of the Ridiculous").
5. Person, interview by author.
6. For other social movements and creative expression, see Reed, *Art of Protest*; Chavez, "*Despierten Hermanas y Hermanos!*" (esp. chap. 5); Gunckel, "The Chicano/a Photographic"; Echols, *Daring to Be Bad*; Roth, *Separate Roads to Feminism*; Moravec, "Toward a History"; Hayes, *Songs in Black and Lavender*; Murray, "Free for All Lesbians"; Kimball, *Women's Culture*. See also Shepard, "Play as World-Making."
7. *GAPOO*, July 24, 1974, SUPEC. See also *VGSC*, May 16, 1974, GLBTHS Periodicals; *GPU News*, August 8, 1977, GLBTHS Periodicals; *GG*, April 1974, CSULB GSU File.
8. See *Gayzette*, February 5, 1976 (talent night); "The Gay Writer's Workshop . . . ," *Gayzette*, May 6, 1976; *Gayzette*, October 20, 1977 (Sons of Walt poetry group).
9. *The Bridge* (San José Gay Liberation), August 6, 1970, GLBTHS Periodicals (coffee

house for meetings, dances, singing, and poetry); Robert Kroll, "Gay Liberation Conference Closes Five Day Symposium," *Berkeley Gazette*, December 31, 1969, Subject File: Berkeley Gay Liberation, ONE Archives (SGP co-opted a campus coffee shop for a cabaret); "All Gay Symposium" (flyer), [ca. 1970], "Organizations, University of California Berkeley—Students for Gay Power and Free Particle," EC; "Gay Sisterhood at UCLA," *LT*, March 1973 (Lesbian Sisterhood hosted coffeehouse after meetings, "Bring an instrument with you if you play"); GSU meeting notice, *DS*, March 11, 1977 ("an evening of entertainment"); "Cultural Nights," *GPU News*, August 6, 1977, GLBTHS Periodicals; "Stanford's G.P.U. News," *BAR*, August 18, 1977; Cultural Night flyer, [ca. 1977], Box 3, Folder: GPU Misc. Materials 1973–77, Series I, Stanford QSR Records; "Homosexuals Escape Their Harassment," *SpD*, September 27, 1977 (GSU "creativity night"); Boneberg, interview by author; "Week's Agenda," *Gayzette*, October 9, 1974.

10. Students also produced films. Gordon advertised by word of mouth and in the campus feminist newspaper to find participants for a planned film about lesbians. See *Feminist News*, March 29, 1973, Box 41, Folder 10, Wagner Papers; Gordon, interview by author.

11. Bennett, "Lesbian Poetry," 106. On the development of a "communal identity" among artists committed to social change and to "arts of transformation," see Collins, "Activists."

12. Writing about Chicana activism of the 1960s and 1970s, Marisela Chavez describes poetry as "one of the most accessible and prolific forms of writing during the movement." Tackling such themes as identity, sexuality, family, relationships with men, white feminism, and politics, poetry had the power to "rouse Chicanos and Chicanas to action both in print and in public performance" (Chavez, "*Despierten Hermanas y Hermanos!*," 288). I have sought to identify student authors where possible, but this thematic assessment includes all poetry shared by students, regardless of its authorship, since the fact that a poem was shared demonstrated that its words had resonance. In addition, the examination of student-authored poetry depends on the availability of organizational newsletters, which constitute a prime source for these texts, and Stanford and UCLA are thus overrepresented here. Writings by gay men are more common than those by lesbians in LGBT student publications, although it is often not possible to determine an author's gender identity—or race, ethnicity, age, or sexual orientation—because the author was identified only by initials or was not identified at all. I have used other sources, including oral histories, to supplement the analysis.

13. Creativity Night advertisement, *SpD*, February 17, 1977.

14. "Homosexuals Escape Their Harassment," *SpD*, September 27, 1977. Similarly, the GPU at Stanford began hosting a "Cultural Night" in 1977, including "live guitar music, poetry, sing-a-longs and folk dancing." An advertisement for the event in their newsletter urged people to "come and add your spirit..." ("Cultural Nights," *GPU News*, August 6, 1977, GLBTHS Periodicals).

15. Laine, "Gay Poetry Reaches Adolescence," 35. See also Steve Abbott, "The Politics of Gay Poetry," *Advocate*, May 13, 1982, 23; Hennessy, "Ten Ways."

16. Bulkin, "Whole New Poetry Beginning Here." For more on lesbian poetry, see Bennett, "Lesbian Poetry."

17. Bennett, "Lesbian Poetry," 105; Steve Abbott, "West," quoted in Abbott and Kikel, "In Search of a Muse," 280.

18. "For My Gay Brothers and Sisters/An Art Exhibit," *CHF Newsletter*, October 16, 1969, Box 1, Folder 3, Thorpe [Thorp] Papers, GLBTHS. On the Committee for Homosexual Freedom, see Sides, *Erotic City*, 90–97; Whittington, *Beyond Normal*.

19. Stein, "Teaching and Researching," 11; "Keynote Speech for the National Stu-

dents Gay Liberation Front Conference," San Francisco, August 21, 1970, Box 1, Folder 52, Thorpe [Thorp] Papers, GLBTHS. The Edgar Allen Poe reference might be to his 1846 short story "The Cask of Amontillado."

20. Harriette Frances, "Not Who I Am," *GG*, April 1974, CSULB GSU File.

21. Andrew Stancliffe, "I Have Too Many Secrets . . . ," *Gayzette*, April 14, 1975.

22. Shaundel Jacobs, "We . . . ," *VGSC*, December 13, 1973, 3, Box: Student Organizations—Gay Lib—History Student Union, Folder: Gay Lib—"The Voice," SFSUSCA.

23. J.D., "I'm Lonely and Empty Here . . . ," *Gayzette*, April 14, 1975. See also A.S. [Andrew Stancliffe], "Speak in Riddles . . . ," *Gayzette*, December 4, 1974; A.S. [Andrew Stancliffe], "Because I'm Still All Alone . . . ," *Gayzette*, April 14, 1975; Steve Johnson, "It Is Time . . . ," *GPU Newsletter*, [ca. early February 1974], SUPEC; Kelly Lee, "Thoughts while Waiting for a Lover," *GPU News*, [ca. July 1977], GLBTHS Periodicals; "There in a Rented Room He Sits . . . ," *GAPOO*, July 24, 1974, SUPEC; A.S. [Andrew Stancliffe], "The Rain's Still Falling," *Gayzette*, December 4, 1974; J.D. [Jonas Dunaway], "Lament," *Gayzette*, April 14, 1975; Superstar, "Bitter," *Gayzette*, May 1, 1975.

24. For example, see PB/GB, "You & Me," *Gayzette*, [ca. April 1976].

25. See J.M.C., "There Is This Old Man of Perhaps 40 Years . . . ," *GPU News*, January 14, 1976, GLBTHS Periodicals; Bill Mitchell, "Further OUT," *GAPOO*, May 15 [likely June 20], 1974, SUPEC; Steve, "I Sit Here Alone on a Beach . . . ," *GAPOO*, May 15 [likely June 20], 1974, SUPEC; M.Z. "Out-Come," *GPU News*, December 17, 1975, GLBTHS Periodicals.

26. "Dear Mom and Dad," *GPU Newsletter*, May 15, 1974 [likely June 1974], SUPEC. See also "It Feels So Good to Release the Truth . . . ," *GPU Newsletter*, May 15, 1974, SUPEC; "Dear Mom & Dad," *GPU Newsletter*, [ca. March 1974], SUPEC; "A Letter to My Family," *Gayzette*, June 10, 1976. The National Gay Student Center's newsletter suggested that readers "might find [such] letters interesting and maybe helpful" in their own situations ("Letters Home," *Interchange*, May–June 1972, 4, copy in author's possession).

27. AS, "Nightfall," *Gayzette*, December 4, 1974; "The Colors Seem to Fly Away Sometime," *Gayzette*, December 4, 1974; W.M., "Closet Fever," *GPU News*, February 1978, GLBTHS Periodicals; "Sisters. Beautiful Sisters . . . ," *GPU Newsletter*, [ca. early April 1974], SUPEC; Apollo, "All That Matters . . . ," *Gayzette*, April 8, 1976.

28. *GPU Newsletter*, April 24–May 1, 1974, GLBTHS Periodicals; Ernie Rael, "As Peter Denied Christ . . . ," *GAPOO*, August 21, 1974, SUPEC.

29. Maureen Kennedy, "Knapsack Slung over My Shoulder . . . ," *LV*, October 1, 1974, ONE Periodicals. See also "Falling from a Lover . . . ," *LV*, October 1, 1974, ONE Periodicals; "Oh Soft Lady," *LV*, [ca. February 1975], Box 1, Folder: Gay People's Union at Stanford Misc. Documents, Corbin Papers, GLBTHS; Kelly Lee, "Thoughts while Waiting for a Lover," *GPU News*, [ca. July 1977], GLBTHS Periodicals.

30. Mellora Termer, "Climax," *LV*, [ca. 1975], GLBTHS Periodicals. For other poems featuring vivid sexual imagery, see Joe Whitney, "Stud" and "Gaypoem," *Gayzette*, April 24, 1975; "Would Like to Touch You Softly . . . ," *LV*, October 15, 1974, ONE Periodicals.

31. Paul Boneberg, "Diamond Hard Words," *Lambda News*, September 1977, 11, GLBTHS Periodicals.

32. Vincent Fanucchi, "Pardon Me, Beautiful, Where Did You Buy Your Tits?," *Lambda News*, September 1977, 10, GLBTHS Periodicals. Fanucchi was one of the winners in a 1978 literary contest at San José State and a member of the GSU. See "Phelan Contest Awards IOUs to Contest Winners," *SpD*, May 3, 1978; "Of Cabbages and Kings," *SpD*, October 17, 1977.

33. Geoffrey Chancre, "Ye Yearre in Reviewe," *Gayzette*, December 4, 1974. Chancre was identified as "a notorious scandalmonger and local journalist and editor who also works for the Department of Psychiatry."

34. Rebecca Lynn Williamson, "The Inward Monitor," *The Bridge*, September 10, 1970, GLBTHS Periodicals.

35. Dave Johnson, "Perversion," *Gayzette*, December 4, 1974. See also Joe Whitney, "America, I Want You to Know ...," *Gayzette*, April 24, 1975.

36. Joe Whitney, "Let Us Be Faggots," *Gayzette*, June 10, 1976.

37. As the editors of the 1975 *Amazon Poetry* collection noted, poetry by lesbians was as diverse as lesbians themselves, featuring themes such as "growing up, sisterhood, sexuality, family, motherhood, work, dying, myth, racism, old age, war, ritual." Noting that "woman identified women" suffered "special oppression," the editors anticipated an intersectional analysis, arguing that lesbian lives are "further circumscribed when we do not meet other standards of contemporary American society—when we are not white or middle class or young." The collection conveyed "both private joy and pain and humor, and a larger context of racial, economic, and social inequality" (Larkin and Bulkin, prefatory note).

38. Wendy Cadden, "To Wendy from Belle," *GPU Newsletter*, [ca. early March 1974], SUPEC; "Sisters. Beautiful Sisters ...," *GPU Newsletter*, [ca. early April 1974], SUPEC ("Straight Sisters, Gay Sisters / Spring is here / Black sisters, Third World Sisters / Spring is here"); "Have Forgotten to Write Nonsensical ... ," *LV*, September 17, 1974, ONE Periodicals(navigating drunken gay men and a lesbian bar on Polk Street in San Francisco); "If You're a General, I'm A.W.O.L.," *LV*, October 15, 1974, ONE Periodicals ("You strut like a General, flashing your eye lines / Like medals for past achievements ... But not in this battle / I'm prone to desert / As *yours* is no honor").

39. Lucy Robinson, "Three Revolutionary Years," 468. See also "Manifesto for Gay Liberation Theatre" and "Pre-Revolutionary Gay Liberation Theater in Berkeley ...," *San Francisco Free Press*, October 16–31, 1969; "A Disorientation Program," *DC*, September 30, 1969; Don Jackson, "Gay Militants Demonstrate for Rights at UC, Berkeley," *Advocate*, December 1969, 1, 3; "Gay Lib Goes to College," *Gay Lib News*, May 31, 1970, Subject File: Gay Liberation Front, Los Angeles Misc., ONE Archives; Ken Camp to Gay Community Services Center, March 21, 1973, CSULB GSU File.

40. "'Lavender Troubadour' Delivers Message of Gay Oppression," *Phoenix*, October 17, 1974; Virgin Beach program, [1975], Box 12, Folder 8, De Cecco Papers, GLBTHS.

41. "A Trilogy on the Meaning of Being Gay," *49er*, October 24, 1975. At the 1976 Gay Awareness Week, events included another play, *Zounds* (Gay Awareness Week '76 program, Daly Papers, Box 11, Daly Papers, GLBTHS).

42. Duplechan, interview by author. Duplechan also wrote another play about a gay man and his straight woman friend.

43. Rosen, *To Live and Die in Berkeley*, copy in University of California, Santa Barbara, Special Research Collections.

44. Konstantin Berlandt, "Restaurant Dialogue between Konstantin Berlandt, Friend, Charles P. Thorp," [ca. 1970], Box: Student Organizations—Gay Lib—History Student Union, Folder: Gay Lib—Manuscript, SFSUSCA.

45. Gordon, interview by author; Person, interview by author; Madame Szwambi, "'The Gang That Wouldn't Shoot *Straight*': Le Theatre Lesbien, Sacramento's Only Lesbian Theater Group" (draft), [1979], Box 2, Folder 6, Gordon Papers.

46. Gordon, interview by author; Person, interview by author. The press release for the conference referred to Le Theatre Lesbien as "Sacramento's GAY WOMEN'S THEATER GROUP" (press release), [ca. January 1973], Subject File: Lesbian Legacy, ONE Archives). Jeanne Córdova, a prime organizer of the UCLA conference, described the event as "a moment of divination and a specific kind of hell" because it sparked numerous conflicts between "warring ideological groups of women." In particular, some lesbian par-

ticipants objected to the involvement of Beth Elliott, a transsexual performer, on the grounds that she was not a woman. See Córdova, *When We Were Outlaws*, 6–7; Michael Colby, "A Brief History of Le Theatre Lesbien," n.d., Gordon Papers.

47. Person, interview by author.

48. Cherie Gordon and Patricia One Person, *Robin Screw: A Modern Satire in Farcical Style*" (draft), 1973, Box 1, Folder 9, Gordon Papers. Le Theatre Lesbien first performed *Robin Screw* at the Off Key ("Le Theatre Lesbien," *Feminist News*, March 29, 1973, Box 41, Folder 10, Wagner Papers).

49. On the Shameless Hussies and lesbian feminist musicians, see Hawthorne, "Australia," 83. Another influence on Le Theatre Lesbien was an Australian television comedy, *Aunty Jack*, on which the title character, played by Grahame Bond, "glowered from her gigantic motorbike wearing the velvet-and-lace dress of a pantomime dame, unmatching football boots, one boxing glove, a wig and a moustache" (Inglis, *This Is the ABC*, 295). Additional influences included the San Francisco Mime Troupe, Monty Python, and Shakespeare (Gordon, interview by author).

50. *Dykes on Parade* program, [1976], Box 1, Folder 21, Gordon Papers. The back of the program described Le Theatre Lesbien as "a non-profit theatre troupe which is dedicated to performing plays which relate to feminist-lesbian issues." The Gordon Papers include a *Dykes on Parade* t-shirt.

51. *Dykes on Parade* poster, [October 30–31, 1976], Box 1, Folder 20, Gordon Papers; "'Dykes on Parade' Show Rates Standing Ovation," *Express*, November 4, 1976, clipping in Box 1, Folder 22, Gordon Papers.

52. *Dykes on Parade* costume list, [1976], Box 1, Folder 14, Gordon Papers; Madame Szwambi, "The Gang That Wouldn't Shoot *Straight*": Le Theatre Lesbien, Sacramento's Only Lesbian Theater Group" (draft) [1979], Box 2, Folder 6, Gordon Papers; *Dykes on Parade* program, [1976], Box 1, Folder 21, Gordon Papers.

53. Quinn, "Working through Culture," 122.

54. "Trustee, Gay Students Exchange Criticism," *Express*, December 2, 1976, "Gays Seek Censure," *Express*, December 2, 1976, clippings in Box 1, Folder 22, Gordon Papers.

55. "Gay Awareness," *SH*, April 11, 1978; Gay Awareness Week, *SH*, April 14, 1978; *Homophobia: A Short and Sassy Comedy* poster, [1978], Flat File Box 2, Gordon Papers; Madame Szwambi, "The Gang That Wouldn't Shoot *Straight*": Le Theatre Lesbien, Sacramento's Only Lesbian Theater Group" (draft) [1979], Box 2, Folder 6, Gordon Papers). According to Michael Colby, the play was a rewritten version of the third act of *From Lesbos to Homophobia* ("A Brief History of Le Theatre Lesbien," n.d., Gordon Papers).

56. "Lesbian Farce to Premiere Here Tomorrow Night," *Express*, April 6, 1978; "Play and Dance Top Off Gay Awareness Week," *Express*, April 13, 1978; Gay Awareness Week schedule, April 10–15, 1978, Box 3, Folder 39, Gordon Papers. According to Gordon, Sacramento City College denied Le Theatre Lesbien's request to use college facilities for the play. In a letter to the student newspaper, she argued that as "an evening student, a former graduate of Sacramento City College," and a community member, taxpayer, and performer, she was entitled to use the facilities and the equipment. She also complained that "once again, Le Theatre Lesbien has been the victim of bigotry and incompetence on the Sacramento City College campus" (April 30, 1978, Box 4, Folder 34, Gordon Papers). On May 18, 1978, the *Express*'s editorial page noted that "because of unanswered questions," Gordon's "letter about the production difficulties experienced by Le Theatre Lesbien is not being run this issue." It did not appear in any subsequent issue. Both Gordon and Person later asserted that Sacramento City College was less friendly to Le Theatre Lesbien's productions than was Sacramento State (Gordon, interview by author; Person, interview by author).

57. Quinn, interview by author.
58. *Cowdykes at the Lavender Corral* flyer, [1979], Box 2, Folder 3, Gordon Papers; *Cowdykes at the Lavender Corral* program, [1979], Box 2, Folder 5, Gordon Papers.
59. Gordon, interview by author.
60. Person, interview by author.
61. Cole, *"Don We Now Our Gay Apparel."* Historian J. Todd Ormsbee distinguishes genderfuck from drag, describing the former as a "self-conscious play and mixing of gendered cultural signs" and "creative act where an individual's masculinity and femininity were mutually emphasized" (*Meaning of Gay*, 224–25).
62. Ormsbee, *Meaning of Gay*, 225.
63. Hillman, "Most Profoundly Revolutionary Act," 173.
64. "Gay Follies" (advertisement), *DN*, May 4, 1973; "Small Segment" (letter to the editor), *DN*, May 9, 1973; Richard Robbins, "Proud to Be Gay" (letter to the editor), *DN*, May 14, 1973.
65. "Drag and Gender Fuck" (flyer), [ca. 1973], Box 1, Folder 26, Thorpe [Thorp] Papers, GLBTHS; Keith St. Clare, interview by Joey Plaster, September 12, 2009, transcript in author's possession; *GPU News* [Stanford], September 3, 1975, GLBTHS Periodicals.
66. Shepard, "Play as World-Making," 181.
67. James T. Harris, "Memories of the Loved and the Lost," *VGSC*, May 16, 1974, 3, ONE Periodicals.
68. Susan Sward, "New Movement at UCLA: Gay Liberation Movement Surfaces Here," *DB*, May 4, 1970.
69. Robert Croonquist, interview by Ina Tiangco, May 2012, Stanford University LGBT Alumni Oral History Interviews, SULDSC; "Gay Pride Week at Stanford," 1974, Series I, Box 2, Folder: Gay People's Union 6/74 Conference and Gay Pride Week, Stanford QSR Records.
70. Duplechan, interview by author.
71. David Cawley, "Drag: Through the Looking Glass," *VGSC*, April 18, 1975, 18, ONE Periodicals. See also David Cawley, "Coming Out in the Dorms," *VGSC*, May 16, 1974, 10, ONE Periodicals.
72. Mark Thompson, "In Drag," *VGSC*, April 18, 1975, ONE Periodicals. On Mathews's life and activism, see Hobson, *Lavender and Red*.
73. "Gay Students Hold Decorous UC Dance," *San Francisco Examiner*, May 23, 1970.
74. GSU Renaissance Costume Ball flyer, November 3, 1972, EC; "Masquerade Dance Caps Gay Awareness Week," *49er*, November 5, 1976; GAYTHINK IV flyer, October 27–29, 1978, GAYTHINK IV news release, August 1978, both in CSULA GSU File. A student criticized the photos that accompanied the CSU Long Beach newspaper's story about the Masquerade Dance, asking why "the drag queens were given all the coverage" and whether the paper was "trying to show an accurate portrayal of gay people at the dance or editorialize its stereotyped idea of gays in order for the rest of the campus to have a few laughs" (*49er*, November 10, 1975). According to Mark Thompson, students also appeared in genderfuck at dances sponsored by the GSCSF (Thompson, interview by author). Randy Alfred, a graduate student at UC Berkeley, attended one GSU Halloween party dressed in an elf costume (Alfred, interview by Roland Schembari, San Francisco, June 13, 1998, Oral History Collection, GLBTHS; Alfred, interview by author).
75. Duplechan, interview by author; "Gay '70's Dance" (flyer), Subject File: University of California, Los Angeles (UCLA)—Gay Students Union, ONE Archives.
76. Hughes-Oldenburg, interview by author.
77. "Gay Dance Turns Sour; New Actions Planned," *Phoenix*, November 11, 1971. One lesbian took complained that at Berkeley's June 1974 Gay Pride Day, "the men are run-

ning everything" (Cecilia Fernandez-Olivia, "Gay Pride Day Festivities Attract Large Crowd of People—Mostly Men," *DC*, June 24, 1974).

78. "Gay Student Coalition Public Forums," *Gay Crusader*, October 1974, GLBTHS Periodicals.

79. Hillman, "Clothes I Wear"; Clawson, "Rest Is All Drag."

80. Aura, interview by author.

81. Quinn, interview by author. Lesbians' challenges to gender presentation sometimes drew critical comments from outsiders. A story about a 1971 lesbian event at Sacramento State College described a few attendees as "dressed in pants of some sort"; one wore a "uniform that looked like it might have come out of General Custer's closet" (Dick Farrell, "Gay Women: Men Inhibit Rap Session," *Sacramento Union*, April 21, 1971, clipping in Box 56, Folder 4, Kepner Papers, ONE Archives).

82. Mentley, interview by author; Gaines, "Cockettes." Mentley also credits his embrace of drag and costume to working in rock music, Sylvester (then known as Ruby Blue) with whom Mentley worked in a Los Angeles performance group, and his studies with a Kabuki master.

83. The person selected for Queen of the "Big Game" would spend the year working on behalf of Associated Students. Big Game week was sponsored by the all-male Californians and the all-women Oskie Dolls. See Suzy Hagstrom, "Queen of the Day to Be Gay?," *DC*, November 5, 1973.

84. Fertig, interview by author.

85. "Dear Dora" remained important to Smith throughout her life: she read it during my interview with her as well as at the Metropolitan Community Church in Rehoboth, Delaware, in 2015 (Smith, "Dear Dora, Dangerous Derek Diesel Dyke"). For more on Smith's career in the Metropolitan Community Church, see Freda Smith, interview by Melissa Wilcox, February 27, 2007, https://lgbtqreligiousarchives.org/oral-histories/elder-freda-smith.

86. "Poets Bring Out Emotions of the Audience," *SH*, May 4, 1973.

87. In *Not in This Family*, Heather Murray contends that "disclosures" were common in 1970s lesbian periodicals, which often published lesbians' short stories and poetry. Such disclosures reflect the "ethos of revelation" that became widespread in gay politics of the time.

Chapter 6. Fostering Cross-Campus Alliances

1. Larry Bernard to "Sisters and Brothers of the Gay Students Council of Southern California," September 30, 1972, GSC File.

2. LGBT faculty also began organizing across campuses regionally and nationally, especially through the Gay Academic Union. At its founding conference, one panel, "Relationship of GAU and Gay Student Organizations," recognized the interconnections of such organizing ("The Universities and the Gay Experience" [conference program], 1974, 31, copy in author's possession). See also D'Emilio, *Making Trouble*, 117–27.

3. While some LGBT described these collaborations as *coalitions*, I prefer *alliances*, drawing on the work of Nella Van Dyke and Holly J. McCammon, who distinguish "organizational alliances" from coalitions of different kinds of organizations focusing on issues in common (*Strategic Alliances*, xiv–xv). On the challenges of coalition work, see Reagon, "Coalition Politics," 359. On the fragility of coalitions in gay and lesbian organizing generally, see Buring, "Gay Activism behind the Magnolia Curtain."

4. Other attempts at forming alliances of LGBT campus-based student organizations in California included Gay Law Students (1972–77), which loosely linked students

from law schools in both Northern and Southern California; a Sacramento-area Inter-Campus Council; the University of California Gay Coalition in the late 1970s; and a statewide alliance in the early 1980s. See "Gay Student Groups Unite," *Mom... Guess What?* December 1979, 5, GLBTHS Periodicals; David Chervin, "Gays and the New Right," *California Aggie*, November 11, 1977; "Consolidating Our Power in the 1980's" (conference program), January 8–10, 1982, EC.

5. See Wesley C. Hogan, *Many Minds, One Heart*; Holsaert et al., *Hands on the Freedom Plow*; Biondi, *Black Revolution on Campus*; Rogers [Kendi], *Black Campus Movement*; Slonecker, "Columbia Coalition"; Evans, *Tidal Wave*; Sue Katz, "Women's Liberation Explosion"; Trine, "Politics of Pleasure"; Baxandall, "Re-Visioning the Women's Liberation Movement's Narrative"; Muñoz and Barrera, "La Raza Unida Party"; Van Dyke, "Crossing Movement Boundaries"; Blackwell, *Chicana Power*; Umemoto, "On Strike!"

6. "Homophile Front News," *Vector*, November 1969, 4; "Homophile Front News," *Vector*, March 1970, 21, 24; Eisenbach, *Gay Power*, 75; Martin [Donaldson], "Student Homophile League," 259. The June–July 1970 issue of *The Ladder* reported that the Student Homophile League had about thirty campus groups involved ("Cross Currents," *The Ladder*, June–July 1970, 37–38). The East Coast Homophile Organization and the North American Conference of Homophile Organizations worked on various regional and national issues, among them bar closings, immigration, gay military personnel, and employment. See D'Emilio, *Sexual Politics, Sexual Communities*.

7. Sprung, *Rutgers Conference on Gay Liberation*; Nichols and Kafka-Hozschlag, "Rutgers University Lesbian/Gay Alliance," 61. The Rutgers Homophile League hosted several of these conferences in the 1970s. See "Conferences," *Interchange*, Fall 1975, 5, Subject File: National Gay Student Center, ONE Archives.

8. "Southeastern Regional Conference," *Interchange*, January–February 1973, 22, copy in author's possession. On faculty and student involvement as well as lesbian concerns about gay men dominating the organizing, see James T. Sears, *Rebels, Rubyfruit, and Rhinestones*. For attempts by the Ann Arbor Gay and Lesbian Front (also known as the GLF, an organization recognized by the University of Michigan student government) to organize a Midwest Gay Liberation Conference in the 1970s, see Dilley, *Gay Liberation to Campus Assimilation*, 30–41.

9. Committee for Homosexual Freedom, "69 Gay Liberation 70," Box 1, Folder 12, Thorpe [Thorp] Papers, GLBTHS; Bois Burk, "Nitty Gritty of the Gay Front," December 1, 1969, Box 1, Folder 15, Burk Papers, GLBTHS; "Gay Lib Conference and Symposium," *San Francisco Free Press*, January 1970.

10. Such one-time meetings nevertheless allowed young organizers to insert their concerns into gay liberation spaces. Gay Youth, organized in Los Angeles around 1972 primarily by high school students, presented a list of demands at a regional gay liberation conference held in 1972. See "Notes on the Southwestern Gay Conference at San Diego," May 13, 1972, Under 21 Caucus to "All Delegates Attending Gay Political Caucus," [ca. May 1972], Bakersfield Southwestern Regional Conference/NCGO amended agenda, July 1972, all in Box 15, Folder 46, L.A. Gay and Lesbian Center Records, ONE Archives; "Gay Youth Workshop" notes, July 1972, Box 15, Folder 50, L.A. Gay and Lesbian Center Records, ONE Archives. For similar age-based efforts in New York, see Stephan Cohen, *Gay Liberation Youth Movement*.

11. Gay Caucus to Congress Steering Committee and Congress Delegates, [ca. August 1971], copy in author's possession.

12. Blumenfeld, interview by author; Blumenfeld, *National Gay Student Center*; "National Student Congress Slates First Gay Caucus," *Advocate*, August 18–31, 1971.

13. "How We Got Started," *Interchange*, March–April 1972, 3–4. GLBTHS Periodicals; Hatfield moved on to work with feminist organizing and was replaced by Sue Lashley ("National Gay Student Center," *Interchange*, May–June 1972, 3, copy in author's possession).

14. *Interchange*, March–April 1972, 3 GLBTHS Periodicals. Informational articles included Warren Blumenfeld, "School Is Not a Very Gay Place to Be," *Interchange*, March–April 1972, 5–7, GLBTHS Periodicals; Anne Hatfield, "Lesbianism: On Being Invisible," *Interchange*, March–April 1972, 9–10 GLBTHS Periodicals; Walt Senterfitt, "The Trials of a Gay Teacher," *Interchange*, January–February 1973, 4–8 copy in author's possession; Warren Blumenfeld, "Are You Recognized?," *Interchange*, January–February 1973, 14–18, copy in author's possession; "Gay Studies," *Interchange*, January–February 1973, 25 copy in author's possession; "Gay Students Win Court Case," *Interchange*, March–April 1974, 2 National Gay Student Center Subject File, ONE Archives; J. Lee Lehman, "Gay Bookstores: An Important Resource for the Gay Student Movement," *Interchange*, Fall 1974, 1. National Gay Student Center Subject File, ONE Archives.

15. "Gay Student Confab Called," *Advocate*, August 19, 1970; "National Gay Groups Here in August," *Vector*, July 1970.

16. "Thorp Plans Gay August," *Phoenix*, July 30, 1970, 4; "Gay Lib," *Vector*, August 1970, 41. Students from San José State's GLF advertised the event in the group's newsletter, urging readers to "have a San Jose turn out" (August 6, 1970, GLBTHS Periodicals).

17. "Gay Students," *Gay Sunshine*, August–September 1970, GLBTHS Periodicals. Thorp's timing was auspicious. Shortly after this conference, a radical caucus challenged attendees at the North American Conference of Homophile Organizations gathering in San Francisco, Thorp among them, to support women's liberation, the Black Panther Party, and a "national gay strike." See Donovan Bass, "Homosexuals Call for Militancy," *San Francisco Chronicle*, August 22, 1970; Dennis Altman, "A Young Australian Speaks His Mind about Gay Liberation," *Vector*, October 1970; "Don't Adjust Your Mind, There's a Fault in Reality," *Agape and Action*, August 25, 1970, GLBTHS Periodicals.

18. Dennis Altman, "A Young Australian Speaks His Mind about Gay Liberation," *Vector*, October 1970.

19. *Proud*, October 13, [probably 1972], CSULB GSU File. The GSC originated as a May 1972 event organized by the GSU at UC Irvine to bring together LGBT student organizations in Southern California; the meeting led to the GSC Campus Rap (*Advocate*, June 7, 1972). Faculty members Jay Hayes (Cal State Fullerton) and Tracy Terrell (UC Irvine) invited their peers in hopes of offering students support (UC Irvine GSU, conference invitation, May 8, 1972, Box 1, Folder 5, Hayes Papers, ONE Archives). Hayes and Terrell followed up with a meeting of teachers at the Claremont Colleges in the fall of 1972 (Jay Hayes, letter to unnamed colleagues, October 30, 1972, Box 1, Folder 5, Hayes Papers, ONE Archives).

20. "The Gay Students Coalition of Southern California," *Interchange*, January–February 1973, 23, copy in author's possession. A 1973 list of gay organizations maintained by the Gay Activists Alliance in New York noted that the GSC included seventeen campus groups. It is the only alliance of separate LGBT student organizations listed, though several "student homophile league" campus groups appear. See Committee Files, National Gay Movement—Lists of Gay Organizations, December 5, 1971–January 1, 1974, Series 1: Committee Files, Box 17, Folder 7, Gay Activists Alliance Records, New York Public Library, Manuscripts and Archives Division.

21. Flyer, May 1972, GSC File. The original members included University of California campuses at Irvine, Los Angeles, Santa Barbara, and Riverside; California State College campuses at Los Angeles, Long Beach, and Fullerton; the California Institute of

the Arts; the California Institute of Technology; the Claremont Colleges; El Camino College; Immaculate Heart College; Occidental College; and the University of Southern California. A few faculty members were active in the coalition. Hayes, who later became active in the Southern California Gay Academic Union, served as the GSC's secretary, maintaining the minutes and mailing bulletins to members. See "Introducing... Gay Students Council of Southern California," [ca. 1972], GSC File.

22. Initially known as the Gay Students Association of Northern California, the group included Chico State and Sacramento State. Nutting saw the organization as offering opportunities for "networking of college student activists" (Nutting, interview by author).

23. Schiller GSCSF Account, 3; "Northern California Students Meet, Form New Council," *Advocate*, June 6, 1973, 22; "Free Gay Students Association, City College of San Francisco" flyer and constitution, [ca. Spring 1972], Box 1, Box 40, Burk Papers, GLBTHS; James Graham, "Gay Groups Organize in SF," *California Aggie*, May 15, 1973.

24. "The Gay Students Coalition," *BAR*, March 6, 1974, 9, GLBTHS Periodicals; "Gay Student Coalition Public Forums," *Gay Crusader*, October 1974, 12; Thompson, interview by author; "Bulletin Board," *Interchange*, Summer 1974, 4, Subject File: National Gay Student Center, ONE Archives (noting formation of the GSCSF by students from San Francisco State, the UCSF Medical Center, City College of San Francisco, Lone Mountain College, the University of San Francisco, and the Hastings College of Law). Associated Students at City College of San Francisco provided some support for the organization in the spring of 1974. See "Spring 1974 Associated Students Budget," *Guardsman*, March 21, 1974, 4; "Coalition Gives Gays a Chance for Sharing," *Guardsman*, June 6, 1974, 1. Some issues of the *Guardsman* (City College of San Francisco) are available at https://archive.org/details/citycollegeofsanfrancisco?tab=collection&page=2&sort=date.

25. "Convocation of So.Cal. GSUs Planned," *Gayzette*, March 5, 1975; gay student organizations meeting program, [1975], Subject File: University of California, Los Angeles (UCLA), ONE Archives; "Intercampus Gay Students Organization Forms," *Gayzette*, April 24, 1975).

26. "Summer Wrapup," *Gayzette*, October 2, 1975; *GPU News*, August 13, 1975, GLBTHS Periodicals; CONFABULATION working agenda, [December 1975], CAGSO File; "What Is PATCHWORK and WHY?," *Patchwork*, January 1976, CAGSO File; GAYTHINK, West Coast Conference program, October 24–26, 1975, Box 246, Kight Papers, University of California, Los Angeles, Special Collections. UCLA's Glenn Erickson may have suggested the shift in focus from Southern California to the entire state. The November 6, 1975, edition of the UCLA GSU newsletter included a list of twenty-six participating GSU organizations, and quoted Erickson as saying, "It seems apparent from this list that we should scrap 'Southern' from our title and rename ourselves something like the 'California Association of Gay Students Organizations' or CAGSO" ("Gay Student Organizations at Other Schools," *Gayzette*, November 6, 1975; Sal Licata, Confabulation invitation letter, [December 1975], CAGSO File).

27. In "The Lavender Leader," Ronni Sanlo argues that while students can sometimes draw on their "communities of origin" for models of leadership styles and approaches, most LGBT students lack the same life experiences within LGBT communities on which to draw; consequently, LGBT student organizations provide important opportunities for developing leadership skills.

28. GSC meeting announcement, [ca. September 9, 1972], GSC File. Meeting needs of "newly gay students" was also a priority for the GSC (GSC meeting notes, May 7, 1972, GSC File.

29. "Gay Students Host Conference," *LT*, April 1973.

30. "Calendar for Southern California GSUs Conference," *Gayzette*, April 14, 1975.

31. Some campus-based LGBT student organizations shared news regarding other campuses. See, for examples, *Octopus*, [ca. mid-1970s], Subject File: Gay Students Union—San Diego State University, ONE Archives; *Gayzette*, October 9, 1975 (encouraging UCLA students to support conference organized by CSU Long Beach GSU).

32. "What Is *PATCHWORK* and WHY?," *Patchwork*, January 1976, CAGSO File. For examples of event announcements, see *Patchwork*, January 22 (Claremont Colleges GSU welcomes Cal Poly Pomona students), February 15 ("non-sexist" dance at San Diego State), April 1, 1976 (Cal State Fullerton GSU meeting about "being Black or Chicano and gay"), CAGSO File.

33. "Campus Happenings," *GSC Newsmagazine*, [December 1972], GSC File (California State Los Angeles GSU open house where eighty-five attendees enjoyed music by El Camino Community College student Maxine Feldman and a screening of the film *Some of Your Best Friends*); "Gay Grams," *VGSC*, May 16, 1974, ONE Periodicals. See also "Solicitations," *Sometimes Regular Newsletter of the Gay Students Council of Southern California*, [ca. Summer 1972], GSC File.

34. *Patchwork*, February 15, 1976, CAGSO File.

35. "News," *GSC Newsmagazine*, April 1973, GSC File (court decision relating to teachers and convictions for sex offenses, Los Angeles mayoral race, local lesbian running for the Los Angeles City school board); "Speak Up: Revolutionary Overdose," *GSC Newsmagazine* [ca. December 1972], GSC File (reprint of political news from the *Lesbian Tide*); *Patchwork*, February 15, 1976, CAGSO File (ACLU gay rights panel held at USC).

36. Hal Offen, "Gay Liberation Growing with BAGL," *VGSC*, April 18, 1975, 10, ONE Periodicals; Harvey Milk, "Gay Groupie Syndrome and the Political Bandwagon," *VGSC*, May 16, 1974, 13, ONE Periodicals; Thompson, interview by author.

37. *Patchwork*, February 15, 1976, CAGSO File.

38. GSC meeting notes, May 21, 1972, GSC File.

39. *Sometimes Regular Newsletter of the Gay Students Council of Southern California*, [Summer 1972], GSC File. The newsletter noted that Cal Tech had "adopted" Pasadena City College and Claremont had teamed up with Cal Poly.

40. Council of Representatives minutes, January 14, 1973, GSC File. It is not clear whether the packet was ever created.

41. Larry Bernard to "Sisters and Brothers of the Gay Students Council of Southern California," September 30, 1972, GSC File; "GSU Denied Recognition," *GSC Newsletter*, [likely December 1972]; Council of Representatives minutes, January 14, 1973, GSC File; "Cal State University Fullerton," *Patchwork*, [1976], ONE Periodicals.

42. "Dr. Lindauer to Teach Peer Counseling," January 30, 1973, GSC File. In October 1972, the GSC newsletter reported that Newt Dieter, a clinical psychologist, had offered to serve as an adviser/consultant to the GSC, leading workshops on counseling or providing other assistance (*Sometimes Regular Newsletter of the Gay Students Council of Southern California*, October 9, 1972, GSC File).

43. Schedule, June 29, 1974, Series I, Box 2, Folder: Gay People's Union 6/74 Conference and Gay Pride Week, Stanford QSR Records.

44. Flyer, [ca. 1974], Subject File: Gay Students Coalition (San Francisco, Calif.), ONE Archives.

45. Meeting notes, May 21, 1972, GSC File; *Sometimes Regular Newsletter of the Gay Students Council of Southern California*, [Summer 1972], GSC File.

46. Campus-based student organizations sometimes socialized with students from other campuses informally. The UCLA GSU newsletter, for example, was filled with such

examples. In 1975, a thanksgiving potluck drew GSU members from both UCLA and USC together, an evening described as "a wonderful expression of the comradeship that can ensure between gays who take the time to care about one another" ("The Turkey Feed at Joe's, It's Good to Have Gay Friends," *Gayzette*, December 4, 1975). See also "Magic Mountain Trip Details," *Gayzette*, May 1, 1975 (organized by students from CSU Northridge); *Gayzette*, May 8, 1975 (beach party with students from UC Irvine); "Interchange," *Gayzette*, May 22, 1975 (end of semester party with CSU Long Beach GSU).

47. GSC meeting announcement, [ca. September 9, 1972], GSC File. See also dance advertisement, *VGSC*, December 13, 1973, 4, GLBTHS Periodicals; CAGSO confabulation agenda, December 29–30, 1975, CAGSO File.

48. "Convocation '72," *Newsmagazine of the Gay Students Council of Southern California*, [ca. November 1972], GSC File. The event was even covered in the *Daily Claremont Collegian*, November 17, 1972, GSC File.

49. Thompson, interview by author.

50. Schiller GSCSF Account, 9.

51. Schiller GSCSF Account, 6. A 1973 GSC meeting sought to "strengthen the gay campus movement" by "offering workshops to improve gay campus organizations and develop expertise in programming and leadership" ("Spring Meet Set," *GSC Newsmagazine*, April 1973, GSC File).

52. GSC meeting notice, *DN*, March 2, 1973; Frank Fitch, "Remember California Hall," *Vector*, February 1973; "Gay Feminist for Board of Education," *LT*, February 1, 1973.

53. "CAGSO Political Caucus??," *Gayzette*, November 20, 1975. The group appears to have created a list of priorities, later reflected in a position paper (CAGSO list of priorities, [ca. 1976], Box 1, Folder 41, Burk Papers, GLBTHS).

54. "We Pee," [ca. 1975], CSULA GSU File; "CAGSO," *Gayzette*, June 10, 1976.

55. CAGSO statement, [ca. 1976], CAGSO File (reprinted in *Patchwork*, February 15, 1976, CAGSO File).

56. Sal Licata, "Sal's Ramblings," *Patchwork*, February 15, 1976, CAGSO File. Bradley subsequently appointed a new liaison to the LGBT community ("Mayor Bradley's New Liaison—Bill Carey, a Man with a Tough Job ahead of Him," *Advocate*, May 5, 1976).

57. Schiller GSCSF Account, 13; Harold Fairbanks, "The Fruiter Did It: Laughing Policeman No Laughing Matter," *Advocate*, December 19, 1973.

58. Thompson, interview by author; "1973 Christopher St. West San Francisco," May–June 1973, GSC File; Jeanne Córdova, "Christopher Street '72," *LT*, June 1972, 5; "Two Big Gay Pride Events," *Gayzette*, June 10, 1976, ONE Periodicals.

59. GSC bulletin, November 20, 1972, GSC File.

60. GSCSF flyer, Spring 1974, Box 140, Folder 11, De Cecco Papers, GLBTHS.

61. Gay Organizations Night invitation, September 25, 1974, Subject File: Gay Students Coalition (San Francisco, Calif.), ONE Archives; "Gay Organization Night," *San Francisco Bay Guardian*, April 13–26, 1974, 14, available at archive.org; "Nearly One Hundred Turn Out for Second Gay Organizations Night," *San Francisco Crusader*, October 1974, 4, GLBTHS Periodicals.

62. Schiller GSCSF Account, 12.

63. Flyer, [ca. 1974], Subject File: Gay Students Coalition (San Francisco, Calif.), ONE Archives; "Press Release, the Gay Students Coalition," *BAR*, March 6, 1974, 9.

64. "Gay Students Coalition—Spring Meetings 1974," *The Gay Students Coalition* (brochure), ca. Fall 1974, both in Subject File: Gay Students Coalition (San Francisco, Calif.), ONE Archives.

65. It is unclear whether the GSCSF lasted beyond 1975. The May 27, 1976, issue

of the *Bay Area Reporter* refers to the Gay Student Coalition of San Francisco City College, but that reference could be to a campus-based organization, not the alliance ("New Group Forms," *BAR*, May 27, 1976, 13). A 1976 article credits students from the GSCSF with completing questionnaires for a study (Bender et al., "Patterns of Self-Disclosure"). Stephen Ken Amerman suggests that coalitions of American Indian organizations working on educational issues in Phoenix were especially important in drawing young people into participation, even into leadership positions ("Let's Get In and Fight!," 630).

66. In 1973, the National Gay Student Center reoriented itself to work along regional lines because national organizing had isolated it from communities in the Washington, D.C., area where the organization was based. See "National Gay Student Center Report," *Interchange*, January–February 1973, 2, copy in author's possession.

67. *GSC Bulletin*, November 20, 1972, GSC File.

68. Schiller GSCSF Account, 14.

69. Thompson, interview by author.

70. As Nella Van Dyke and Ronda Cress suggest in their study of Ohio's gay and lesbian movement, in the 1970s gender was "the dominant organizing identity for women, as lesbian feminists identified with the women's movement and the label *lesbian* itself became the epitome of feminist resistance" (""Political Opportunities and Collective Identity," 520).

71. A 1975 survey by the National Gay Student Center found that while 74 percent of all gay student groups "mixed" men and women, there was a "considerable predominance of men" at several campuses, including Harvard-Radcliffe, Rutgers, New York University, and UC Davis. The GSCSF was noted as predominantly students from City College of San Francisco and San Francisco State. See "NGSC Gay Student Groups Survey," in Lehman, *Gays on Campus*, 23.

72. Carole Mathews, letter to the editor, *LT*, June 1974, 28–29

73. Schiller GSCSF Account, 8.

74. Council of Representatives minutes, August 20, 1972, GSC File. It is not clear whether the meeting actually took place.

75. Executive board minutes, October 20, 1972, endorsement policy and list of resolutions, [ca. 1972], both in GSC File.

76. "A Word about Our Third Chairperson," [late spring 1973], *GSC Bulletin*, May–June 1973, 1, both in GSC File. The GSCSF also frequently fielded questions about how many women would be at meetings (Schiller GSCSF Account, 8).

77. Ron Norman, editorial, *Patchwork*, February 15, 1976, CAGSO File.

78. Susan Sachs, "Gay Student Reps Attend Convention," *DB*, April 4, 1979.

79. Gay and Lesbian Student Coalition meeting notice, *BAR*, May 10, 1979, 19; Gay Awareness Week flyer, May 7–13, 1979, Series IV, Box 1, Folder: Gay Awareness Week 1979, Stanford QSR Records; Northern Caucus of the California Coalition of Gay and Lesbian Student Organizations delegate photo, [ca. May 1979], Series VIII, Box 3, Folder: GPU Scrapbook, Stanford QSR Records.

80. According to Blake Sloneker, evidence from Columbia University in 1968 suggests that a successful model of coalition building among diverse organizations, especially between white student radicals and black separatists, needed to emphasize "both unity and difference." The creation of student communes on campus—distinct movement spaces—"facilitated the temporary reconciliation of political and social differences" so that political debates could occur and students could "recognize the legitimacy of other views in the name of commune solidarity" (Slonecker, "Columbia Coalition," 969). LGBT student alliances had only temporary common spaces and thus

lacked the opportunity to forge such bonds. On gender, race, and class fractures within the Memphis Gay Coalition, see Buring, "Gay Activism behind the Magnolia Curtain."

81. Staggenborg, "Social Movement Communities."

82. J. Lee Lehman, "Lobbying," in "Changes in Gay Students Rights" (National Gay Student Center), [ca. 1977], 1, EC.

Chapter 7. Engaging Politics

1. Randy Shilts, "Gay Campus Movement: Trading Pickets for Proms," *Advocate*, September 8, 1976, 6. According to Shilts's article Sacramento State professor Martin Rogers attributed the drop in interest on that campus to the visibility and impact of early organizing, which had provoked a backlash of "outside pressure."

2. "The Campus Mood Is Mellow," *Advocate*, September 8, 1976, 23. Only half of the respondents to an *Advocate* survey of LGBT student organizations reported involvement in political activity, and most of their work focused on "social services and educational functions." About 60 percent of responding groups received student government funding ("Survey Results," *Advocate*, September 8, 1976, 6).

3. I recognize that the distinction between "on-campus" and "off-campus" organizing is somewhat artificial, particularly at nonresidential or commuter schools, a category that includes community colleges and most California State University campuses. However, I distinguish campus-specific areas of focus from those that were primarily off campus to highlight the interconnectedness of such venues.

4. Barbara Bryant, as an undergraduate student at UC Berkeley in the late 1960s, recalled gay liberation as an "immediate personal salvation," eventually finding her way to feminism by way of "women who were lesbian feminists." She enacted this shift in political framework as a graduate student at Sacramento State, where she became involved in the emerging Women's Studies Program alongside other lesbian students. Bryant, interview by author.

5. SGP meeting notes, November 1969, SPC; "Other News from the Revolutionary Front," Box 1, Folder 15, Burk Papers, GLBTHS.

6. "New Student Homosexual Group Stands for 'Gay Power' Instead of Fear," *DC*, November 18, 1969. One early SGP organizer claimed that the group was "working on the first step in Gay Liberation," which was "confronting the truth about our own homosexuality, and confronting our parents with that truth" ("Closet Queen? Der Blue Max Peeks through Ivy," *Berkeley Tribe*, November 27–December 5, 1969, available at https://www.jstor.org/stable/community.28033774).

7. "New Life for Gay Students," *Berkeley Barb*, September 29, 1972.

8. "Gays Expanding on Campus," *DC*, October 12, 1972.

9. "Gay People's Union of U.C. Berkeley" flyer, 1977, Folder: Berkeley U.C., EC.

10. Women's Collective raps, [ca. 1976], Series III, Box 1, Folder: Rap Topic Outlines, Stanford QSR Records.

11. Dave Johnson, "Affiliation: The Real Issue," *DB*, April 10, 1974; "Gay Group Fights for Affiliation," *DB*, April 3, 1974; "SLC-GSU Affiliation Tabled," *DB*, April 5, 1974. UCLA chancellor Charles Young held veto power over the decision to recognize the GSU and had expressed concerns about the group's political activity. See "SLC Affiliation Vote Open to Veto," *DB*, April 3, 1974; Kathy Bartolo, "Chancellor Defends UC Academic Plan," *DB*, April 17, 1974; "Affiliation with Gays Approved by SLC," *DB*, April 12, 1974; "Gay Rights and the Socialist Campaign," *DB*, May 22, 1974.

12. Charter, October 10, 1974, Subject File: University of California, Los Angeles (UCLA)—Gay Students Union, ONE Archives.

13. D. K. Hughes-Oldenburg, "Gays Gaining Power," *StD*, February 5, 1976.

14. "Johnson Speaks on Gays," *DB*, October 3, 1974.

15. "GSU Chairman Attacks Therapy," *DB*, November 25, 1974.

16. Dave Johnson, "Homophobia Comes out of the Closet," *DB*, May 30, 1974; Dave Johnson, "The Gay Experience at UCLA," *DB*, March 6, 1974; Dave Johnson, "Affiliation: The Real Issue," *DB*, April 10, 1974. The *Advocate* described Johnson as not afraid to take action, which included issues such as challenging sexism and resisting police brutality ("Activist Dave Johnson: He Knocks the 'Stars' and Looks Beyond," *Advocate*, July 31, 1974, 14).

17. Duplechan, interview by author. Johnson told Duplechan that "not every cocksucker is my gay brother" even though there was a "political component to being gay." Johnson also lent Duplechan books on gay liberation. Another UCLA student, Bob Walsh, also respected Johnson's leadership of the GSU because of "its upfrontness, its unabashed enthusiasm for the bold and unconventional," which drew Walsh into "the orbit of gay activism" (Donald Warman, "Bob and John: Two for the Revolution," *NewsWest*, January 9–22, 1976, 12, ONE Periodicals).

18. "Gay Libbers Accuse Daily of Censorship," *SpD*, March 23, 1971; *The Bridge* (San José GLF), March 26, 1971, GLBTHS Periodicals; GLF, "Gay Is Good," *SpD*, March 24, 1971.

19. Letter to the editor, *DC*, January 20, 1970.

20. The issues that prompted the Women's Liberation protest included an all-male karate class, the lack of free child care, employment discrimination, the absence of courses on the history of women, "restriction[s] on women in dorms," and the lack of on-campus access to birth control. See "Women Invade Men's Locker Room," *DC*, January 8, 1970; "Liberated Women Stopped at Harmon," *DC*, January 9, 1970; "Women to Protest Again at Gym," *DC*, January 13, 1970; editorial, *DC*, January 12, 1970; "Women's Liberation Marches to Harmon," *DC*, January 14, 1970.

21. "Gay Pickets Rap Trappers," *Berkeley Barb*, January 23–29, 1970; SGP meeting notes, January 10, 14, 1970, Reel 27, SPC; "SGP Charges Illegal Means by Police," *DC*, January 16, 1970; "Gays Organize Politically," *DC*, January 16, 1970; "Homosexuals Plan Protest, Daily Picketing at UC Gym," *Berkeley Gazette*, January 23, 1970, Subject File: Berkeley Gay Liberation, ONE Archives; "Students for Gay Power March on Harmon," *DC*, January 22, 1970; "Berkeley Gays Get It Together," *Radical Homosexual Rag*, January 25 and February 1, 1970, Miscellaneous Gay Liberation Titles, Reel 1, GLBTHS; Harmon Gym protest flyer, January 22, 1970, Folder: Students for Gay Power, EC; "'Gay Power' Frustrated at the Gym Door," *Berkeley Gazette*, January 24, 1970, Subject File: Berkeley Gay Liberation, ONE Archives; "Gay Liberation—A Human Being Is a Human Being," unidentified clipping, Organizations—UC Berkeley, EC; SGP Meeting Minutes, January 28, 1970, Organizations—Students for Gay Power, EC. After the protest, Konstantin Berlandt wrote that Harmon Gym should be renamed St. Stephen's Baths after Stephen McClave, director of the Gay Liberation Theater: "The dark gray castle has become a palace of lights shining for us. This is our temple, our shelter in the forest, our free space / I met another animal who looked like me / He came with a gun / His eyes looked like mine / He had a helmet on" ("Gimme Shelter," *DC*, February 25, 1970).

22. "Students for Gay Power March on Harmon," *DC*, January 23, 1970; "Gay Pickets Rap Trappers," *Berkeley Barb*, January 23–29, 1970.

23. "Interview: Two Gays Rap about Themselves, Their Group," *DC*, February 27, 1970.

24. "Sex Role Program Exposed," *DB*, January 29, 1975; "Students Demand to Stop 'Gender Program,'" *Advocate*, March 12, 1975. One of the program coordinators, Peter M.

Bentler, sprang to its defense: "The gay libbers group is worried that we are stamping out homosexual behavior. Sexual behavior per se is essentially an irrelevant consideration." Instead, the program sought to help children develop "social skills" for better interaction with peers and family: "In spite of today's open society and in disagreement with what some people might think, the boys I know clinically were very unhappy being rejected or called names by others. To overlook such humiliation is a real disservice to the child" ("Sex Role Program Exposed," *DB*, January 29, 1975).

25. "GIP, CADOC Meets Amicably; Rally/Parade Today," *Gayzette*, February 5, 1975.

26. Rod Thorsen, "A Note from CADOC," *Gayzette*, February 5, 1975. Although GSU members participated in this coalition, the organization denied affiliation ("GSU Defends Relationship with CADOC," *Gayzette*, February 12, 1975).

27. "CDAC Presses GIP for Full Disclosure," *Gayzette*, January 29, 1975; "UCLA Demo against Psycho-Conditioning," [ca. January 1975], Box 3, Folder 9, Steele Papers, ONE Archives. UCLA student John Toy's participation in the protest got him in trouble with the Reserve Officer Training Corps, which had provided him with a scholarship. "They told me to stay out of politics," which he took to mean he needed to leave the GSU. Instead, he left the corps. See Donald Warman, "Bob and John: Two for the Revolution," *NewsWest*, January 9–22, 1976, 12, ONE Periodicals.

28. "Gays 'Come Out' on Campus Today," *DC*, October 26, 1976; "Blue Jeans, Gays Come out of Closet," *SpD*, December 1, 1976; "Gay Denim Day," *Chico Wildcat*, February 15, 1977; "National Gay Blue Jeans Day Bringing 'Ostracism' to Heterosexuals," *DB*, October 14, 1977; "Gay 'Blue Jeans' Day Returns," *SpD*, October 13, 1977; Blue Jeans Day notice, *SH*, October 14, 1977; "Blue Jeans Day" (letter to the editor), *Phoenix*, October 10, 1977 (San Francisco State); National Gay Blue Jeans Day advertisement, *MD*, April 13, 1978 (Cal Poly San Luis Obispo). In 1974, the Rutgers University Homophile League organized "National Gay Day," urging gay students to wear jeans for a "survey" of their number on campus (Don Kelsey, "Straights Get a Taste of Stereotypes," *Advocate*, May 22, 1974).

29. Philip McGowen, letter to the editor, *Chico Wildcat*, February 3, 1977.

30. "Gays 'Come Out' on Campus Today," *DC*, October 26, 1976.

31. "National Gay Blue Jeans Day 'a Success,'" *DB*, October 17, 1977. The following year, National Gay Blue Jeans Day, coordinated by the National Gay Task Force on April 14, drew participants from the University of Colorado at Boulder, the University of Hawai'i, Arizona State University, and the University of Florida. See "'Gay Blue Jean Day' Proclaimed for Today," *SpD*, April 14, 1978; letter to the editor, *StD*, May 15, 1978; Gay Awareness Week advertisement, *DC*, May 7, 1979; "National Gay Blue Jeans Day Is April 14," Box 36, Folder 71, National Gay and Lesbian Task Force Records, Cornell University Library, Division of Rare and Manuscript Collections; "National Gay Task Force Announces National Gay Blue Jeans Day," *Alternative* (New York), March 30, 1978; "Gay Blue Jeans Day" (press release), April 4, 1978, "Why Blue Jeans Day" (press release), April 7, 1978 (University of Colorado, Boulder), "Blue Jeans Day" flyer, April 14, 1978 (University of Hawai'i), John L. Myers to National Gay Task Force, May 31, 1978 (Arizona State University Gay Services noting Gay Blue Jeans Day and "cancellation" of "Free Spirit" student organization status after the event), all in Box 139, Folder 25, National Gay and Lesbian Task Force Records, Cornell University Library, Division of Rare and Manuscript Collections; Clawson, "Coming Out of the Campus Closet" (University of Florida). On the history of the National Gay and Lesbian Task Force, see D'Emilio, "Organizational Tales: Interpreting the NGLTF Story," in *World Turned*, 99–119; Duberman, "Feminism and Gay Men," in *Left Out*, 285–95.

32. Randy Brown, "Yesterday's 'Blue Jeans Day' Gets Mixed Student Reaction," *SpD*, December 3, 1976. The following year, home economics major Lee Vistrauss inadvertently wore jeans on Blue Jeans Day and subsequently wrote to the *Spartan Daily* that "just the thought of being associated with homosexuals makes me nauseous. Gays always seem to be complaining about the ignorance, by others, of their rights. What about the personal rights of those who are stared at and snickered at because they happened to be wearing blue jeans and did not realize the hidden meaning of that action," a reaction that seems to indicate that Vistrauss had missed the point of the event (*SpD*, April 18, 1978).

33. Chris Raymond, "Blue Jeans" (letter to the editor), *DB*, October 20, 1977. Negative reactions were common on campuses across the country: announcing the 1978 event, the National Gay Task Force asked participants to share news of "any special reaction" (NGTF media director to "Friends," March 30, 1978, Box 139, Folder 25, National Gay and Lesbian Task Force Records, Cornell University Library, Division of Rare and Manuscript Collections). A Gay Services staff member at Arizona State University attributed the negative responses on that campus to the "conservative nature of Arizona's political climate" (Gay Services staff member to National Gay Task Force, May 31, 1978, Box 139, Folder 25, National Gay and Lesbian Task Force Records, Cornell University Library, Division of Rare and Manuscript Collections).

34. Fanucchi quoted in Carol Sarasohn, "Of Cabbages and Kings," *SpD*, October 17, 1977.

35. May, "History of Student Governance." For contemporaneous reflections on student government as a pathway to student power, see Alexander, "Rethinking Student Government for Larger Universities"; Shaffer, "Students in the Policy Process." At Sacramento State, Associated Students president Steve Whitmore and vice president Tom Goff claimed in 1969 that "student government is perhaps the most immediately affected by the new militancy on campus," especially in moving beyond "a sandbox of operations" and into "real pressure" on administration (Steve Whitmore and Tom Goff, "Student Politicians Ask Help of Electorate in Making Student Government Effective," *SH*, September 15, 1969).

36. "I don't mean to start a trend of homosexuals getting awards," Associated Students president Steve Rasco told the student newspaper, "but I look at it like this: the gay students did the most to upgrade their status on campus and in the community. They worked at it, why shouldn't they get it?," ("Club of the Year: Gay Students Union," *49er*, September 17, 1974).

37. "Gays Get Shaft from Bishop," *SH*, October 31, 1972; gay studies motion, Student Senate meeting, October 26, 1972, gay studies resolution, Student Senate meeting, October 30, 1972, both in Series 7, Box 35, Folder: AS SSC Minutes, 1972–73, Associated Students Records, CSUSSCUA.

38. Matthew Savoca, "GSU" (letter to the editor), *SpD*, September 12, 1977.

39. Michael Cassidy to Bob Brunsting, December 7, 1970, Box 2, Folder: Activities Board Correspondence, [ca. 1965–75], Associated Students Collection, San Diego State University, Special Collections and University Archives; Joseph Cornish, letter to the editor, *DS*, October 24, 1974; Rosalie McCordic, "Gay Sex Seminar Gets A.S. Funds," *DS*, December 3, 1974.

40. "Conference on Gay Life Due at Cal State," *Los Angeles Times*, October 29, 1977.

41. David Landis, "New AS UC Budget Discussed," *DC*, October 18, 1976; Kyle Counts and Brian Williams, "Quoting Bible vs. Gays," *DC*, December 1, 1976.

42. Black Students Union, Sharon Tinsley, Jolie Johnson, and Roy Jeter, "Farewell— Slanderous Opportunist," *DN*, May 23, 1974; Andy Rogers, letter to the editor, *DN*, June

3, 1974; "Council Allocated Large Budgets, Money Gone, 20 Groups Remain," *DN*, June 5, 1974.

43. Gay Caucus and the Gay Studies Board, "Supports Coalition" (letter to the editor), *SH*, May 2, 1973. The Women's Caucus described the coalition as having "brought together a collective of diverse interests that have been traditionally under-represented in campus governments" ("Women's Caucus Backs Coalition," *SH*, May 1, 1973).

44. "Personal Opinion ... Student Elections," *Gayzette*, April 29, 1976. See also "Student Leaders Give Views on Gay Issues," *DB*, February 6, 1978.

45. "Student Government Campaigning Underway for 44 Candidates," *DB*, April 24, 1978; GSU advertisement, *DB*, April 26, 1978. Junior Mosley, a candidate for homecoming king at Los Angeles City College, wrote to the GSU that he was "aware of the [organization's] importance" and that he believed "a person (male or female) should not be judged on there [*sic*] sexual preference." See Junior Mosely to GSU, October 25, 1979, and "Gay Students Vote for Junior Mosley" (flyer), Subject File: Los Angeles City College GSU, ONE Archives.

46. SGP meeting minutes, February 4, 1970 (microfilm), SPC.

47. SGP meeting minutes, April 4, 1970, Organizations—Students for Gay Power, EC. In the spring of 1970, the SGP and its faculty and staff allies placed a referendum on the ballot seeking "full academic and civil rights for homosexuals" on campus; the measure passed overwhelmingly, 2,359–420 (GSU newsletter, June 8, 1970, SPC); "Cal Backs Gay Lib," *Berkeley Barb*, June 12, 1970; "Gay Lib: Students Ask for Vote" (flyer), [ca. spring 1970], Reel 27, SPC).

48. Gay Students Alliance newsletter, Spring 1976, Folder: City College, San Francisco, EC; "Baker Urges Equal Future for All Grads," *Advocate*, July 7, 1971, 12; Johansen, "Out of Silence." For a contemporary analysis of gay men and student government leadership, see Goodman, "Lived Experiences."

49. "Gay Runs for Senate," *DC*, December 2, 1970; "AS UC Senate Candidates," *DC*, December 1, 1970; "AS UC Election Results," *DC* December 11, 1970; "Senator Discusses Gay Lib; Gays Face Problems of Oppression," *DC*, April 4, 1971. Wilford was among the students who "reconstituted" the GSU as "an action-oriented group" in the fall of 1970 ("Gay Students Meeting Tonight," *DC*, November 24, 1970).

50. Dave Cash, candidate statement, *DC*, November 16, 1971; John Phelan, "Coalition Claims AS UC Accomplishments," *DC*, November 17, 1971; "DC Endorsements," *DC*, November 19, 1971; Dave Cash, "Harassment for Gay People" (letter to the editor), *DC*, November 16, 1972.

51. "Gay Feminist Chosen as Council Member," *SpD*, February 21, 1975; "AS UCLA Elections Loom," *Gayzette*, May 1, 1975 (five GSU members had put their names in for elections to the Student Legislative Council and "a healthy host of sympathetic candidates lined up to woo GSU votes"); Scott Lanon, "Slates Face Off in Week's Campaign; Barbs Traded," *DN*, April 23, 1973; Richard Robbins platform, *DN*, April 30, 1973; "Haight Wins; Clark, Norris Runoff," *DN*, May 3, 1973.

52. Richard Thomas to Germane, April 11, 1975, Series I, Box 3, Folder: GPU Correspondence 1974, Stanford QSR Records; Richard Thomas to GPU distribution list, September 4, 1975, Series I, Box 3, Folder: Stanford Libraries Locked Stack Policy 1975–1976, Stanford QSR Records; Richard Thomas, memo, September 4, 1975, Box 1, Folder 4, Gay and Lesbian Alliance at Stanford University Records, ONE Archives; Richard Thomas, "Gay Lib Books Isolated by Library Here," *StD*, September 29, 1975; "Locked Stack Policy Reviewed," *StD*, October 3, 1975; Richard Thomas, "Books as Symbols," *StD*, October 6, 1975; Kim Hatamiya, "Libraries Revise Policy," *StD*, April 20, 1976.

53. The GSU and other LGBT student organizations specifically called out the Re-

serve Officer Training Program (ROTC) because of the military's antigay positions ("Newsline: Rights for UCLA?," *Advocate*, January 12, 1977, 43).

54. SGP newsletter, [ca. January 1970], EC; GSU newsletter, October 10, 1970, GLBTHS Periodicals. However, one critic at UC Berkeley objected to pressuring employers not to discriminate against homosexuals on the grounds that doing so "would aid and encourage gays to become a part of the counter-revolutionary industrial complex" (GSU newsletter, January 20, 1971, Subject File: Gay Student Union, University of California Berkeley, ONE Archives; "Senator Discusses Gay Lib; Gays Face Problems of Oppression," *DC*, April 4, 1971).

55. Richard A. Thomas to Daniel Poston, October 10, 1975, Series I, Box 2, Folder: CPPC Stanford QSR Records; "Gay Rights," *StD*, November 5, 1975; William M. Kays to James Lyons, February 20, 1976, Series III, Box 25, Folder St.4.2, Lyman Papers, SULDSC.

56. Richard A. Thomas to Thomas Ehrlich, November 12, 1975, Series I, Box 2, Folder: CPPC Stanford QSR Records; Richard Thomas, "Placement Center Harms Gays," *StD*, November 12, 1975.

57. Richard A. Thomas to Dan Poston, January 18, 1976, Series I, Box 2, Folder: CPPC, Stanford QSR Records.

58. "COSS Holds Off Decision on Gay Job Discrimination," *StD*, October 30, 1975; "COSS Asks Lyman for Gay Hiring Statement," *StD*, December 4, 1975; "Committee to Decide Gay Employment Issue," *StD*, February 10, 1976; "COSS Indecisive on Gay Controversy," *StD*, February 11, 1976.

59. Such reframing also occurred on other campuses. At UC Berkeley, in 1970, when the SGP became the GSU, the group's newsletter declared itself the "Weekly Voice of a Revolution in Human Rights" (GSU newsletter, May 18, 1970, SPC). The organizers of San José State's GSU stressed that it was working on behalf of "the human rights and dignity of all students, no matter what their sexual orientation might be" ("Gay Students Working for Human Rights," *SpD*, April 25, 1974).

60. "Human Rights Policy," attached to Richard A. Thomas to James W Lyons, April 7, 1976, Series III, Box 25, Folder St.4.2, Lyman Papers, SULDSC; Richard A. Thomas statement, [ca. April 1976], Series I, Box 2, Folder: CPPC, Stanford QSR Records.

61. "Human Rights Rally Set for Tomorrow," *StD*, May 24, 1976; "Human Rights Policy," *StD*, May 25, 1976; "Students March to Support Proposed Human Rights Policy," *StD*, May 26, 1976; *GPU News*, July 21, 1976, GLBTHS Periodicals.

62. In "To Stamp Out the Oppression of All Black People," Kevin Quin documents student involvement in Los Angeles's Association of Black Gays Angeles during the 1970s. The students who participated included Ron Grayson, who attended the People's College of Law, and Maxwell Royce Harris, "an art student." The Association of Black Gays also engaged local educational institutions through consciousness-raising sessions and workshops at Long Beach State College and other institutions. See also Mumford, "Trouble with Gay Rights," 66–68.

63. *Radical Homosexual Rag*, January 25, 1970, GLBTHS Periodicals.

64. "Gay-In at Griffith" (letter to the editor), *DB*, April 6, 1971.

65. *GPU Newsletter*, [ca. late March 1974], SUPEC.

66. GSU meeting notice, *DC*, April 20, 1971 (GSU to march with Gay Contingent at antiwar march in San Francisco); Z[elima] Williams, "Dual Struggle" (letter to the editor), *SpD*, May 6, 1971 (reflecting on GLF participation in San Francisco antiwar march).

67. Goen-Salter, interview by author (reflecting on involvement in off-campus communities as a "feminism of practice" in Oakland); Mahaney, interview by author (on fluidity between community-based and campus organizing for lesbian students and faculty).

68. Bryant, interview by author. Such community institutions were important gathering spaces for lesbian students in the late 1970s and early 1980s. As Lisa Orta recalled, feminist bookstores were the "locus of lesbian and feminist activity at the time" (interview by author).

69. *GPU News*, October 29, 1975, GLBTHS Periodicals.

70. Palo Alto Unified School District Board of Education meeting minutes, November 4, 1975, Subject File: Stanford–Palo Alto Board of Education, ONE Archives. Hughes-Oldenburg did not recall this meeting when asked about it (interview by author).

71. *GPU News*, November 12, 1975, SUPEC; Palo Alto Unified School District Board of Education meeting minutes, November 18, 1975, Subject File: Stanford–Palo Alto Board of Education, ONE Archives; "Gay Hiring Policy to Be Re-Examined," *StD*, November 18, 1975; *GPU News*, December 3, 1975, GLBTHS Periodicals; GPU/Gay Committee of Concern flyer, [ca. December 1975], Box 1, Folder: Gay People's Union at Stanford Misc. Documents, Corbin Papers, GLBTHS.

72. *GPU News*, March 17, 1976, GLBTHS Periodicals.

73. Dave Steward, "A Commissioner Speaks," *Lambda News*, December 1977, GLBTHS Periodicals; Chris Georges, "Ad Controversy Mounts," *SpD*, September 19, 1977; "Round About and Little Tid Bits," *Lambda News*, February 1978, GLBTHS Periodicals; Lori Hayes, "Gays Can Advertise," *SpD*, February 1, 1978; "Santa Clara County," *South Bay Chronicle* (supplement to *Bay Area Reporter*), February 16, 1978; "San Jose Gays Win Transit Fight," *South Bay Chronicle* (supplement to *Bay Area Reporter*), March 16, 1978.

74. Leo Laurence, journalist and activist involved in both the Committee for Homosexual Freedom and the GLF in Berkeley, recalled that "our leaflets, our newsletters and everything else . . . were printed at the UC Berkeley campus in the offices" by both faculty and students. One faculty member in particular "had keys, he had access, he could get into an office at midnight and crank stuff out." See Laurence, interview by author; "Deny Gays Affirmative Action Seat," *SpD*, September 24, 1974; "Gay Plan Nears Approval," *SpD*, October 3, 1974; "Gay Editorial Blasted," *SpD*, October 4, 1974.

75. "Brown Bill Nears Passage," *Gayzette*, May 8, 1975.

76. "California's Senate Votes Bill Repealing Sexual Prohibitions," *New York Times*, May 2, 1975. The bill was popularly known as the Brown Bill after Willie Brown, who represented San Francisco in the Assembly and later served as the city's mayor. Brown had first proposed the legislation in 1969 and was one of its most ardent supporters (Richardson, *Willie Brown*, 237–39).

77. David Judson, "Gay Union Seeks to Create Positive Campus Atmosphere," *DB*, October 5, 1978; Susan Sachs, "School Groups Here May Not Endorse Political Issues," *DB*, October 19, 1978. The Student Leadership Council passed and published a statement opposing Proposition 6 ("Statement of Opposition to Proposition Six," *DB*, November 6, 1978). Campus religious leaders published a statement of opposition to Proposition 6 as well ("We the Ministers, Priests and Rabbis of the University Religious Conference at UCLA Oppose Proposition 6," *DB*, November 2, 1978).

78. "A Threat to Human Rights," *GPU News*, [ca. October 1977], GLBTHS Periodicals; No on the Briggs Initiative Committee mailing, September 1978, Subject File: Briggs No on 6 Committee, ONE Archives; John Dos Santos and Richard Willey, "'Homophobia': Learn What It Is and How to Fight It," *DB*, September 19, 1978.

79. Gay People's Union meeting notice, *DS*, October 4, 1978.

80. GPU Steering Committee meeting minutes, December 7, 1977, Series I, Box 3, Folder: GPU Steering Committee 1977, Stanford QSR Records.

81. "Benefit Run 4 Rights" flyer, September 30, 1978, Subject File: Briggs No on 6, ONE Archives.

82. "Crucial Events and Fun Dances" (flyer), [ca. November–December 1977], Subject File: University of Southern California (USC)—Gay Student Union, ONE Archives.

83. "Scrap Prop. 6" (flyer), October 26, [1978], Subject File: Briggs Found Loose 1 of 4, ONE Archives.

84. Press release, March 12, 1978, Subject File: unmarked folder related to Briggs, ONE Archives.

85. "Briggs Initiative Night" (advertisement), *DB*, May 10, 1978.

86. Unknown speaker, notes of comments delivered at the concert, [ca. November 1978], Briggs Initiative Collection.

87. LA Regional CCABI meeting minutes, [n.d.], workshops and meetings schedule, [1977], both in Briggs Initiative Collection.

88. "Briggs Initiative 'Badly Drafted,' States Vasconcellos in Speech," *SpD*, September 19, 1978.

89. Campus Outreach Task Force of the Inland Empire No on 6 Committee to faculty and staff, October 1978, Subject File: Briggs No on 6 Committee, ONE Archives.

90. "Call for Action," September 24, 1977, Briggs Initiative Collection.

91. Bay Area Coalition against the Briggs Initiative meeting notes, October 23, December 11, 1977, Briggs Initiative Collection; "Briggs Initiative Faces Tough Fight in San Francisco," *Phoenix*, May 11, 1978; Waters, "He's Still Rising."

92. Calendar, [1977], Briggs Initiative Collection.

93. "Briggs Initiative Faces Tough Fight in San Francisco," *Phoenix*, May 11, 1978; "Prof to Battle Briggs on TV," *Phoenix*, September 21, 1978; "Gay Professor Teams with Milk against Briggs," *Zenger's/Golden Gater*, October 17, 1978.

94. Paul Boneberg, "For Human Rights," *Lambda News*, October 1977, GLBTHS Periodicals.

95. Cinde Chorness, "Lesbian Alliance a 'Political Force,'" *SpD*, October 13, 1977.

96. Katherine Hamilton, "Prop. 6 Foes Plan Campaign with Education," *SpD*, September 21, 1978.

Conclusion

1. "Gay Rights Reach Nation," *Plexus*, October 1979, 1, GLBTHS Periodicals.

2. Organizer's Handbook, National March on Washington for Lesbian and Gay Rights, 1979, National March on Washington for Lesbian and Gay Rights Records, Box 1, Folder 1, ONE Archives.

3. D'Emilio, "1979 March's Place"; Ghaziani, *Dividends of Dissent*.

4. "Endorsers of the National March on Washington, October 1979," clipping in Subject File: Los Angeles City College, ONE Archives.

5. Kenna Himes, "Rally Supports Gay Rights, Condemns Oppression," *DN*, October 16, 1979.

6. "CSLA Gays March in Washington Protest," *UT*, October 15, 1979.

7. Organizer's Handbook, National March on Washington for Lesbian and Gay Rights, 1979, National March on Washington for Lesbian and Gay Rights Records, Box 1, Folder 1, ONE Archives; Boneberg, interview by author. Boneberg became an important HIV/AIDS activist in the 1980s (Boneberg, interview by Scott Schaefer).

8. Echelman, "Everybody Assumes."

9. Bryant, interview by author; Goen-Salter, interview by author; Duplechan, interview by author.

BIBLIOGRAPHY

Archival Sources

California State University, Sacramento, Donald & Beverly Gerth Special Collections and University Archives
    AR Files
    Associated Students Records (RG 7)
    Records of the Office of the President (RG 88)
    University Archives
    Sally Roesch Wagner Papers (MSS 2000/31)
    Women's Studies Program Records (RG 21)
Columbia Center for Oral History Research, Columbia University, New York
    LGBTQ Columbia University Oral History Project. https://www.ccohr.incite.columbia.edu/lgbtq-columbia-university-oral-history.
Cornell University Library, Division of Rare and Manuscript Collections, Ithaca, N.Y.
    National Gay and Lesbian Task Force Records (Collection 7301)
GLBT Historical Society, San Francisco
    Bois Burk Papers (Collection 1989-07)
    Arthur Corbin Papers (Collection 1995-20)
    Jo Daly Papers (Collection 1998-13)
    John De Cecco Papers (Collection 2001-17)
    San Francisco LGBT Groups Ephemera Collection (Collection GRP EPH)
    San Francisco LGBT General Subjects Collection (Collection SUB EPH)
    Phyllis Lyon and Del Martin Papers (Collection 1999-13)
    Oral History Collection (Collection GLBT-OH)
    Periodicals Collection (Collection GLBT-PER)
    Poster Collection (Collection GLBT-POSTER)
    George Raya Papers (Collection 1990-09)
    Daniel A. Smith and Queer Blue Light Videotapes (Collection 1999-52)
    Charles Thorpe [Thorp] Papers (Collection 1987-02)
Lavender Library, Sacramento, Calif.
    Cherie Gordon Collection
New York Public Library, Manuscripts and Archives Division
    Gay Activists Alliance Records (MssCol 1121)
ONE National Gay & Lesbian Archives, USC Libraries, University of Southern California, Los Angeles
    Don Amador Papers (Coll2011.016)
    Paul C. Ballard Papers (Coll2014-029)
    California Proposition 6 Briggs Initiative Collection (Coll2011-018)
    Jeanne Córdova Papers (collection Coll2008-064)

    Gay and Lesbian Alliance at Stanford University Records (Coll2014-069)
    Gay Liberation Front (GLF) Los Angeles Records (Coll2012-031)
    Barbara Gittings and Kay Tobin Lahusen Collection (Coll2008-069)
    Joseph P. Hayes Papers (Coll2014-071)
    Jim Kepner Papers (Coll2011-002)
    L.A. Gay and Lesbian Center Records (Coll2007-010)
    Lesbian and Gay Academic Union Records (Coll2011-041)
    Mattachine Society Project Collection (Coll2008-016)
    National March on Washington for Lesbian and Gay Rights Records (Coll2013.087)
    Periodicals Collection
    Gary Steele Papers (Coll2014-032)
    Subject Files (Coll2012.001)
    UCLA Gay Awareness Week Records (Coll2013-054)
San Diego State University, Special Collections and University Archives, San Diego
    Associated Students Collection
San Francisco State University, Special Collections and Archives, San Francisco
    Holloway Historians: Oral History Transcripts
    University Archives
    Women's Studies Records
San José State University, Special Collections and Archives, San José University Archives
    San José State University Office of the President, Hobert W. Burns Records (MSS.2009.06.02)
    San José State University Women's Studies Program Records (MSS.2005.08)
Stanford University Libraries, Department of Special Collections and University Archives, Stanford, Calif.
    Stanford University Queer Student Resources Records (SC 252)
    Richard W. Lyman Papers (SC 0215)
    Stanford University LGBT Alumni Oral History Interviews (SC 1164)
    Stanford University Publications and Ephemera Collection (SC 4000-7750 GAPOO)
University of California, Berkeley, Bancroft Library
    Social Protest Collection (BANC MSS 86/157)
    University Archives
    Gay Bears Collection (CU 484)
    Records of the Office of Student Activities (CU 14)
    Queer Resource Center Records (CU 486)
    Women's Resource Center Library Ephemera Collection (CU 515)
University of California, Los Angeles, Special Collections
    Morris Kight Papers (Collection 354)
    University Archives
    Office of the Chancellor, Administrative Files of Franklin D. Murphy (Record Series 401)
University of Richmond, Student Center for Equity and Inclusion, Richmond, Va.
    LGBTQIA History at UR. https://inclusion.richmond.edu/resources/lgbtqia/history/index.html.
Virginia Tech, Special Collections and University Archives, Blacksburg
    LGBTQ History at Virginia Tech. http://digitalsc.lib.vt.edu/VTLGBTQ.

Interviews Conducted by the Author

Alfred, Randy. San Francisco, September 11, 2006.
Aura, Jan. Culver City, Calif., June 14, 2014.
Beardsley, Scott. San Francisco, May 19, 2014.
Benemann, William. San Francisco, January 10, 2009.
Blackburn, John. San Francisco, October 1, 2007.
Blumenfeld, Warren. Ames, Iowa, July 11, 16, 2006.
Boneberg, Paul. San Francisco, June 9, 2008.
Bryant, Barbara. Berkeley, Calif., September 24, 2010.
Capron, Bear. Palo Alto, Calif., May 7, 2014.
Coleman, Tom. Los Angeles, July 15, 2008.
Corbin, Arthur. San Francisco, June 26, 2014.
Dunbar, Bob. San Francisco, August 18, 2014.
Duplechan, Larry. Los Angeles, March 6, 2014.
Fertig, Jack. San Francisco, July 16, 2009.
Goen-Salter, Sugie. San Francisco, April 8, 2014.
Gordon, Cherie. Stockton, Calif., August 5, 2012.
Hughes-Oldenburg, Donna. August 14, 2014.
Laurence, Leo. San Diego, August 7, 2009.
Mahaney, Ruth. San Francisco, July 26, 2006.
Mentley, Lee. Murphys, Calif., July 6, 2012.
Murley, Jay. San Diego, September 12, 2008.
Nutting, Spencer. August 2, 2014.
Orta, Lisa. Oakland, Calif., October 4, 2019.
Person, Matrisha. San Francisco, August 24, 2012.
Poswall, John. Sacramento, Calif., July 11, 2006.
Quinn, Therese. May 28, 2020.
Raya, George. Sacramento, Calif., June 4, 2006, July 22, 2010.
Reese, Preston. Gold River, Calif., June 6, 2006.
Rogers, Martin. San Francisco, January 10, April 10, 2010.
Sivertsen, Wiggsy. San José, Calif., July 11, 2006.
Smith, Freda. Sutter Creek, Calif., July 23, 2010.
Spring, Don. Los Angeles, September 10, 2008.
Strachan, David. San Francisco, August 20, 2014.
Thompson, Mark. Los Angeles, September 23, 2007.
Whitney, Joe. Fort Bragg, Calif., June 20, 2014.

Other Sources

Abbott, Steve, and Rudy Kikel. "In Search of a Muse: The Politics of Gay Poetry." In *A Gift of Tongues: Critical Challenges in Contemporary Poetry*, edited by Marie Harris and Kathleen Aguero, 267–85. Athens: University of Georgia Press, 1987.

Acuña, Rodolfo F. *The Making of Chicana/o Studies: In the Trenches of Academe*. New Brunswick, N.J.: Rutgers University Press, 2011.

Alexander, William A. "Rethinking Student Government for Larger Universities." *Journal of Higher Education* 40, no. 1 (January 1969): 39–46.

Allison, April, with Terry Stein and Anita Skeen. "A Rich Heritage: The History of Lesbians and Gay Men at MSU." In *Moving Forward: Lesbian and Gay Men and Michigan State University: A Report of the University-Wide Task Force on Lesbian and Gay Issues*, 1:49–81. East Lansing: Michigan State University, 1992.

Amerman, Stephen Kent. "'Let's Get in and Fight!': American Indian Political Activism in an Urban Public School System, 1973." *American Indian Quarterly* 27, nos. 3–4 (2003): 607–38.

Armstrong, Elizabeth. *Forging Gay Identities: Organizing Sexuality in San Francisco, 1950–1994*. Chicago: University of Chicago Press, 2002.

Arrow, Michelle. *The Seventies: The Personal, the Political and the Making of Modern Australia*. Sydney: NewSouth Publishing, University of New South Wales, 2019.

Bailey, Beth. *Sex in the Heartland*. Cambridge: Harvard University Press, 1999.

Bailey, Beth, and David Farber, eds. *America in the Seventies*. Lawrence: University Press of Kansas, 2004.

Baim, Tracy, ed. *Gay Press, Gay Power: The Growth of LGBT Community Newspapers in America*. Chicago: Prairie Avenue, 2012.

Barney, David D., comp. *Gay and Lesbian History at the University of Kansas: Lawrence Gay Liberation Front, 1971–1975*. Lawrence: Student Assistance Center, University of Kansas, 1992.

Bartolotto, Juliane Maria. "An Early History of Women's Studies at California State University, Long Beach: 1968–1976." Master's thesis, California State University, Long Beach, 1996.

Batza, Katie. *Before AIDS: Gay Health Politics in the 1970s*. Philadelphia: University of Pennsylvania Press, 2018.

Baxandall, Rosalyn. "Re-Visioning the Women's Liberation Movement's Narrative: Early Second Wave African American Feminists." *Feminist Studies* 27, no. 1 (Spring 2001): 225–45.

Beck, Brittney L. "'A Different Kind of Activism': The University of Florida Committee on Sexism and Homophobia, 1981–1992." *American Educational Research Journal* 56, no. 4 (2019): 1353–79.

Beemyn, Brett. "The Silence Is Broken: A History of the First Lesbian, Gay, and Bisexual College Student Groups." *Journal of the History of Sexuality* 12, no. 2 (2003): 205–23.

Beins, Agatha. *Liberation in Print: Feminist Periodicals and Social Movement Identity*. Athens: University of Georgia Press, 2017.

Bell, Jonathan, ed. *Beyond the Politics of the Closet: Gay Rights and the American State since the 1970s*. Philadelphia: University of Pennsylvania Press, 2020.

Bell, Jonathan. *California Crucible: The Forging of Modern American Liberalism*. Philadelphia: University of Pennsylvania Press, 2012.

Bender, V. Lee, Yvonne Davis, Oliver Glover, and Joy Stapp. "Patterns of Self-Disclosure in Homosexual and Heterosexual College Students." *Sex Roles* 2, no. 2 (1976): 149–60.

Bennett, Paula. "Lesbian Poetry in the United States, 1890–1990: A Brief Overview." In *Professions of Desire: Lesbian and Gay Studies in Literature*, edited by George E. Haggerty and Bonnie Zimmerman, 98–110. New York: Modern Language Association of America, 1995.

Binkley, Sam. *Getting Loose: Lifestyle Consumption in the 1970s*. Durham: Duke University Press, 2007.

Biondi, Martha. *The Black Revolution on Campus*. Berkeley: University of California Press, 2012.

Blackwell, Maylei. *Chicana Power: Contested Histories of Feminism in the Chicano Movement*. Austin: University of Texas Press, 2011.

Blumenfeld, Warren. "Gays on Campus." *Gay Men's Liberation and Last Motive* 32, no. 2 (1972): 22–24.

Blumenfeld, Warren. *The National Gay Student Center*. New York: National Task Force on Student Personnel and Homosexuality, 1972.

Boggs, George R., and Lawrence A. Galizio, eds. *College for All Californians: A History of the California Community Colleges*. New York: Teachers College Press, 2021.

Boneberg, Paul. Interview by Scott Schaefer. "AIDS at 30: Interview—What Were the Earliest Days of the Epidemic Like?" KQED, June 7, 2011. https://cdn.KQED.org/wp-content/uploads/sites/10/2011/06/Boneberg.mp3.

Boxer, Marilyn J. "Women's Studies as Women's History." *Women's Studies Quarterly* 30, nos. 3–4 (Fall 2002): 42–51.

Boyd, Nan Alamilla. *Wide Open Town: A History of Queer San Francisco to 1965*. Berkeley: University of California Press, 2003.

Boyd, Nan Alamilla, and Horacio N. Roque Ramírez, eds. *Bodies of Evidence: The Practice of Queer Oral History*. New York: Oxford University Press, 2012.

Brantley, Allyson P. "'Shouldn't You Be Boycotting Coors?': Ephemera, Boycotting Counterpublics, and the Campaign against Coors Beer." *Radical History Review* 2019, no. 134 (May 2019): 142–67.

Braukman, Stacy Lorraine. "Anticommunism and the Politics of Sex and Race in Florida, 1954–1965." Ph.D. diss., University of North Carolina, Chapel Hill, 1999.

Broaddus, Toni. "Commentary: Vote No If You Believe in Marriage: Lessons from the No on Knight/No on Proposition 22 Campaign." *Berkeley Women's Law Journal* 15 (2000): 1–13.

Broadhurst, Christopher J. "Campus Activism in the 21st Century: A Historical Framing." *New Directions for Higher Education* 167 (Fall 2014): 3–15.

Brown, Elspeth. "Canada's First Gay Student Activist Group." Notches Blog, February 5, 2019. http://notchesblog.com/2019/02/05/canadas-first-gay-student-activist-group/.

Bulkin, Elly. "Heterosexism and Women's Studies." *Radical Teacher* 17 (November 1980): 25–31.

Bulkin, Elly. "'A Whole New Poetry Beginning Here': Teaching Lesbian Poetry." *College English* 40, no. 8 (1979): 874–88.

Buring, Daneel. "Gay Activism behind the Magnolia Curtain: The Memphis Gay Coalition, 1979–1991." *Journal of Homosexuality* 32, no. 1 (1996): 113–35.

Burton, William, with Barry Loveland. *Out in Central Pennsylvania: The History of an LGBTQ Community*. University Park: Pennsylvania State University Press, 2020.

Bye, Susan, Felicity Collins, and Sue Turnbill. "Aunty Jack, Norman Gunston and ABC Television Comedy in the 1970s." *ACH: The Journal of the History of Culture in Australia* 26 (2007): 131–52.

Cain, Patricia A. "Litigating for Lesbian and Gay Rights: A Legal History." *Virginia Law Review* 79, no. 7 (October 1993): 1551–1641.

Cain, Timothy Reese, and Michael S. Hevel. "'Gay People Pay Activity Fees Too': The Committee on Gay Education's Pioneering Legal Victories at the University of Georgia." *Review of Higher Education* 45, no. 1 (Fall 2021): 61–91.

California State Colleges, Inglewood, Office of the Chancellor. *Experimental College Developments in the California State Colleges*. November 1969. ED052676. https://eric.ed.gov/?id=ED052676.

Callan, Patrick M. "Higher Education in California: Rise and Fall." In *Higher Education in the American West*, edited by Lester F. Goodchild, Richard W. Jonsen, Patty Limerick, David A. Longanecker, 233–56. New York: Palgrave Macmillan, 2014.

Calvert, Robert, Jr., and William A. Draves. *Free Universities and Learning Referral Centers, 1978*. Washington, D.C.: U.S. Department of Health, Education, and Welfare, Education Division, National Center for Education Statistics, 1979.

Canaday, Margot. *The Straight State: Sexuality and Citizenship in Twentieth Century America*. Princeton: Princeton University Press, 2009.

Casey, Maurice. "Radical Politics and Gay Activism in the Republic of Ireland, 1974–1990." *Irish Studies Review* 26, no. 2 (2018): 217–36.

Center for the Study of Gender and Sexuality at the University of Chicago. "Closeted/Out in the Quadrangles: A History of LGBTQ Life at the University of Chicago." 2015. http://gendersexuality.uchicago.edu/projects/closeted/.

Chavez, Marisela Rodriguez. "*Despierten Hermanas y Hermanos!*: Women, the Chicano Movement, and Chicana Feminisms in California, 1966–1981." Ph.D. diss, Stanford University, 2004.

Chen, Susan Y. F. "Slowly but Surely: My Search for Family Acceptance and Community Continues." In *The Very Inside: An Anthology of Writing by Asian and Pacific Islander Lesbian and Bisexual Women*, edited by Sharon Lim-Hing, 79–84. Toronto: Sister Vision, 1994.

Chica, Christina Marie. "Toward a Sociology of Global Comparative Placemaking." *Sociology Compass* 15, no. 8 (2021): 1–16.

Christ, Carol T. "Anniversary Lecture: The American University and Women's Studies." *Tulsa Studies in Women's Literature* 16, no. 1 (Spring 1997): 13–25.

Clawson, Jessica. "Coming Out of the Campus Closet: The Emerging Visibility of Queer Students at the University of Florida, 1970–1982." *Educational Studies* 50, no. 3 (2014): 209–30.

Clawson, Jess. "'Existing and Existing in Your Face': Hiram Ruiz and the Pedagogy of Gay Liberation Front in Tallahassee, Florida, 1970–71." *Journal of Curriculum Theorizing* 29, no. 2 (2013): 143–48.

Clawson, Jessica. "Queers on Campus: LGBTQ Visibility at Three Public Universities in Florida, 1970–1985." Ph.D. diss., University of Florida, 2014.

Clawson, Jess. "'The Rest Is All Drag': Trans-gressive Women on Higher Education History." In *Women's Higher Education in the United States: New Historical Perspective*, edited by Margaret A. Nash, 277–95. New York: Palgrave Macmillan, 2018.

Cohen, Robert. *When the Old Left Was Young: Student Radicals and America's First Mass Student Movement, 1929–1941*. New York: Oxford University Press, 1997.

Cohen, Stephan. *The Gay Liberation Youth Movement in New York: "An Army of Lovers Cannot Fail."* New York: Routledge, 2007.

Cole, Shaun. *"Don We Now Our Gay Apparel": Gay Men's Dress in the Twentieth Century*. Oxford: Berg, 2000.

Coley, Jonathan S. *Gay on God's Campus: Mobilizing for LGBT Equality at Christian Colleges and Universities*. Chapel Hill: University of North Carolina Press, 2018.

Collins, Lisa Gail. "Activists Who Yearn for Art That Transforms: Parallels in the Black Arts and Feminist Art Movements in the United States." *Signs: Journal of Women in Culture and Society* 31, no. 3 (2006): 717–52.

Corbett, Kathryn L., and Kathleen Preston. *From the Catbird Seat: A History of Women's Studies at Humboldt State University, 1971–1996*. Eureka, Ca.: Eureka, 1998.

Córdova, Jeanne. *When We Were Outlaws: A Memoir of Love and Liberation*. Midway, Fl.: Spinsters Ink, 2011.

Delgado, Richard. "Storytelling for Oppositionists and Others: A Plea for Narrative." *Michigan Law Review* 87, no. 8 (1989): 2411–41.

D'Emilio, John. "The Campus Environment for Gay and Lesbian Life." *Academe* 76, no. 1 (1990): 16–19.

D'Emilio, John. *Making Trouble: Essays on Gay History, Politics and the University*. New York: Routledge, 1992.

D'Emilio, John. "The 1979 March's Place in History." *Gay and Lesbian Review*, March–April 2005, 33–34.

D'Emilio, John. *Sexual Politics, Sexual Communities: The Making of a Homosexual Minority in the United States, 1940–1970.* Chicago: University of Chicago Press, 1983.

D'Emilio, John. *The World Turned: Essays on Gay History, Politics and Culture.* Durham: Duke University Press, 2002.

D'Emilio, John, and Estelle B. Freedman. *Intimate Matters: A History of Sexuality in America.* 2nd ed. Chicago: University of Chicago Press, 1997.

Denby, Eric. "Fighting for Inclusion: The Origin of Gay Liberation at the University of Michigan." Master's thesis, Western Michigan University, 2015.

Deverell, William, and David Igler, eds. *A Companion to California History.* West Sussex, Eng.: Wiley Blackwell, 2014.

Diggs, Marylynne. "Romantic Friends or a 'Different Race of Creatures?': The Representation of Lesbian Pathology in Nineteenth-Century America." *Feminist Studies* 21, no. 2 (1995): 317–40.

Dilley, Patrick. *Gay Liberation to Campus Assimilation: Early Non-Heterosexual Student Organizing at Midwestern Universities.* New York: Palgrave Macmillan, 2019.

Dilley, Patrick. *Queer Man on Campus: A History of Non-Heterosexual College Men, 1945–2000.* New York: Routledge/Falmer, 2002.

Dong, Harvey. "The Origins and Trajectory of Asian American Political Activism in the San Francisco Bay Area, 1968–1978." Ph.D. diss., University of California, Berkeley, 2002.

Dong, Harvey. "Third World Liberation Comes to San Francisco State and UC Berkeley." *Chinese America: History and Perspectives* (2009): 95–106, 157.

Douglass, John Aubrey. *The California Idea and American Higher Education: 1850 to the 1960 Master Plan.* Stanford: Stanford University Press, 2000.

Downs, Jim. *Stand by Me: The Forgotten History of Gay Liberation.* New York: Basic Books, 2016.

Duberman, Martin. *Has the Gay Movement Failed?* Oakland: University of California Press, 2018.

Duberman, Martin. *Left Out: The Politics of Exclusion: Essays 1964–2002.* Cambridge: South End Press, 2002.

DuBois, Ellen. "Women's Studies in the Thicket of Academe in the 1970s: Liz Kennedy in Buffalo." *Feminist Formations* 24, no. 3 (2012): 79–83.

Echelman, Adam. "'Everybody Assumes That It's Like the Rest of California and It's Not': Rural LGBTQ Students and Administrators Describe Campus Strife." *Cal Matters*, June 15, 2023. https://calmatters.org/education/higher-education/2023/06/rural-lgbtq-college-students/.

Echols, Alice. *Daring to Be Bad: Radical Feminism in America, 1967–1975.* Minneapolis: University of Minnesota Press, 1989.

Edgecomb, Sean. "History of the Ridiculous, 1960–1987." *Gay and Lesbian Review Worldwide* 14, no. 3 (May–June 2007): 21–23.

Eisenbach, David. *Gay Power: An American Revolution.* New York: Carroll and Graf, 2006.

Enke, Anne. *Finding the Movement: Sexuality, Contested Space and Feminist Activism.* Durham: Duke University Press, 2007.

Enszer, Julie R. "The Whole Naked Truth of Our Lives: Lesbian Feminist Print Culture from 1969 through 1989." Ph.D. diss., University of Maryland, College Park, 2013.

Eskridge, William N., Jr. *Gaylaw: Challenging the Apartheid of the Closet.* Cambridge: Harvard University Press, 1999.

Eskridge, William N., Jr. "Challenging the Apartheid of the Closet: Establishing Conditions for Lesbian and Gay Intimacy, Nomos, and Citizenship, 1961–1981." *Hofstra Law Review* 25, no. 3 (Spring 1997): 817–970.

Evans, Sara M. "Sons, Daughters, and Patriarchy: Gender and the 1968 Generation." *American Historical Review* 114, no. 2 (2009): 331–47.

Evans, Sara M. *Tidal Wave: How Women Changed America at Century's End*. New York: Free Press, 2004.

Eymann, Marcia A., and Charles Wollenberg, eds. *What's Going On?: California and the Vietnam Era*. Berkeley: University of California Press, 2004.

Faderman, Lillian, and Stuart Timmons. *Gay L.A.: A History of Sexual Outlaws, Power Politics and Lipstick Lesbians*. New York: Basic Books, 2006.

Farley, Tucker. "Speaking, Silence, and Shifting Listening Space: The NWSA Lesbian Caucus in the Early Years." *NWSA Journal* 14, no. 1 (Spring 2002): 29–50.

Faulkenbury, T. Evan, and Aaron Hayworth. "The Carolina Gay Association, Oral History, and Coming Out at the University of North Carolina." *Oral History Review* 43, no. 1 (Winter–Spring 2016): 115–37.

Fejes, Fred. *Gay Rights and Moral Panic: The Origins of America's Debate on Homosexuality*. New York: Palgrave Macmillan, 2008.

Ferreira, Jason Michael. "All Power to the People: A Comparative History of Third World Radicalism in San Francisco, 1968–1974." Ph.D. diss., University of California, Berkeley, 2003.

Foley, Michael Stewart. *Front Porch Politics: The Forgotten Heyday of American Activism in the 1970s and 1980s*. New York: Hill and Wang, 2013.

Foulkes, Sara Beth. "Coalitions, Collaborations, and Conflicts: The History of Women's Studies at San Diego State University from 1969–1974." Master's thesis, San Diego State University, 2007.

Franklin, V. P. "Hidden in Plain View: African American Women, Radical Feminism, and the Origins of Women's Studies Programs, 1967–1974." *Journal of African American History* 87, no. 4 (Autumn 2002): 433–45.

Freeman, Susan K. "Building Lesbian Studies in the 1970s and 1980s." In *Breaking the Wave: Women, Their Organizations, and Feminism, 1945–1985*, edited by Kathleen Laughlin and Jacqueline Castledine, 229–45. New York: Routledge, 2010.

Freeman, Susan K. "Learning Alternatives: Student-Led Gay and Lesbian Studies in the U.S., 1969–1989." Paper Presented at the Berkshires Conference of Women's Historians, 2010.

Gaines, Malik. "The Cockettes, Sylvester and Performance as Life." In Gaines, *Black Performance on the Outskirts of the Left: A History of the Impossible*, 135–78. New York: New York University Press, 2017.

Gallo, Marcia M. *Different Daughters: A History of the Daughters of Bilitis and the Rise of the Lesbian Rights Movement*. New York: Carroll and Graf, 2006.

García, Mario T. *The Chicano Generation: Testimonios of the Movement*. Oakland: University of California Press, 2015.

Gerth, Donald K. *The People's University: A History of the California State University*. Berkeley, Calif.: Berkeley Public Policy Press, 2010.

Gewirtzman, Doni. "'Make Your Own Kind of Music': Queer Student Groups and the First Amendment." *California Law Review* 86, no. 5 (October 1998): 1131–68.

Ghaziani, Amin. *The Dividends of Dissent: How Conflict and Culture Work in Lesbian and Gay Marches on Washington*. Chicago: University of Chicago Press, 2008.

Giardina, Carol. "The Making of the Women's Liberation Movement, 1953–1970." Ph.D. diss., City University of New York, 2004.

Gold, Ben K. *An Analysis of A.A. Degrees Awarded at Los Angeles City College, 1964–1978.* June 1979. Research Study 79-9; ERIC Report 171353. https://ericed.gov/?id=ED171353.

Gold, Ben K. *Institutional Research at Los Angeles City College: A Thirty-Five Year Perspective.* March 29, 1982. ERIC Report 215724. https://eric.ed.gov/?id=ED215724.

Gomez, Letitia. "*No Te Rajes*—Don't Back Down! Daring to Be Out and Visible." In *Queer Brown Voices: Personal Narratives of Latina/o LGBT Activism*, edited by Uriel Quesada, Letitia Gomez, and Salvador Vidal-Ortiz, 121–38. Austin: University of Texas Press, 2015.

Goodchild, Lester F., Richard W. Jonsen, Patty Limerick, and David A. Longanecker, eds. *Higher Education in the American West.* New York: Palgrave Macmillan, 2014.

Goodman, Michael Anthony. "The Lived Experiences of Openly Gay Undergraduate Men in Elected Student Government: A Phenomenological Queering." Ph.D. diss., University of Maryland, College Park, 2020.

Graves, Karen L. "The History of Lesbian, Gay, Bisexual, Transgender, Queer Issues in Higher Education." In *Higher Education: Handbook of Theory and Research*, edited by M. Paulson, 127–73. Cham, Switz.: Springer International, 2018.

Graves, Karen L. "'So You Think You Have a History?': Taking a Q from Lesbian and Gay Studies in Writing Education History." *History of Education Quarterly* 52, no. 4 (November 2012): 465–87.

Gunckel, Colin. "The Chicano/a Photographic: Art as Social Practice in the Chicano Movement." *American Quarterly* 67, no. 2 (June 2015): 377–412.

Hall, Jacqueline Dowd. "'To Widen the Reach of Our Love': Autobiography, History and Desire." *Feminist Studies* 26, no. 1 (Spring 2000): 230–47.

Hall, Simon. *American Patriotism, American Protest: Social Movements since the Sixties.* Philadelphia: University of Pennsylvania Press, 2011.

Hall, Simon. "Framing the American 1960s: A Historiographical Review." *European Journal of American Culture* 31, no. 1 (2012): 5–23.

Hall, Simon. "Protest Movements in the 1970s: The Long 1960s." *Journal of Contemporary History* 43, no. 4 (2008): 655–72.

Hanhardt, Christina B. "Queer History." *American Historian* 20 (May 2019): 18–23.

Hanhardt, Christina B. *Safe Space: Gay Neighborhood History and the Politics of Violence.* Durham: Duke University Press, 2013.

Hawthorne, Susan. "Australia." In *Lesbian Histories and Cultures: An Encyclopedia*, edited by Bonnie Zimmerman, 82–85. New York: Garland, 2000.

Hayes, Eileen M. *Songs in Black and Lavender: Race, Sexual Politics and Women's Music.* Urbana: University of Illinois Press, 2010.

Hennessy, Christopher. "Ten Ways of Looking at Gay Poetry." *Gay and Lesbian Review*, October 2005, 10–12.

Higginson, Reid Pitney. "When Experimental Was Mainstream: The Rise and Fall of Experimental Colleges, 1957–1979." *History of Education Quarterly* 59, no. 2 (2019): 195–226.

Hillman, Betty Luther. "'The Clothes I Wear Help Me to Know My Own Power': The Politics of Gender Presentation in the Era of Women's Liberation." *Frontiers: A Journal of Women's Studies* 34, no. 2 (2013): 155–85.

Hillman, Betty Luther. "'The Most Profoundly Revolutionary Act a Homosexual Can Engage In': Drag and the Politics of Gender Presentation in the San Francisco Gay Liberation Movement, 1964–1972." *Journal of the History of Sexuality* 20, no. 1 (January 2011): 153–81.

Hobson, Emily. *Lavender and Red: Liberation and Solidarity in the Gay and Lesbian Left.* Oakland: University of California Press, 2016.

Hogan, Kristen. "Women's Studies in Feminist Bookstores: 'All the Women's Studies Women Would Come In.'" *Signs: Journal of Women in Culture and Society* 33, no. 3 (2008): 595–621.

Hogan, Wesley C. *Many Minds, One Heart: SNCC's Dream for a New America*. Chapel Hill: University of North Carolina Press, 2007.

Holsaert, Faith S., Martha Prescod Norman Noonan, Judy Richardson, Betty Garman Robinson, Jean Smith Young, and Dorothy M. Zellner, eds. *Hands on the Freedom Plow: Personal Accounts by Women in SNCC*. Chicago: University of Illinois Press, 2010.

Horn, Alice Y. "Unifying Differences: Lesbian of Color Community Building In Los Angeles and New York, 1970s–1980s." Ph.D. diss., Claremont Graduate University, 2011.

Howard, Clayton. *The Closet and the Cul-de-Sac: The Politics of Sexual Privacy in Northern California*. Philadelphia: University of Pennsylvania Press, 2019.

Howard, John. *Men Like That: A Southern Queer History*. Chicago: University of Chicago Press, 1999.

Howe, Florence, ed. *The Politics of Women's Studies: Testimony from Thirty Founding Mothers*. New York: Feminist Press of the City University of New York, 2000.

Howe, Florence. "The Proper Study of Womankind: Women's Studies." In *Sisterhood Is Forever: The Women's Anthology for a New Millennium*, edited by Robin Morgan, 70–84. New York: Washington Square, 2003.

Hunter, Nan D. "Expressive Identity: Recuperating Dissent for Equality." *Harvard Civil Rights–Civil Liberties Law Review* 35, no. 1 (Winter 2000): 1–55.

Hurewitz, Daniel. "Between Liberation and Oppression: Gay Politics and Identity." In *A Companion to California History*, edited by William Deverell and David Igler, 322–38. West Sussex, Eng.: Wiley Blackwell, 2014.

Hurewitz, Daniel. *Bohemian Los Angeles and the Making of Modern Politics*. Berkeley: University of California Press, 2007.

Inglis, Ken. *This Is the ABC*. Carlton, Vic.: Melbourne University Press, 1983.

Johansen, Bruce. "Out of Silence: FREE, Minnesota's First Gay Rights Organization." *Minnesota History* 66, no. 5 (Spring 2019): 186–201.

Johnson, David K. *The Lavender Scare: The Cold War Persecution of Gays and Lesbians in the Federal Government*. Chicago: University of Chicago Press, 2004.

Johnson, E. Patrick. *Sweet Tea: Black Gay Men of the South*. Chapel Hill: University of North Carolina Press, 2008.

Johnson, Phylis A., and Michael C. Keith. *Queer Airwaves: The Story of Gay and Lesbian Broadcasting*. London: Sharpe, 2001.

Johnson, Susan Lee. "'My Own Private Life': Toward a History of Desire in Gold Rush California." *California History* 79, no. 2 (Summer 2000): 316–46.

Katz, Jonathan Ned. *The Invention of Heterosexuality*. New York: Dutton, 1995.

Katz, Jonathan Ned. *Love Stories: Sex between Men before Homosexuality*. Chicago: University of Chicago Press, 2001.

Katz, Sue. "Women's Liberation Explosion at Boston University (1969–70)." *Sixties: A Journal of History, Politics* 7, no. 1 (2014): 77–81.

Kenney, Moira. *Mapping Gay L.A.: The Intersection of Place and Politics*. Philadelphia: Temple University Press, 2001.

Killens, John O. "The Artist and the Black University." *Black Scholar* 1, no. 1 (November 1969): 61–65.

Kimball, Gayle, ed. *Women's Culture: The Women's Renaissance of the Seventies*. Metuchen, N.J.: Scarecrow, 1981.

Kissack, Terence. "Freaking Fag Revolutionaries: New York's Gay Liberation Front, 1969–1971." *Radical History Review* 62 (1995): 104–34.

Kleinberg, Seymour. *Alienated Affections: Being Gay in America*. New York: St. Martin's, 1980.

Koehler, Elizabeth M. "*Healy v. James* and Campus Gay Groups: The Expansion of Associational Freedoms on Campus." *Free Speech Yearbook* 36 (1998): 72–85.

Koskovich, Gerard. "Private Lives, Public Struggles." *Stanford Magazine*, June 1993, 33–40.

Kruse, Kevin M., and Julian E. Zelizer. *Fault Lines: A History of the United States since 1974*. New York: Norton, 2019.

Kunzel, Regina. "Queer History, Mad History, and the Politics of Health." *American Quarterly* 69, no. 2 (2017): 315–19.

Kunzel, Regina. "Review Essay: The Power of Queer History." *American Historical Review* 123, no. 5 (December 2018): 1560–82.

Kutula, Judy. *After Aquarius Dawned: How the Revolutions of the Sixties Became the Popular Culture of the Seventies*. Chapel Hill: University of North Carolina Press, 2017.

Laine, Barry. "Gay Poetry Reaches Adolescence." *Christopher Street* 1, no. 6 (December 1976): 34–42.

Langman, Lauren. "Cycles of Contention: The Rise and Fall of the Tea Party." *Critical Sociology* 38, no. 4 (July 2012): 469–94.

Larkin, Joan, and Elly Bulkin. Prefatory note to *Amazon Poetry: An Anthology of Lesbian Poetry*, edited by Joan Larkin and Elly Bulkin. Brooklyn, N.Y.: Out and Out, 1975.

Lassiter, Matthew D. "Inventing Family Values." In *Rightward Bound: Making America Conservative in the 1970s*, edited by Bruce Schulman and Julian F. Zelizer, 13–28. Cambridge: Harvard University Press, 2008.

Lauter, Paul, and Florence Howe. "What Happened to the 'Free University'?" *Saturday Review*, June 20, 1970, 80–82.

Lehman, J. Lee, ed. *Gays on Campus*. Washington, D.C.: United States National Student Association, 1975.

Leighton, Jared. "'All of Us Are Unapprehended Felons': Gay Liberation, the Black Panther Party, and Intercommunal Efforts against Police Brutality in the Bay Area." *Journal of Social History* 52, no. 3 (2019): 860–85.

Lekus, Ian Keith. "Queer and Present Dangers: Homosexuality and American Anti-War Activism during the Vietnam War." Ph.D. diss., Duke University, 2003.

Liddle, Kathleen. "More Than a Bookstore: The Continuing Relevance of Feminist Bookstores for the Lesbian Community." In *Lesbian Communities: Festivals, RVs, and the Internet*, edited by Esther Rothblum and Penny Sablove, 145–59. Binghamton, N.Y.: Harrington Park Press, 2005.

Liebert, Robert. "The Gay Student: A Psychopolitical View." *Change* 3, no, 6 (October 1971): 38–44.

Lieser, Jordan. "Ronald Reagan's Good University: Rising Conservatism and the 'Berkeley Issue' in the Age of Campus Unrest." *Journal of the West* 59, no. 4 (2020): 11–38.

Litkowski, Thomas. *Free Universities and Learning Referral Centers, 1981*. Washington, D.C.: National Center for Education Statistics, 1983.

Loftin, Craig M. *Masked Voices: Gay Men and Lesbians in Cold War America*. Albany: State University of New York Press, 2012.

Luckenbill, Dan. *With Equal Pride: Gay and Lesbian Studies at UCLA: Catalog of an Exhibit, University Research Library, January–March 1993*. Los Angeles: Department of Special Collections, University Research Library, UCLA, 1993.

MacKay, Anne. *Wolf Girls at Vassar: Lesbian and Gay Experiences, 1930–1990*. New York: St. Martin's, 1993.

Malcolm, David. "A Curious Courage: The Origins of Gay Rights Campaigning in the National Union of Students." *History of Education* 27, no. 1 (2018): 73–86.

Marine, Susan B. *Stonewall's Legacy: Bisexual, Gay, Lesbian and Transgender Students in Higher Education*. Hoboken, N.J.: Wiley, 2011.

Mariposa Film Group, dir. *Word Is Out: Stories of Some of Our Lives*. New Yorker Film Group, 1977.

Mariscal, George. *Brown-Eyed Children of the Sun: Lessons from the Chicano Movement, 1965–1975*. Albuquerque: University of New Mexico Press, 2005.

Marshall, Daniel. "Young Gays: Toward a History of Youth, Queer Sexualities and Education in Australia." *La Trobe Journal* 87 (May 2011): 60–73.

Martin, Robert A. [Stephen Donaldson]. "Student Homophile League: *Founder's Retrospect*." In *Homosexuality in Government, Politics and Prisons*, edited by Wayne Dynes and Stephen Donaldson, 258–61. New York: Garland, 1992.

May, Walter P. "The History of Student Governance in Higher Education." *College Student Affairs Journal* 28, no. 2 (2010): 207–20.

Mayernick, Jason. "The Gay Teachers Association of NYC and LGB Students: 1974–1985." *Teachers College Record* 122, no. 9 (September 2020): 1–30.

McDaniel, Judith. "My Life as the Only Lesbian Professor." In *The Lesbian Path: 37 Lesbian Writers Share Their Personal Experiences, Viewpoints, Traumas, and Jots*, edited by Margaret Cruikshank, 196–202. Monterey, Calif.: Angel Press, 1980. First published as "Is There Room for Me in the Closet? Or, My Life as the Only Lesbian Professor." *Heresies: A Feminist Publication on Art and Politics* 2, no. 3 (Spring 1979): 36–39.

McGirr, Lisa. *Suburban Warriors: The Origins of the New American Right*. Princeton: Princeton University Press, 2001.

McMillian, John. "'Our Founder, the Mimeograph Machine': Participatory Democracy in Students for a Democratic Society's Print Culture." *Journal for the Study of Radicalism* 2, no. 2 (Fall 2008): 85–110.

McMillian, John. *Smoking Typewriters: The Sixties Underground Press and the Rise of Alternative Media in America*. Oxford: Oxford University Press, 2011.

McNaron, Toni. "Poisoned Ivy: Lesbian and Gay Academics from the 1960s through the 1980s." In *Feminist Waves, Feminist Generations: Life Stories from the Academy*, edited by Hokulani K. Aikau, Karla A. Erickson, and Jennifer L. Pierce, 67–86. Minneapolis: University of Minnesota Press, 2007.

Meeker, Martin. *Contacts Desired: Gay and Lesbian Communications and Community, 1940s–1970s*. Chicago: University of Chicago Press, 2005.

Moravec, Michelle. "Toward a History of Feminism, Art, and Social Movements in the United States." *Frontiers* 33, no. 2 (2012): 22–54.

Morris, Bonnie J. "In Their Own Words: Oral Histories of Festival Artists." *Frontiers* 19, no. 2 (1998): 53–71.

Mumford, Kevin J. "The Trouble with Gay Rights: Race and the Politics of Sexual Orientation in Philadelphia, 1969–1982." *Journal of American History* 98, no. 1 (2011): 49–72.

Muñoz, Carlos, Jr. *Youth, Identity, Power: The Chicano Movement*. Rev. and updated ed. New York: Verso, 2007.

Muñoz, Carlos, Jr., and Mario Barrera. "La Raza Unida Party and the Chicano Student Movement in California." *Social Science Journal* 19, no. 2 (April 1982): 101–19.

Murray, Heather. "Free for All Lesbians: Lesbian Cultural Production and Consumption in the United States during the 1970s." *Journal of the History of Sexuality* 16, no. 2 (May 2007): 251–75.

Murray, Heather. *Not in This Family: Gays and the Meaning of Kinship in Postwar North America*. Philadelphia: University of Pennsylvania Press, 2010.

Nash, Margaret A., and Jennifer A. R. Silverman. "'An Indelible Mark': Gay Purges in Higher Education in the 1940s." *History of Education Quarterly* 55, no. 4 (November 2015): 441–59.

Nelson, Jennifer. *More Than Medicine: A History of the Feminist Women's Health Movement*. New York: New York University Press, 2015.

Nguyen, Thai-Huy, and Marybeth Gasman. "Activism, Identity and Service: The Influence of the Asian American Movement on the Educational Experiences of College Students." *History of Education* 44, no. 3 (2015): 339–54.

Nichols, David, and Morris J. Kafka-Hozschlag. "The Rutgers University Lesbian/Gay Alliance, 1969–1989: The First Twenty Years." *Journal of the Rutgers University Libraries* 51, no. 2 (December 1989): 55–95.

"Note: Freedom of Political Association on the Campus: The Right to Official Recognition." *New York University Law Review* 46 (1971): 1149–80.

Oberlin College Alumni Association. *Into the Pink: An Oral History of Lesbian, Gay and Bisexual Students at Oberlin College from 1937–1991*. Oberlin, Ohio: Oberlin College Alumni Association, 1996.

Ormsbee, J. Todd. *The Meaning of Gay: Interaction, Publicity and Community among Homosexual Men in 1960s San Francisco*. Lanham, Md.: Lexington, 2010.

Pelfrey, Patricia. *A Brief History of the University of California*. Berkeley: University of California Press, 2004.

Pellegrini, Ann. "A Gay Purge at Harvard." *Gay and Lesbian Review*, March–April 2003, 10–12.

Porion, Stéphane. "Reassessing a Turbulent Decade: The Historiography of 1970s Britain in Crisis." *Études Anglaises* 69, no. 3 (2016): 301–20.

Prescott, Heather Munroe. "College Mental Health since the Early Twentieth Century." *Harvard Review of Psychiatry* 16, no. 4 (2008): 258–66.

Quin, Kevin C. "'To Stamp Out the Oppression of All Black People': Ron Grayson and the Association of Black Gays, 1975–1979." *Journal of African American History* 104, no. 2 (2019): 227–49.

Quinn, Therese Maura. "Working through Culture: Students and Museum Workers Talk Back." Ed. D. diss., University of Illinois at Chicago, 2001.

Rafferty, Max. "Should Gays Teach School?" *Phi Delta Kappan* 29, no. 2 (October 1977): 91–92.

Reagon, Bernice Johnson. "Coalition Politics: Turning the Century." In *Home Girls: A Black Feminist Anthology*, edited by Barbara Smith, 356–68. New York: Kitchen Table Women of Color Press, 1983.

Reed, T. V. *The Art of Protest: Culture and Activism from the Civil Rights Movement to the Streets of Seattle*. Minneapolis: University of Minnesota Press, 2005.

Reichard, David A. "Animating Ephemera through Oral History: Interpreting Visual Traces of California Gay College Student Organizing from the 1970s." *Oral History Review* 39, no. 1 (Winter–Spring 2012): 37–60.

Reichard, David A. "Behind the Scenes at *The Gayzette*: The Gay Student Union and Queer World Making at UCLA in the 1970s." *Oral History Review* 43, no. 1 (2016): 98–114.

Reichard, David A. "'We Can't Hide and They Are Wrong': The Society for Homosexual

Freedom and the Struggle for Recognition at Sacramento State College, 1969–1971." *Law and History Review* 28, no. 3 (2010): 629–74.

Reti, Irene, ed. *Out in the Redwoods: Documenting Gay, Lesbian, Bisexual and Transgender History at the University of California, Santa Cruz, 1965–2003*. Santa Cruz, Calif.: Regional Oral History Project, 2004.

Retter, Yolanda. "Lesbian (Feminist) Los Angeles, 1970–1990: An Exploratory Ethnohistory." Paper presented at Queer Frontiers, National Lesbian, Gay and Bisexual Student Conference, University of Southern California, March 23–26, 1995. Accessed August 15, 2023. https://web.archive.org/web/20121008211403/http://www.usc.edu/libraries/archives/queerfrontiers/queer/papers/retter.html.

Retter, Yolanda. "On the Side of Angels: Lesbian Activism in Los Angeles, 1970–1990." Ph.D. diss., University of New Mexico, 1999.

Retzloff, Tim. "Outcast, Miscast, Recast: A Documentary History of Lesbians and Gay Men at the University of Michigan." In *From Invisibility to Inclusion: Opening Doors for Lesbians and Gay Men at the University of Michigan*, 110–34. Ann Arbor: Affirmative Action Office, University of Michigan, 1991.

Rhoads, Robert A. *Freedom's Web: Student Activism in an Age of Cultural Diversity*. Baltimore: Johns Hopkins University Press, 1998.

Rhoads, Robert A. "Student Activism, Diversity, and the Struggle for a Just Society." *Journal of Diversity in Higher Education* 9, no. 3 (2016): 189–202.

Richardson, James. *Willie Brown: A Biography*. Berkeley: University of California Press, 1996.

Rivera, Rhonda R. "Our Straight-Laced Judges: The Legal Position of Homosexual Persons in the United States." *Hastings Law Journal* 50, no. 4 (1999): 1015–1178.

Rivers, Daniel Winunuwe. *Radical Relations: Lesbian Mothers, Gay Fathers, and Their Children in the United States since World War II*. Chapel Hill: University of North Carolina Press, 2013.

Robinson, Ken, dir. *Some of Your Best Friends*. San Francisco: Frameline, 1972.

Robinson, Lucy. "Three Revolutionary Years: The Impact of the Counter Culture on the Development of the Gay Liberation Movement in Britain." *Cultural and Social History* 3 (2006): 445–71.

Rofes, Eric. "After California Votes to Limit Marriage: A Call for Direct Action and Civil Disobedience." *Social Policy* 30, no. 4 (Summer 2000): 31–35.

Rogers, Ibram H. [Ibram X. Kendi]. *The Black Campus Movement: Black Students and the Racial Reconstitution of Higher Education, 1965–1972*. New York: Palgrave Macmillan, 2012.

Rohrer, Meghan, and Joseph Plaster, eds. *Vanguard Revisited: The Queer Faith, Sex and Politics of the Youth of San Francisco's Tenderloin*. San Francisco: Wilgefortis, 2016.

Rojas, Fabio. *From Black Power to Black Studies: How a Radical Social Movement Became an Academic Department*. Baltimore: Johns Hopkins University Press, 2007.

Romesburg, Don, ed. *The Routledge History of Queer America*. New York: Routledge, 2018.

Ronner, Amy D. "The Crucible, Harvard's Secret Court, and Homophobic Witch Hunts." *Brooklyn Law Review* 73, no 1 (Fall 2007): 217–98.

Rose, Albin Michael. "Historical Perspectives on the Midwestern Gay and Lesbian Academic Community: Stonewall and the Ivory Tower." Master's thesis, Michigan State University, 1995.

Rose-Mockry, Katherine G. "'We're Here and We're Not Going Away': How the Lawrence Gay Liberation Front Challenged Norms and Changed the Culture for the Gay Community at the University of Kansas in the 1970s." Ph.D. diss., University of Kansas, 2015.

Rosen, Mike. *To Live and Die in Berkeley: A Verse Play in Three Acts*. Berkeley, Calif.: privately printed, 1970.

Ross, Mathew, and Fred Mendelsohn. "Homosexuality in College: A Preliminary Report of Data Obtained from One Hundred Thirty-Three Students Seen in a University Student Heath Service and a Review of Pertinent Literature." *AMA Archives of Neurology and Psychiatry* 80, no. 2 (1958): 253–63.

Roth, Benita. *Separate Roads to Feminism: Black, Chicana, and White Feminist Movements in America's Second Wave*. New York: Cambridge University Press, 2004.

Rothblum, Esther D. "Lesbians in Academia." *NWSA Journal* 7, no. 1 (Spring 1995): 123–30.

Roy, Emilie E. "The Personal Is Historical: The Impact of Lesbian Identity on the Sonoma County Women's Movement and Beyond." Master's thesis, Sonoma State University, 2009.

Rushkin, Kate. "Pat Parker: Creating Room to Speak and Grow." *Sojourner*, October 1985, 28–29.

Ryan, Angela. "Counter College: Third World Students Reimagine Public Higher Education." *History of Education Quarterly* 55, no. 4 (2015): 413–40.

Sahl, Ted. *From Closet to Community: A Quest for Gay and Lesbian Liberation in San José and Santa Clara County*. Campbell, Calif.: Ted Sahl Gallery, 2002.

Sahli, Nancy. "Smashing: Women's Relationships before the Fall." *Chrysalis* 8 (Summer 1979): 17–27.

Salper, Roberta. "San Diego State 1970: The Initial Year of the Nation's First Women's Studies Program." *Feminist Studies* 37, no. 3 (2011): 656–82.

Sanlo, Ronni L. "The Lavender Leader: An Inqueery into Lesbian, Gay, Bisexual, and Transgender Student Leadership." In *Developing Non-Hierarchical Leadership on Campus: Case Studies and Best Practices in Higher Education*, edited by Charles L. Outcalt, Shannon K. Faris, and Kathleen N. McMahon, 211–21. Westport, Conn.: Greenwood, 2000.

Schacter, Jane. "Sexual Orientation, Change and the Courts." *Drake Law Review* 54, no. 4 (Summer 2006): 861–83.

Schiavi, Michael. *Celluloid Activist: The Life and Times of Vito Russo*. Madison: University of Wisconsin Press, 2011.

Schulman, Bruce J. "Islands in Time; Or, How I Learned to Stop Worrying and Love the Decade." *Reviews in American History* 49, no. 2 (2021): 322–37.

Schulman, Bruce J. *The Seventies: The Great Shift in American Culture, Society and Politics*. New York: Free Press, 2001.

Schulman, Bruce J., and Julian E. Zelizer, eds. *Rightward Bound: Making the American Conservative in the 1970s*. Cambridge: Harvard University Press, 2008.

Scott, Craig. "Lust, Language, and Legislation: Long Beach California 1914." *Ex Post Facto* 19 (Spring 2010): 93–101.

Scott, James C. *Weapons of the Weak: Everyday Forms of Peasant Resistance*. New Haven: Yale University Press, 1985.

Sears, Clare. *Arresting Dress: Cross-Dressing, Law and Fascination in Nineteenth-Century San Francisco*. Durham: Duke University Press, 2015.

Sears, James T. *Behind the Mask of the Mattachine: The Hal Call Chronicles and the Early Movement for Homosexual Emancipation*. New York: Harrington Park, 2006.

Sears, James T. *Lonely Hunters: An Oral History of Lesbian and Gay Southern Life, 1948–1968*. Boulder, Colo.: Westview, 1997.

Sears, James T. *Rebels, Rubyfruit and Rhinestones: Queering Space in the Stonewall South*. New Brunswick, N.J.: Rutgers University Press, 2001.

Secor, Cynthia. "Lesbians: The Doors Open." *Change: The Magazine of Higher Learning* 7, no. 1 (1975): 13–17.

Self, Robert O. *American Babylon: Race and the Struggle for Postwar Oakland*. Princeton: Princeton University Press, 2005.

Self, Robert O. "Sex in the City: The Politics of Sexual Liberalism in Los Angeles, 1963–1979." *Gender and History* 20, no. 2 (August 2008): 288–311.

Shaffer, Jay C. "Students in the Policy Process." *Journal of Higher Education* 41, no. 5 (May 1970): 341–49.

Shah, Nayan. *Stranger Intimacy: Contesting Race, Sexuality, and the Law in the North American West*. Berkeley: University of California Press, 2011.

Shand-Tucci, Douglass. *The Crimson Letter: Harvard, Homosexuality, and the Shaping of American Culture*. New York: St. Martin's, 2003.

Shepard, Benjamin. "Play as World-Making: From the Cockettes to the Germs, Gay Liberation to DIY Community Building." In *The Hidden 1970s: Histories of Radicalism*, edited by Dan Berger, 177–94. New Brunswick, N.J.: Rutgers University Press, 2010.

Sides, Josh. *Erotic City: Sexual Revolutions and the Making of Modern San Francisco*. New York: Oxford University Press, 2009.

Sides, Josh. "Sexual Revolutions and Sexual Politics." In *A Companion to California History*, edited by William Deverell and David Igler, 416–27. West Sussex, Eng.: Wiley Blackwell, 2014.

Silverman, Victor, and Susan Stryker, dirs. *Screaming Queens: The Riot at Compton's Cafeteria*. San Francisco: Frameline, 2005.

Slonecker, Blake. "The Columbia Coalition: African-Americans, New Leftists, and Counterculture at the Columbia University Protest of 1968." *Journal of Social History* 41, no. 4 (2008): 967–96.

Smallwood, Andrew P. "The Intellectual Creativity and Public Discourse of Malcolm X: A Precursor to the Modern Black Studies Movement." *Journal of Black Studies* 36, no. 2 (2005): 248–63.

Snyder, Thomas D., and Charlene M. Hoffman. *State Comparisons of Education Statistics, 1969–70 to 1996–97*. Washington, D.C.: U.S. Department of Education, Office of Educational Research and Improvement, National Center for Education Statistics, 1998.

Smith, Freda. "Dear Dora / Dangerous Derek Diesel Dyke." In *Dear Dora / Dangerous Derek Diesel Dyke*. Sacramento, Calif.: Suzy Seeker Press, 1973. Also published in *Lesbian Tide*, April 1973, 15–17.

Smith, Freda. "Dear Dora, Dangerous Derek Diesel Dyke." YouTube, September 28, 2015. https://www.youtube.com/watch?v=mjdweIsodbI.

Soldatenko, Michael. *Chicano Studies: The Genesis of a Discipline*. Tucson: University of Arizona Press, 2009.

Sprung, Jerry. *Rutgers Conference on Gay Liberation*. New York: National Task Force on Student Personnel and Homosexuality, 1972.

Staggenborg, Suzanne. "Social Movement Communities and Cycles of Protest: The Emergence and Maintenance of a Local Women's Movement." *Social Problems* 45, no. 2 (May 1998): 180–204.

Staley, Kathryn. "Gay Liberation Comes to Appalachian State University, 1969–1979." *Appalachian Journal* 39, nos. 1–2 (Fall 2011–Winter 2012): 72–91.

Stanley, William R. "The Rights of Gay Student Organizations." *Journal of College and University Law* 10, no. 3 (1983): 397–418.

Stein, Marc. *City of Sisterly and Brotherly Loves: Lesbian and Gay Philadelphia, 1945–1972*. Philadelphia: Temple University Press, 2004.

Stein, Marc. *Rethinking the Gay and Lesbian Movement*. 2nd ed. New York: Routledge, 2023.

Stein, Marc. "Students, Sodomy, and the State: LGBT Campus Struggles in the 1970s." *Law and Social Inquiry* 48, no. 2 (2022): 531–60.

Stein, Marc. "Teaching and Researching the History of Sexual Politics at San Francisco State, 1969–1970. *California History* 98, no. 4 (2021): 2–29.

Stewart-Winter, Timothy. *Queer Clout: Chicago and the Rise of Gay Politics*. Philadelphia: University of Pennsylvania Press, 2016.

Streitmatter, Rodger. *Unspeakable: The Rise of the Gay and Lesbian Press in America*. Boston: Faber & Faber, 1995.

Stryker, Susan. *Transgender History: The Roots of Today's Revolution*. Rev. ed. New York: Seal, 2017.

Sueyoshi, Amy. "Redefining Higher Education: Reflection on Queer Ethnic Studies." *Ethnic Studies Review* 42, no. 2 (2019): 225–31.

Suran, Justin David. "Coming Out against the War: Antimilitarism and the Politicization of Homosexuality in the Era of Vietnam." *American Quarterly* 53, no. 3 (2001): 452–88.

Sweat, Jeffrey Wayne. "Crossing Boundaries: Identity and Activism in Gay-Straight Alliances." Ph.D. diss., University of California, Davis, 2004.

Syrett, Nicholas L. "The Boys of Beaver Meadow: A Homosexual Community at 1920s Dartmouth College." *American Studies* 48, no. 2 (2007): 9–18.

Syrett, Nicholas L. *Company He Keeps: A History of White College Fraternities*. Chapel Hill: University of North Carolina Press, 2009.

Teal, Donn. *The Gay Militants*. New York: Stein and Day, 1971.

Tijerina-Revilla, Anita. "Are All Raza Womyn Queer? An Exploration of Sexual Identity in a Chicana/Latina Student Organization." *NWSA Journal* 21, no. 3 (Fall 2009): 46–62.

Trine, Mari Kimberly. "The Politics of Pleasure: Sexuality in Radical Movements for Liberation and the Women's Liberation Movement, 1968–1975." Ph.D. diss., University of Minnesota, 2000.

Trow, Katherine Bernhardi. *Habits of Mind: The Experimental College Program at Berkeley*. Berkeley, Calif.: Institute of Governmental Studies, 1988.

Turner, Jeffrey A. *Sitting In and Speaking Out: Student Movements in the American South, 1960–1970*. Athens: University of Georgia Press, 2010.

Ullman, Sharon R. *Sex Seen: The Emergence of Modern Sexuality in America*. Berkeley: University of California Press, 1997.

Ullman, Sharon R. "'The Twentieth Century Way': Female Impersonation and Sexual Practice in Turn-of-the-Century America." *Journal of the History of Sexuality* 5, no. 4 (1995): 573–600.

Umemoto, Karen. "'On Strike!': San Francisco State College Strike, 1968–69: The Role of Asian-American Students." *Amerasia Journal* 15, no. 1 (1989): 3–41.

Uyeda, Ann Yuri. "All at Once, All Together: One Asian American Lesbian's Account of the 1989 Pacific Lesbian Network Retreat." In *The Very Inside: An Anthology of Writing by Asian and Pacific Islander Lesbian and Bisexual Women*, edited by Sharon Lim-Hing, 109–21. Toronto: Sister Vision, 1994.

Van Dyke, Nella. "Crossing Movement Boundaries: Factors That Facilitate Coalition Protest by American College Students, 1930–1990." *Social Problems* 50, no. 2 (2003): 226–50.

Van Dyke, Nella, and Ronda Cress. "Political Opportunities and Collective Identity." *Sociological Perspectives* 49, no. 4 (2009): 503–26.

Van Dyke, Nella, and Holly J. McCammon, eds. *Strategic Alliances: Coalition Building and Social Movements*. Minneapolis: University of Minnesota Press, 2010.

Vázquez, Irene E. "Black and Brown Tumbling the Walls Together: African Americans and Mexican Americans Accessing Higher Education through Intersectoral Points of Contact and Interactions." *Kalfou* 2, no. 1 (Spring 2015): 71–87.

Verge, Arthur. "World War II." In *A Companion to California History*, edited by William Deverell and David Igler, 311–21. West Sussex, Eng.: Wiley Blackwell, 2014.

Vida, Ginny, ed. *Our Right to Love: A Lesbian Resource Book*. Englewood Cliffs, N.J.: Prentice-Hall, 1978.

Walters, David Martin [pseud.]. *Homophiles of Penn State*. New York: National Task Force on Student Personnel and Homosexuality, 1972.

Ward, Michael, and Mark Freeman. "Defending Gay Rights: The Campaign against the Briggs Amendment in California." *Radical America* 13, no. 4 (September 1979): 11–26.

Warner, Michael. "Publics and Counterpublics." *Public Culture* 14, no. 1 (Winter 2002): 49–90.

Waters, Rob. "He's Still Rising." *SF State Magazine*, Spring–Summer 2017. https://magazine.sfsu.edu/archive/archive/spr-17/along-came-jones.html.

Weiler, Kathleen. "The Case of Martha Deane: Sexuality and Power at Cold War UCLA." *History of Education Quarterly* 47, no. 4 (November 2007): 470–96.

Werner, Steve. "The Gay Student Group." In *Gays on Campus*, edited by J. Lee Lehman, 29–33. Washington, D.C.: United States National Student Association, 1975.

White, C. Todd. *Pre-Gay L.A.: A Social History of the Movement for Homosexual Rights*. Urbana: University of Illinois Press, 2009.

Whitt, Jan. "A 'Labor from the Heart': Lesbian Magazines from 1947–1994." *Journal of Lesbian Studies* 5, nos. 1–2 (2001): 229–51.

Whittington, Gale Chester. *Beyond Normal: The Birth of Gay Pride*. 2010. E-book.

Wilk, Rona M. "'What's a Crush?' A Study of Crushes and Romantic Friendships at Barnard College, 1900–1920." *OAH Magazine of History* 18, no. 4 (July 2004): 20–22.

Wilson, Jennifer. "'I'm Not a Man. I Don't Want to Destroy You': Tolstoy College and LGBTQ Studies in the Vietnam War Era." *Journal of Social History* 52, no. 4 (Summer 2019): 1355–76.

Wright, William. *Harvard's Secret Court: The Savage 1920 Purge of Campus Homosexuals*. New York: St. Martin's, 2005.

Yeager, Ken. "Wiggsy Sivertsen." Queer Silicon Valley. Accessed January 4, 2022. https://www.queersiliconvalley.org/wiggsy-sivertsen/.

Zelnik, Reginald, and Robert Cohen. *The Free Speech Movement: Reflections on Berkeley in the 1960s*. Berkeley: University of California Press, 2002.

Zimmerman, Bonnie. "A Lesbian-Feminist Journey through Queer Nation." *Journal of Lesbian Studies* 11, nos. 1–2 (2007): 37–52. Also published in *Twenty-First Century Lesbian Studies*, edited by Noreen Giffney and Katherine O'Donnell, 37–52. New York: Harrington Park, 2007.

INDEX

Abbott, Steve, 62
ACLU: Cal Poly San Luis Obispo, 123n66, 123n69; Cal State Fullerton, 34; Cal State Long Beach, 52; Fullerton College, 34; general legal support, 122n64; attorney Jay Murley, 34, 36, 52, 119n16, 123n65; Sacramento State College, 36; San José State College, 34; Women's Caucus, 54
administrators, 10; as allies to students, 59; experimental colleges, 41; general resistance to LGBT student activists, 7, 11, 27, 29–30; official recognition of student groups, 28; publicity, 31; Sacramento State College, 36; Stanford, 92; UC Berkeley, 24, 28; UCLA, 25, 28
Advocate: archival access, 109n15; critique of campus organizations, 85; critique of GSU, 124n77; Leo Laurence, 14, 27, 36, 116n1, 159n74
African American civil rights movement, 8, 75, 98
Alamilla Boyd, Nan, 3
All in the Family, 11, 107n69, 107n71
Alliance of Black Gays, 57
alliances, 146n3; challenges faced, 81–82; cross-campus, 4–6, 74–75, 84; leadership and organizing experience, 77–78; peer mentoring, 79–80; political work, 81; racialized and gendered experiences, 83, 152n80. *See also* coalitions
allies, 75, 86, 123n65; faculty, 46, 52; graduate students, 44; organizing, 1–2, 7, 12, 28–29, 98, 157n47; Proposition 6, 94–95; Sacramento City College, 68–69; West Los Angeles College, 16; women's centers, 17
Anderson, Wendell, 13
Angels of Light, 70–71
anti-cross-dressing laws, 3
anti-war movement, 2, 5; teach-ins, 41; organizing, 98, 158n66

Asian American students, 23, 112n60, 113n64. *See also* students of color
Asian American studies, 41; experimental college, 128n49
Associated Students: Bakersfield College, 32; Cal Poly San Luis Obispo, 32, 34, 123n68; Cal State Fullerton, 32; Cal State Long Beach, 57–58, 90, 156n36; Cal State Northridge, 90; City College of San Francisco, 149n24; Los Angeles City College, 15; Sacramento State College, 46, 90, 118n11, 132n92, 156n35; San Francisco State College, 17, 44; San José State, 32, 90, 121n46; UC Berkeley, 21, 91, 146n83; UC Santa Barbara, 90; University of Southern California, 32. *See also* student government
Association of Black Gays, 158n62
attorneys, 28, 34–35, 52, 121n46, 123n66
Aura, Jan, 19, 44, 71; Jan Field, 129n56, 134n22, 138n69
awareness weeks, 6, 55–56, 59; Gay Awareness Weeks, 55, 85; Gay and Lesbian Awareness Weeks, 55, 138n72; Gay Pride Day, 56, 138n73, 139n78, 145n77; Women's Weeks, 54–55

backlash, 5, 85, 139n78, 153n1; Ken Boegert, 32; Jim Hull, 32; Mike Ruskovich, 32–33; against transsexual performer Beth Elliott, 143n46; Thomas Weissbluth, 33, 122n54
Bailey, Beth, 2
Bakersfield College, 120n33; Associated Students, 32; *Renegade Rip*, 110n31; student organizing, 16, 28–29
ballot initiatives, 94
bars, clubs and coffeehouses, 3, 24, 61, 67, 143n38, 147n6; dating, 14, 61; harassment, 39, 123n65; organizing, 8, 19, 22, 34–35, 113n65, 117n8, 140n9; police raids, 3, 106n52

179

Bay Area Coalition against the Briggs Initiative, 95, 160n91; Cleve Jones, 95
Bay Area Reporter (BAR), 56, 151n65, 159n73; archival access, 108n10
Beardsley, Scott, 21, 25, 113n67
Bell, Jonathan, 4–5
Benemann, William, vii, 163
Bennett, Paula, 62, 141n11, 141n16
Berkeley Barb, 13; archival access, 108n7
Berkeley Gazette, archival access, 109n13
Berkeley Tribe, archival access, 153n6
Berlandt, Konstantin, 67, 154n21
Bernard, Larry, 29–30, 33, 47, 74, 122n58
bisexuality: as educational program topic, 37, 53; participation in GPUs and GSUs, 7, 19, 22, 25, 34, 114n91, 116n114; exclusion from other organizing spaces, 9, 17–18, 32, 83
Black Cat, 3
Black Panther Party, 148n17
Black Power movements, 2–4, 42
Black students, 8, 23, 105n44, 112n62, 152n80; Cal State Long Beach, 49; Larry Duplechan, 20, 98–99, 143n42, 154n17; El Camino College, 55; Los Angeles City College, 20, 48; San Francisco State College, 23, 128n48; UC Berkeley, 67; UCLA, 71, 80. *See also* Association of Black Gays; students of color
Black Students Unions, 90, 92, 156n42; UC Santa Barbara, 90
Black studies, 41–42, 132n92
Blackburn, John, 23, 57, 111n51, 114n87, 139n91
Blanco, Cesar, 38
Blumenfeld, Warren, 5; National Gay Student Center, 18, 28, 37, 76, 116n1, 121n44; LGBT student organizing, 22, 118n11
Boneberg, Paul, 95, 97, 160n7; "Diamond Hard Words," 65
Bottini, Ivy, 54, 57
Briggs, John, 5, 30, 34, 56, 94–95; California Assembly, 34, 56; debate with Harvey Milk, 95
Briggs Initiative, 5, 94; against gay rights, 7, 24; Anita Bryant, 7, 24, 56, 69; California Conference to Defeat the Briggs Initiative, 95; campaign against, 27, 94–95. *See also* Proposition 6
Broshears, Rev. Ray, 35
Brown, Jerry, 94
Brown, Rita Mae, 52, 54, 58, 60
Bryant, Barbara, 153n4, 159n68; Sacramento State College, 44, 46, 51, 93, 98, 111n37; UC Berkeley, 6, 21, 98

Burns, Hobert, 29, 31, 44, 46, 51, 93, 98, 111n37
Butz, Otto, 30, 118n11, 119n19
Byrd, Greg, 14

California Aggie (UC Davis), 146n4; archival access, 127n38
California Association of Gay Student Organizations (CAGSO), 77–78, 80, 151n53; Ron Norman, 83–84
California Association of Sex Educators, Tye Ray, 39
California Polytechnic State University, San Luis Obispo (Cal Poly San Luis Obispo, Cal Poly SLO), 77, 124n77; Associated Students, 32, 34, 123n68; Everett Chandler, 29, 120n35; President Robert Christensen, 36, 129n49–129n50; Marianne Doshi, 32; Pete Evans, 32; Gerald Jones, 33; recognition legal cases, 34
California State Fullerton (Cal State Fullerton): ACLU, 34; Associated Students, 32; Bob Gardner, 56; *Daily Titan*, 33, 120n26; experimental college, 41; Gay Awareness Week, 55; Jay Murley, 34, 119n16, 123n65; recognition legal cases, 30, 34, 36, 119n19; Donald Shields, 30, 33–34, 36, 121n45
California State Long Beach (Cal State Long Beach, CSU Long Beach): Associated Students, 57–58, 90, 156n36; Black Students, 49; "Celestial Hop" and "Roll Me Over in the Clover Rock" dances, 23; Gay Awareness Week, 55–56, 143n41, 145n74; Gay Pride Week, 135n42, 139n94; Halloween dance on the *Queen Mary*, 23, 71; Lee Mentley, 14, 72, 110n22, 146n82. *See also* Forty Niner/49er/Daily 49er
California State Los Angeles (Cal State Los Angeles), 15, 109n20, 135n42; dances, 71; experimental college, 41; *University Times*, 109n20
California State Northridge (Cal State Northridge, CSU Northridge, CSUN), 41, 50–51, 127n39, 150n46; *Daily Sundial*, 109n21; experimental college, 41; Gay '70s Dance, 23; GSU, 90, 94.
California legislature, 72
California State University Chancellor's office, 34, 120n37, 128n48
camaraderie among organizers, 74
campus-based student organizations, 27, 118n11, 146n4, 150n46
campus newspapers, 10, 15, 18–19, 21, 29,

180   INDEX

107n69; letters to the editor, 15, 27, 57; opposition to LGBT students, 48, 88; support for LGBT students, 16, 32, 48–49, 61, 67, 87, 94, 132n97
Capron, Bear, 13, 108n7
Carolina Gay Association at University of North Carolina, Chapel Hill, 105n44
Carpenter, Edgar, 68
Cash, Dave, 21, 50, 91
Chavez, Marisela, 141n12
Chicana/Chicano students, 49, 55, 141n12, 150n32; Alternative Coalition, 90–91. *See also* students of color
Chicano studies, 41, 132n92
Chicano movement, 2, 141n12
Chico Wildcat (Chico State University), archival access, 110n33
Christian: colleges, 2, 31, 107n68; student organizing, 122n54
City College of San Francisco, 57, 77, 149n23–149n24, 152n71
civil rights, 5–6, 8, 157n47; American Psychiatric Association, 134n20; legislation, 49; movement, 82; programs and presentations about, 39, 56, 81
coalitions, 35, 75, 83, 90, 146n3, 151n65; coalition building, 152n80. *See also* alliances
Coalition for Human Rights, 95
Cockettes, 70, 72, 146n82
Cold War, 3, 7–8, 106n53
Coley, Jonathan, 107n68
collectives and caucuses, 2, 14, 17–18, 74–75, 133n11, 157n43; ACLU Women's Caucus, 54; CAGSO, 151n53; Chico State University, 83; collective defense, 4; Gay Caucus of the Gay Studies Board, 157n43; Gay Caucus of the National Student Association, 75–76; Northern Caucus of the California Coalition of Gay and Lesbian Student Organizations, 152n79; Sacramento State College Women's Caucus, 15, 90; San Francisco State University's Symposium '76, 56; San José State Lesbian Caucus, 19; Stanford Women's Caucus, 71, 83, 114n91, 135n41, 136n48, 153n10; Charles Thorp, 148n17; UC Berkeley, 53, 136n48; UC Davis, 83; UCLA, 134n22; UC Santa Barbara Women's Caucus, 50; USC, 80; young organizers, 147n10. *See also* Men's Collective; Women's Collective
College of the Redwoods, 28
College of the Sequoias, 28, 30

Collegian (Los Angeles City College), 48, 109n17, 133n4; archival access, 109n15. *See also* Jackson Smith
Collins, John J., 16, 120n33
Columbia University, 130n72; coalition building, 152n80; "gay lounge," 114n81; gay students' experiences, 130n72; Student Homophile League, 13, 75, 107n2
coming out, 1, 24–25, 61, 79, 116n114; family response, 20; letter in school paper, 122n62; poetry, 63–64; UC Santa Barbara program, 50, 134n18. *See also* National March on Washington for Lesbian and Gay Rights
Committee for Homosexual Freedom, 4, 8, 14, 109n13, 159n74
community activism: allies, 31, 75, 80; Cal Poly San Luis Obispo, 35; Cal State Long Beach, 53; Cal State Los Angeles, 57; grassroots organizing, 5–6, 92–93; speakers' bureaus, 50–51; Stanford, 25–26; UC Berkeley, 86–87; UCLA, 43, 55, 78; women's studies programs, 44
community colleges, 24, 30, 55, 68, 150n33; archives, 10; Bakersfield College, 16, 28–29, 32, 120n33; City College of San Francisco, 57, 77, 149n23–149n24, 152n71; demographics, 106n62; El Camino College, 55, 78, 148n21, 155n33; Foothill Community College, 24; Fullerton College, 28; Lone Mountain College, 70, 77, 149n24; Los Angeles City College (LACC), 109n17; organizing, 21, 153n3; Sacramento City College, 55, 68–69, 77, 144n56; West Los Angeles College, 16, 18. *See also* junior colleges
Compton's Cafeteria, 3
conferences, 6, 75, 94; confabs, 55, 78–79; 1971 Conference on Gay Liberation, 75; Jeanne Córdova, 143n46; East Coast Homophile Organization and the North American Conference of Homophile Organizations, 147n6; Gay Academic Union, 55–57, 146n2; Gaythink, West Coast Conference, 149n26; North American Conference of Homophile Organizations, 148n17; Rutgers Student Homophile League, 75, 147n7; Southeastern Regional Conference, 147n8; Southern California GSUs, 150n30; Stanford GPU, 150n43; UC Irvine, 148n19; UCLA, 143n46; youth participation, 147n10. *See also* awareness weeks
consciousness-raising, 38–39, 49, 125n7, 158n62
Cole, Shaun, 69, 145n61

INDEX 181

Cooper, Shelly, 49, 51–52, 135n30
Corbin, Arthur, 22, 93
Córdova, Jeanne, 43, 143n46
Corrigan, Theresa, 17, 44–45
Council on Religion and the Homosexual, 3
counselors and counseling centers, 20, 25, 150n42. *See also* peer counseling
Crawford, Jesse, 15
creative expression, 14, 60–61, 67, 69, 73, 140n6
creative writing, 62, 70. *See also* poetry
Cronenwalt, Steve, 51, 70
Crookshanks, Ivan, 30
CSU Long Beach. *See* Cal State Long Beach
CSU Los Angeles (CSULA). *See* Cal State Los Angeles
CSU Monterey Bay, 11
CSU Northridge (CSUN). *See* Cal State Northridge
curriculum, 2, 40; changes and reform, 37, 42–44, 48, 85, 125n4, 131n81; women's studies, 45. *See also* experimental colleges

Daily Bruin (UCLA), 19–20, 49–50, 55, 83, 87, 115n108, 126n21–126n22; archival access, 108n10; Richard Gollance, 40–41, 127n34
Daily Californian (UC Berkeley), 86, 88; archival access, 110n33
Daily Claremont Collegian, 151n48
Daily Nexus (UC Santa Barbara), archival access, 110n26
Daily Sundial (Cal State Northridge), archival access, 109n21
Daily Titan (Cal State Fullerton), 33; archival access, 120n26
Daily Trojan (USC): archival access, 117n8; Gay Liberation Forum, 33; Del Whan letter, 122n62
dances and dancing, 6, 9, 114n94; Cal State Long Beach, 71, 145n74; Cal State Los Angeles, 71; community and campus ties, 52; drag and/or genderfuck, 70; political, 24, 85, 94–95; Vito Russo, 58–59; Sacramento State College, 90, 110n36, 135n42; San Francisco State University, 56, 71; San José State Lesbian Feminist Alliance, 24; space for, 16, 140n9; UC Berkeley, 71, 145n77; UCLA Lesbian Sisterhood, 54–55; USC, 35, 69, 94–95; West Coast Lesbian Conference, 138n69; women organizers, 23, 68
Daughters of Bilitis (DOB) 3, 8–9; "Blanche Baker Memorial Scholarship," 8; Rita Mae Brown, 52, 54, 58, 60; Sally Gearhart, 45, 54, 60, 95, 130n76; Phyllis Lyon, 53, 60; Del Martin, 53–54, 60
D'Emilio, John, 7, 104n9, 106n52, 109n14, 125n4, 146n2, 147n6, 155n31
demands for LGBT related courses, 41, 75, 105n40, 147n10
Democratic Party, 5
denials of recognition, 2, 28–29, 31–36, 86, 98, 123n66. *See also* recognition legal cases
Dilley, Patrick, 105n38, 105n40, 107n68, 114n94, 147n8
DiLuzio, Giovanni, 18
discrimination, 92–93, 154n20, 158n54; GSU membership, 32, 89, 91–93, 97; protection from, 4, 78, 80, 89, 91–93, 97. *See also* homophobia
DIY (do-it-yourself): education, 37, 85, 87, 98; healthcare practices, 125n3; library, 40; posting flyers and tabling, 48; raps, 39
Doshi, Marianne, 32
Doty, Andrew, 13
drag; dances and Halloween parties, 23, 71, 145n74; Betty Luther Hillman, 69–70; Tede Mathews, 71; Todd Ormsbee, 69, 145n61; *The Gay Follies*, 70
drag ball, 3, 107n71
Duberman, Martin, 4, 155n31
Dumke, Chancellor Glenn, 24, 31, 33, 120n37
Duplechan, Larry, 20, 98–99, 143n42, 154n17; *Optimistic Voices*, 67; UCLA GSU, 22, 71, 87–88, 114n84
Dykes on Parade, 68, 144n50. *See also* Le Theatre Lesbien
Dymally, Mervyn, 94

El Camino College, 55, 78, 148n21, 155n33
electoral politics, 5
Erickson, Glenn, 14, 133n11, 149n26
ethnic studies, 5; demands for, 42, 75; experimental college at UCLA, 42
Evans, Pete, 32
experimental colleges, 41, 127n39–127n40; advertisement for, 129n55, 129n59; Dave Allison, 42; Asian American studies, 128n49; Martha Biondi, 42; Black communities, 128n48; budget, 128n40; Cal State Fullerton, 41; Cal State Los Angeles, 41; Cal State Northridge, 41; courses, 42, 45, 120n23, 128n47–128n49, 129n58; Jeanne Córdova, 43; LGBT organizing, 6, 37, 41–43; Rosalio

182 INDEX

Muñoz, 42; San Francisco State University, 41–43, 127n40, 128n47–128n48; San José State College, 41; student-run, 6, 37, 127n40; UC Berkeley, 41; UC Davis, 41; UCLA, 42, 129n55; USC Gay Liberation Forum, 120n23; women's studies, 6, 127n38
Express (Sacramento City College), 138n73

faculty: advisers, 11, 16, 20, 25, 29, 48, 57; critiques about organizing, 147n8; Barry Dank (Cal State Long Beach), 127n33; Gay Academic Union, 19, 146n2, 148n21; LGBT faculty promoting curriculum reform, 6–7, 125n4, 132n94, 133n9, 148n19, 158n67, 159n74; Sacramento State College Society for Homosexual Freedom, 18; Sacramento State College Women's Caucus, 15; Student Homophile League, 13, 75, 107n11; support for Students for Gay Power, 157n47; targeted as subversive, 8; Del Whan letter, 122n62
Farber, David, 2, 104n10
feminism: as liberation struggle, 4, 158n67; conservative backlash against, 5; drag, 71–72; and gay rights discourse, 18, 56, 71–72, 153n4; Gay Students Coalition of San Francisco, 71; Sugie Goen-Salter, 44, 98, 158n67; poetry and expression, 141n12; Sacramento State College Society for Homosexual Freedom, 18; Sacramento State College Women's Studies program, 45–46; women's studies programs, 43–44. *See also* lesbian feminism
Fertig, Jack, 21, 72
film, 6, 37, 81, 135n42, 137n53, 141n10; Nancy Adair, 53; *The Laughing Policeman*, 80; Vito Russo, 58; screenings, 52–53; *Some Of Your Best Friends*, 53, 118n9; 135n42; 137n54; 150n33; *Word Is Out*, 53, 137n55
Florida, 2; University of, 155n31
Foothill Community College, 24
Forty Niner/49er/Daily 49er (Cal State Long Beach), 145n74, 156n36; archival access, 111n43; Shelly Cooper, 135n30; *Gay Power . . . Can Accomplish a Lot!*, 133n14; Gay Awareness Week, 143n41; Gay Pride Week, 139n94; Masquerade Dance, 145n74
Frances, Harriette, "Not Who I Am," 63
fraternity brothers, 8
freedom, 21, 58, 83; Scott Beardsley, 21; in loco parentis surveillance, 98; in poetry, 64, 73; in theater, 67; Charles Thorp, 62. *See also* liberation
Fullerton College, 28; recognition legal cases, 34

Gallo, Marcia, 8
Gay Activist Alliance, 49
Gay Blue Jeans Days, 89, 155n28, 155n31
Gay Community Services Center, 14, 39, 113n67, 116n109; Morris Kight, 39, 50, 89, 122n62, 136n50
gay student organizing, 36, 122n54
gay and lesbian liberalism, 4
gay and lesbian movement, 2, 74–75, 84, 152n70; California's LGBT college student organizing, 1, 7, 36, 86–88, 93–94, 98; terminology, 107n65
Gay Academic Union, 111n51, 139n85, 146n2, 148n21;; San Francisco State, 19, 54, 56, 114n87, 125n4
Gay Awareness Weeks. *See* awareness weeks
Gay and Lesbian Alliance at UC Santa Cruz, 95
Gay Liberation at Sacramento State College (SSC), "gay orientation," 39
Gay Liberation Forum at USC, 28, 40, 117n8–117n9, 120n23, 122n62; Larry Bernard, 29–30; denial of recognition, 29–30, 32–33, 119n20; "gay college dance"; legal counsel, 34–35; Sal Licata, 40; Randy Schrader, 14, 29, 53
Gay Liberation Front (GLF) in Los Angeles, 4, 14–15, 109n15; Morris Kight, 39, 50, 54, 89, 122n62
Gay Liberation Front (GLF) in Berkeley, 67, 86
Gay Liberation Front (GLF) at Sacramento State College, 52. *See also* Society for Homosexual Freedom
Gay Liberation Front (GLF) at San Francisco State College, 4, 14, 62, 110n22
Gay Liberation Front (GLF) at San José State College: advertising controversy, 88; Warren Blumenfeld, 28, 37, 76; Hobert Burns, 31, 119n19, 120n37, 120n39, 121n41; legal counsel, 121n46, 122n66; Robert Martin, 119n19; Ronald Reagan, 30–31, 115n100; *Vector*; Zelima Williams, 20, 88, 158n66; Paul Wysocki, 21. *See also* Gay Student Union (GSU) at San José State College
Gay Peoples Union (GPU) at CSU Chico, 25, 89; "Gay Switchboard," 24–25

INDEX 183

Gay People's Union (GPU) at Sacramento City College: Robert Lynch, 68–69

Gay People's Alliance of Western Washington University, 25, 116n114

Gay People's Union (GPU) at Stanford: Scott Beardsley, 21, 25, 113n67; Benefit Gay Show, 24; Arthur Corbin, 22, 111n44; goals, 37–38; Michael Hughes, 37; Lesbian Collective, 18; James Mitchell, 37; office in the Old Firehouse, 22; peer counseling, 25; Richard Thomas, 40, 92–93; "women's nights," 25

Gay Pride: Committee for Homosexual Freedom, 4; CSU Long Beach Week, 55, 57–58, 67, 139n94; Los Angeles City College Week, 20; Sacramento Parade, 69; San José State College Day, 56, 139n78; Stanford GPU goals, 37–38; Stanford Week, 56, 79, 145n69; UC Berkeley, 145n77; UC Santa Barbara Week, 140n98. *See also* awareness weeks

gay rights: ACLU, 123n65, 150n35; backlash against, 85; ballot initiative, 94; blue jeans in support of, 89; CAGSO, 80; and gay awareness weeks, 69; mental illness stigma, 135n41; National March on Washington for Lesbian and Gay Rights, 2, 27, 97; protest for, 92; opposition to Vietnam War, 93; and students of color, 105n44. *See also* human rights

Gay Sisterhood (UCLA), 19, 43, 55, 112n58, 138n69; Jan Aura, 19, 44, 71. *See also* Lesbian Sisterhood

Gay Students Coalition of the San Francisco Bay Area (GSCSF), 77, 81–82, 84, 151n65, 152n71; Jan Aura, 19, 44, 71; "Coming Out on Campus" workshop, 79; participation of women, 82; social events, 80–81, 145n74

Gay Students Council of Southern California (GSC), 47, 74–75, 151n48; Larry Bernard, 29–30, 33, 47, 74, 122n58

Gay Student Union (GSU) at LACC: Tony Lopez, 20; Freda Marshall, 20, 113n64

Gay Student Union (GSU) at Cal Poly San Luis Obispo: ACLU, 123n66, 123n69; Aethelred's bar, 35; Associated Students; President Robert Christensen, 36, 121n49–121n50; Mike Hurtado, 34; Robert E. Kennedy, 34–35, 123n70–123n71; "Legal Defense Drive," 34; Scott Plotkin, 34, 123n71; Ron Pursley, 35; San Luis Obispo County Young Republicans, 36; Margo Terrill, 35

Gay Student Union (GSU) of the Claremont Colleges, 82, 95, 150n32

Gay Student Union (GSU) at College of the Sequoias, 30. *See also* Ivan Crookshanks

Gay Student Union (GSU) at Cal State LA (CSULA GSU), 109n20, 145n74; Gay Awareness Week, 135n42

Gay Student Union at Cal State Long Beach (CSULB GSU): *Gay Power . . . Can Accomplish a Lot!*, 133n14; "Run for Rights" fundraiser, 94; Marguerite Silicero, 18, 20, 39

Gay Student Union (GSU) at Cal State Northridge, 90, 94

Gay Student Union (GSU) at San José State College: Paul Boneberg, 160n7; Vincent Fanucchi, 65, 89, 142n32; Proposition 5–6, 94–96, 159n77; Matthew Savoca, 94–95; *See also* Gay Liberation Front (GLF) at San José State College

Gay Student Union (GSU) at Sacramento State College: ACLU, 34; "creativity night" (1977), 61; Jay Murley, 36; Donald Shields, 30, 33–34, 36, 121n45. *See also* Society for Homosexual Freedom

Gay Student Union (GSU) at UC Berkeley: Barbara Bryant, 6, 21, 98, 153n4; Dave Cash, 21, 50, 91, 157n50; Jack Fertig, 21, 72; "Gay Lounge," 22, 114n81; renamed as Gay People's Union, 86; Rod Gordillo, 86; Lisa Orta, 1, 21, 44, 159n68; peer counseling, 22; "Renaissance Costume Ball," 71, 145n74; Student Legislative Council (SLC), 23, 38, 66, 87, 91, 157n51; Steve Wilford, 91, 157n49

Gay Student Union (GSU) at UCLA: "Being Black and Gay," 39; Cesar Blanco, 38; "Closet Crackers," 25; Scott Beardsley, 21, 25; Steve Cronenwalt, 51, 70; Larry Duplechan, 20, 22, 67, 71, 87–88, 98, 114n84, 143n42, 154n17; *Gayzette*, 129n55, 129n59, 132n86; hotline, 6, 115n108; Dave Johnson, 49, 66, 87, 89, 153n11, 154n16; peer counseling, 25; Don Spring, 1, 21, 113n76; Gary Steele, 22, 43, 89, 124n2, 129n59, 132n86, 155n27; Sunset Canyon Recreation Center, 23; Alan Turri, 25, 115n108; Joe Whitney, 56, 66, 142n30, 143n36

Gay Students Union (later People's) at UC Santa Barbara: *The Gay Follies*, 70; Gay Pride Week, 140n98; hotline, 6, 25; peer counseling program, 25; renamed as Gay

People's Union, 27, 50; Richard Robbins, 70, 91
Gay Student Union (GSU) at West LA College, 18; Preston Reese, 16
Gay studies, in experimental colleges, 42, 43; at Sacramento State, 45–47, 90; 129n55; Jim Kepner, 129n60
Gayzette (UCLA): archival access, 108n10; CADOC, 155n26; CAGSO, 151n53; California Assembly Bill 489, 94; GSU, 129n55, 129n59, 132n86; Gay studies, 129n55, 129n60; UCLA Medical School, 135n26; Geoffrey Chancre, 142n33; Don Spring, 113n76; social events among Southern California college students, 1149n25, 150n31, 150n46; Student Legislative Council, 38, 157n51; protests, 39, 155n27; Women's studies courses, 129n62
Gearhart, Sally, 45, 54, 60, 95, 130n76
gender identity, 9, 13, 17, 37, 53, 61, 89
genderfuck, 6, 53, 61, 69–72, 145n61, 145n74; Steve Cronenwalt, 70; Shaun Cole, 69; Larry Duplechan, 71; Jack Fertig, 21, 72; Lee Mentley, 14, 72, 110n22, 146n82; Therese Quinn, 71
GLBT Historical Society in San Francisco, 10, 125n14
Goen-Salter, Sugie, 44, 98, 158n67
Gordon, Cherie, 60, 68–69, 140n2, 140n4, 141n10, 143n46, 144n48
Grahn, Judy, 52, 60
GSC Bulletin, 79, 81. *See also* California Association of Gay Student Organizations
GSC Newsmagazine, 78. *See also* California Association of Gay Student Organizations
Guardsman (City College of San Francisco), 149n24
guerrilla or street theater, 67, 72
guest speakers, 8, 25, 39, 60. 80

Hamilton, Paula, 111n51
Hanhardt, Christina, 4, 104n22
Harris, James B., 70
Hastings College of Law, 77, 149n24
Hennigan, Shannon, 45, 129n56
HIV and AIDS, 7, 125n3, 160n7
Hobson, Emily, 105n35, 105n41, 106n63; "collective defense," 4
Homobrontosaurus, 60, 67, 140n2. *See also* Le Theatre Lesbien
Homophobia, 69, 144n55. *See also* Le Theatre Lesbien
homophobia: accusations of, 17; challenging, 28, 49, 85, 88–90, 133n14; critique of, 66, 73; Out and About, 107n71; women's center, 17
homosexuality: letters against, 116n3, 140n98; Briggs Initiative, 5; John D'Emilio, 7–8; discourse of illness, 29; creative works, 72; denials of recognition, 29–30; education, 37, 40–42, 46, 48, 53, 127n33, 128n46, 128n48, 128n59, 130n76, 77 and 78; gay liberation, 153n6; treated as sickness, 8, 32, 48; politics, 7, 86
hotlines or switchboards, 6, 25, 115n108, 118n10
human rights, 7, 78, 80, 83, 85, 90; campus organizing and programs, 56, 80, 92, 158n59; Coalition for Human Rights, 95
Hurewitz, Daniel, 3

in loco parentis surveillance, 98
Inland Empire No on 6 Committee, 95, 160n89
Interchange (Washington, D.C.), 37, 76, 124n2, 148n13, 148n20, 152n66

Johnsgard, Keith W., 32
Johnson, Dave, 49, 66, 87, 89, 153n11, 154n16. *See also* Gay Student Union (GSU) at UCLA
junior colleges, 4. *See* community colleges

Kennedy, Maureen, 65
Kennedy, Robert E., 34–35, 123n70–123n71
Kight, Morris, 39, 50, 89, 122n62, 136n50
Koehler, Elizabeth, 36
Kunzel, Regina, 107n64, 134n20, 135n41

Laine, Barry, 62
Latinos Unidos (de Los Angeles), 39, 57, 71, 95; Tony Guevera, 39
Laurence, Leo, 14, 27, 36, 116n1, 159n74
Lavender Library and Archives in Sacramento, 10
lavender scares, 8
lawyers, 34. 81, 122n64, 123n66. *See* attorneys
Le Theatre Lesbien: history of, 60–61, 67–68, 140n4; influences, 144n49; members, 140n2; poster, 69; press release, 143n46; program, 144n50; and Sacramento City College, 144n56. *See also* Dykes on Parade, *The Homobrontosaurus*; *Homophobia*, *Robin Screw*

INDEX   185

leadership, 11–12, 17, 77–78, 154n17, 157n48; "The Lavender Leader," 149n27; and Proposition 6, 159n77; race and gender demographics, 7; students of color leadership, 20, 151n65; women's, 82–83; workshops, 151n51

lesbian feminism, 6–7, 52, 56, 58, 61, 68, 71, 81, 86; future of, 87, 115n106. *See also* feminism

Lesbian Feminist Alliance at San José State College, 16, 19, 24, 54, 95, 126n24; Jacqua Miller, 39; Women's Center, 39; Nancy Robertson, 91

Lesbian Sisterhood (UCLA): formerly Gay Sisterhood, 19, 43, 55, 112n58, 138n69; Lesbian Rap Group, 24; Lesbian Sisters radio show, 50; meetings, 126n18, 140n9; Women's Health Week, 52; Women's Resource Center collaboration, 19, 39, 52, 54–55, 126n22

lesbian student organizing, 7, 15, 19, 39, 44, 111n39, 112n58; in women's studies programs, 5, 9, 40, 44–46, 60, 68, 86

Lesbian Tide, 35, 40, 82, 137n53, 150n35; archival access, 112n58

Lesbian Visions (Stanford University), 102

Lesbian Union at UC Berkeley, 111n53; peer counseling, 25

letter writing; Kenneth Pascoe, 31, 121n41; Orpha Strong Wright, 31; Bertha Wirtz, 31, 120n39. *See also* backlash

LGBT: breadth of experiences across community, 1–2, 149n27; use of term, 9

liberation: archives, 108n10; gay, 1; gay movement, 84, 113n65, 132n92. *See also* freedom

libraries: Gay Academic Union, 126n29; limited library resources about gender and sexuality, 40; Powell Library (UCLA), 23, 39; San José State College Women's Center, 126n27; struggles over, Stanford, 91; student generated, USC, 79

lobbyists, 3–4, 54, 92–94

local school boards, 7, 80; Los Rios Community College District Board, 68–69; Palo Alto Board of Education, 93–94

Loftin, Craig, 8, 106n53

Lone Mountain College, 70, 77, 149n24

Lopez, Tony, 20

Los Angeles, California: anti-LGBT state backlash, 3; Association of Black Gays, 158n62; backlash against, 58; Ivy Bottini, 54; Tom Bradley, 80; Gay Liberation Front, 4, 14–15, 93; Gay Students Coalition, 80; growth and change through LGBT student organizing, 3–4, 30, 53; Lesbian Sisters, 50; Morris Kight, 39, 50, 54, 89; LAPD, 39; regional group of the California Coalition, 95

Los Angeles City College (LACC), 7, 27, 48, 54, 77, 97, 109n17; *Collegian*, 109n15, 109n17, 133n4; Gay Pride Week, 20

Los Angeles Gay Community Services Center, 14

Los Angeles Times, 18, 56

Lynn Williamson, Rebecca: "The Inward Monitor," 66

Lyon, Phyllis, 53, 60

Mahaney, Ruth, 45, 130n78, 131n85, 158n67

Marshall, Freda, 20, 103n5, 113n64

Martin, Del, 8, 53–54, 60

Massachusetts Daily Collegian, archival access, 113n78

Master Plan of 1960, 4

Mattachine Society, 3, 43, 56, 106n56

McNaron, Toni, 44, 106n53

media: coverage of LGBTQ, 11; local, 89; public events, 52;use of organizing, 49, 81. *See also* newsletters and newspapers; radio

Mentley, Lee, 14, 72, 108n11, 110n22, 146n82

Metropolitan Community Church (MCC), 35, 73, 77, 117n8, 133n11, 146n85

Mexican American Youth Organization (MAYO), 5

Milk, Harvey: against Briggs Initiative, 5, 95; assassination of, 5, 97; commemorations of, 97; public discussions with, 53; published support of student activists, 78

Moore, Charles, 46, 132n91, 132n94

Mudgett, Mrs. William A., 13

Murley, Jay, 34, 36, 52, 119n16, 123n65

Music: Margie Adams, 53; Gwen Avery, 53; Backwater Rising, 71; Cal State Los Angeles, 150n33; Claremont Colleges concert, 95; Cal State Long Beach symposium, 135n42, 136n48; Maxine Feldman, 53, 136n49; 150n33; Richard Gonzales, 57; Joan Hand, 60; Lee Mentley, 146n82; musicians, 52–53, 55, 60; Purple Earthquake, 71; Malvina Reynolds, 53; Sacramento State College festival, 133n50; Shameless Hussies, 68; Stanford Cultural Night, 141n14; Symposium '76, 56; Le Theatre Lesbien,144n49; Linda Tillery, 53; Holly Near, 53; UC Berkeley concert, 136n48; Mary Watkins, 53, 136n48; West Coast Lesbian Con-

ference, 138n69; Cris Williamson, 53; women's music, 53, 95, 136n51
Mustang Daily (Cal Poly San Luis Obispo), archival access, 118n10

Narver, Lee, 13
National Gay Student Center, 18, 28, 37, 76, 116n1, 121n44, 152n66, 152n71; Warren Blumenfeld, 5; *Interchange*, 37, 76, 124n2, 148n13, 148n20, 152n66; J. Lee Lehman, 30, 40, 76, 84, 118n13, 121n44; Steve Werner, 28, 33, 76
National March on Washington for Lesbian and Gay Rights, 2, 27, 97
newsletters and newspapers: backlash against LGBT students, 27, 32, 57; critique of administrators, 11; DIY educational goals, 39-40, 87; mainstream and alternative, 31; organizations, 142n26; student organizing through advertisements, 15, 88, 109n20, 113n77, 114n91, 115n106, 113n108, 124n72, 137n54; student-produced publications, 9-10, 38, 40, 48-49, 77; students and readers writing opinion pieces, 15, 27, 32, 38, 57, 59, 87, 94, 122n58
Nutting, Spencer, 77, 111n53, 149n22

off-campus: events, 7, 25, 153n3, 158n67; organizations to support students, 34; political work, 26, 28, 36, 51, 75, 94-96; women's studies programs, 44
office spaces for LGBT student organizations, 22-23, 47, 67, 98, 114n84; 114n87; 116n114; 117n4; 133n11
ONE Archives at USC, 10
ONE, Incorporated; Dorr Legg, 39
ONE Letter (USC), archival access, 123n65
One Person, Patricia. *See* Matrisha Person
oral histories,2,.98;, 161-163; methods discussion, xvi, 10, 141n12
Orange County, California, 5, 30, 34, 90, 119n16
Ormsbee, Todd, 69, 145n61
Orta, Lisa, 1, 21, 44, 159n68
Out and About (CSU Monterey Bay), 107n71

Palmer, Cynthia, 16
Parker, Pat, 52-53, 60, 136n47
Patchwork, 78, 80, 149n26, 150n32. *See also* California Association of Gay Student Organizations
peer counseling, 6, 22, 25; training, 25, 79, 150n42

Person, Matrisha, 18, 46, 60, 140n2. *See also Dykes on Parade*; Le Theatre Lesbien; Patricia One Person; Matty Wallace
Phoenix (San Francisco State University), archival access, 111n39
poetry: Geoffrey Chancre's "Ye Yearre in Reviewe," 66, 142n33; Chicana/o activism, 141n12; Vincent Fanucchi's "Pardon Me, Beautiful, Where Did You Buy Your Tits?," 65, 89, 142n32, 156n34; gender and ethnic identity, 66, 141n11-141n12, 143n37, 146n87; Shaundel Jacobs' "We," 63; as queer creative practice, 61-66; political organizing, 6, 85, 141n12; public readings, 52-53, 85, 95, 136n46, 140n9; Freda Smith's "Dear Dora," 72-73; symposium and cultural nights, 135n42, 141n14
police raids, 3, 106n52
policies, campus: discriminatory, 89; homophobic, 85-86, 91-92, 96; sexist, 88
political: caucus, 80; clubs, 4; dances and dancing, 24, 85, 94-95; DIY, 125n3; Emily Hobson, 105n41; off-campus work, 26, 28, 36, 51, 75; poetry and organizing, 6, 85, 141n12; work, 81
politics: drag, 71; and education, 54; electoral, 5; and gay liberation, 6, 24, 39, 50, 85, 128n48, 146n87; Gay Liberation Student Conference, 76; gender and women's liberation, 98; and homosexuality, 7, 86; liberal, 3-4; in poetry, 63, 66; Reserve Officer Training Corps, 155n27
posters and fliers, 21, 57, 62, 69, 77, 110n22, 144n51
Pride (organization), 107n71
Proposition 6, 5, 94-95; *See also* Briggs Initiative
Proposition 22, 11, 107n70
protests, 4, 6, 39, 56, 61, 81, 88-89, 92-93, 154n21, 155n27
Pursley, Ron, 35

queer, use of term, 87
Queer Blue Light Videotapes, 120n33
Quinn, Therese, 68-69, 71-72, 146n81

race and ethnicity: conflicts in campus organizing, 7, 14, 87, 90, 92, 98, 138n71, 152n80; identity and activist students, 1, 3, 5, 8, 17, 18, 20, 24, 42, 48, 61, 66, 111, 105n44, 141n12

INDEX 187

radio, 31; campus stations, 48–50, 134n17; national network with other colleges, 134n18; public service announcements, 50
Rael, Ernie, 64
raps and discussion groups, 17, 24–25, 37, 39, 126n24
Raya, George, 1, 20, 54
reactionary resistance, 7, 27, 29, 36, 97–98, 116n2–116n3
Reagan, Ronald, 30–31, 115n100
Renegade Rip (Bakersfield College), archival access, 110n31
Reese, Preston, 16
Robin Screw, 68. *See also* Le Theatre Lesbien
Roe, Rev. Richard, 13; United Campus Ministries, 13, 92; "Homosexuality and Ethical Choices," 13
Rogers, Martin, 18, 32, 46–47, 51, 53, 153n1
romantic friendships, 7
Romesburg, Don, 9, 107n64
Rosen, Mike; *To Live and Die in Berkeley: A Verse Play in Three Acts*, 67
Russo, Vito, 58

Sacramento, California, 15, 17, 67, 69, 143n46
Sacramento Bee, 17
Sacramento City College, 55, 77; *Express*, 138n73; Gay Awareness Week, 69; Le Theatre Lesbien, 68, 144n56
Sacramento State College: Associated Students, 46, 90, 118n11, 132n92, 156n35; Barbara Bryant, 44, 46, 51, 93, 98, 111n37; Colloquium on Lesbian Women: Myth and Reality, 60; Barbara Bryant, 44, 46, 51, 93, 98, 111n37; Otto Butz, 30, 118n11, 119n19; Edgar Carpenter, 68; Gay Awareness Week, 69, 144n56; Gay Caucus, 15, 90; recognition legal cases, 32–34; George Raya, 1, 20, 54; Martin Rogers, 18, 32, 46–47, 51, 53, 153n1; Randy Shilts, 153n1; Freda Smith, 15, 18, 44, 46, 52, 72, 134n17; *State Hornet*, 49, 52; Women's Caucus, 15, 90; women's studies programs, 44–45, 48. *See also* Gay Liberation Front at Sacramento State College; Gay Student Union at Sacramento State College; Society for Homosexual Freedom at Sacramento State College
San Francisco, California, 3, 36, 77; bar raids, 106n52; gay community, 80; Gay Liberation Front, 3–4, 14, 39; growth and change through LGBT student organizing, 3–4, 30, 53; Tenderloin, 93, 104n22
San Francisco Bay Guardian, archival access, 151n61
San Francisco Free Press, archival access, 109n13
San Francisco State College (later San Francisco State University): Associated Students, 17, 44; Black students, 23, 128n48; John Blackburn, 23, 57, 111n51; Communiversity, 128n48; experimental college, 41–43, 127n40, 128n47–128n48; David Cawley, 70–71; Gay Liberation Front (GLF), 4, 14, 62, 110n22; Sally Gearhart, 45, 54, 60, 95, 130n76; Ruth Mahaney, 45, 130n78, 158n67; *Phoenix*, 111n39; Mark Thompson, 71, 78, 80, 82, 145n74; Charles Thorp, 8, 62, 67, 76, 148n17; Women Studies, 44–45, 130n75; Women and Gender Studies, 130n77; *Zenger's/Golden Gater*, 111n38. *See also* Gay Students Coalition of the San Francisco Bay Area (GSCSF)
San José State College (later San José State University): experimental college, 41; Gay Blue Jeans Day, 89, 155n28, 155n31, 156n32; Keith W. Johnsgard, 32; recognition legal cases, 31–32; Lesbian and Gay Awareness Week, 138n72; Max Rafferty, 119n22; *Spartan Daily*, 110n30; Dudley Swim, 29; Rebecca Lynn Williamson, 66; Oscar Wilde dance, 23. *See also* GSU at San José State College; Lesbian Feminist Alliance
Santa Clara Human Relations Commission, 94
Schiller, Gregg, 80–82
Schrader, Randy, 14, 29, 53
self-determination, 32, 88, 98, 123n70
self-help trainings, 6
Shilts, Randy, 85, 88, 96, 132n88, 132n94, 139n91; City College of San Francisco, 56–57; Sacramento State College, 153n1. *See also Advocate*
Sides, Josh, 4, 104n22, 109n13
Silicero, Marguerite, 18, 20, 39
Sivertsen, Wiggsy, 20, 30, 120n37
Smith, Freda, 15, 18, 133n11; "Dear Dora," 72–73, 146n85; interview with Melissa Wilcox, 146n85; Women's Studies Board with Barbara Bryant, 44, 46, 52
Smith, Jackson, 48, 133n4
social concern over homosexuality, 8

Society for Homosexual Freedom at Sacramento State College, 1, 5, 18, 52, 68; recognition legal case, 32–33; George Raya, 1, 20, 54. *See also* Gay Liberation Front at Sacramento State College; Gay Student Union at Sacramento State College
Society for Individual Rights (SIR), 3, 8, 36, 76, 108n6
Some of Your Best Friends, 53, 118n9, 137n54, 150n33
Sonoma State University, 77
sorority sisters, 8
Spartan Daily (San José State College), 110n30
speakers' bureaus, 7, 35, 49–51, 61, 94, 134n21
Spring, Don, 21–22, 113n76
Stanford Daily (Stanford University), archival access, 108n3
Stanford University: ad hoc committee on Human Rights, 92; administrators, 92; Keith Archuleta of the Black Students Union, 92; Bear Capron, 13; community activism, 25–26; Arthur Corbin, 22, 93; Robert Croonquist, 70; Cultural Night, 141n14; Gay Awareness Week, 83; Gay Pride Week, 56, 79, 145n69; GPU goals, 37–38, 138n73; Donna Hughes-Oldenburg, 71, 93, 159n70; *Lesbian Visions*, 102; library, 91; Men's Collective, 18; *Stanford Daily*, 108n3; Student Homophile League, 2, 107n1, 108n6; Women's Caucus, 71, 83, 114n91, 135n41, 136n48, 153n10; Women's Collective, 18, 71, 87, 93. *See also* GPU at Stanford
State Hornet, 49, 52. *See also* Sacramento State University
Steele, Gary, 22, 43, 89, 124n2, 129n59, 132n86, 155n27
Stein, Marc, 4, 9, 103n8, 107n65, 110n22
Stonewall Rebellion of June 1969, 4, 97, 105n40
Strachan, David, 17–18
Stryker, Susan, 107n66
student government, 10, 50, 78; candidates and forums, 91–92, 96; experimental colleges, 41; funding issues, 56–57; leadership of, 147n48; legal support, 34; newsletters, 38; pushback against women, 17; Richard Robbins, 70, 91; Nancy Robertson, 91; support for LGBT organizing, 11, 16, 32, 56, 85, 90–91; Steve Wilford, 91, 157n49. *See also* Associated Students
Student Homophile League, 147n6, 148n20;

Columbia University, 13, 75, 107n2; Rutgers University, 75; Stanford University, 2, 107n1, 108n6; UC Berkeley, 107n1
Student Legislative Council at UCLA, 23, 38, 66, 87, 91, 157n51
Students for Gay Power at UC Berkeley, 20, 38, 86, 134n21, 140n9, 154n21, 157n47. *See also* GSU at UC Berkeley
student movements, 5, 27, 85, 98, 105n44; anti-fascist movements, 2
Student Non-Violent Coordinating Committee (SNCC), 75
students of color, 7, 9, 17–18, 20, 82–83, 106n62. *See also* Asian American students; Black students; Chicana/Chicano students
Supreme Court of California, 34

Tavern Guild, 3
Tay Bush Inn, 106n52
tearooms, 14
Terebinski, Nina, 16
theater, 6, 20, 61, 67–70, 72
Theater of the Ridiculous, 140n4
Le Theatre Lesbien, 61, 69, 143n46, 144n49; *Dykes on Parade*, 144n50; Cherie Gordon, 60, 140n2, 144n56; *The Homobrontosaurus*, 67, 140n2; *Homophobia*, 69; *Robin Screw*, 68; *See also* Cherie Gordon; Matrisha Person; Therese Quinn
Thompson, Mark, 71; on activism, 82; on dances and parties, 80, 145n74; editor of the Voice, 78
Thorp, Charles: background, 8, 62; Konstantin Berlandt, 67; Gay Liberation Student Conference, 62, 76, 148n17
transgender, 7, 97; and LGBT term, 9
transexual, 53, 143n46, 107n66
trustees: Hobert Burns, 31; California State College System, 29; private colleges, 30; publicity of, 31; resistance from, 7, 29–30; USC, 30, 32–33, 36, 119n20, 122n62
Turri, Alan, 25

University of California system, 4
University of California, Berkeley (UC Berkeley): administrators, 24, 28; Associated Students, 21, 91, 146n83; Konstantin Berlandt, 67, 154n21; Black students, 67; Barbara Bryant, 6, 21, 98; Gay Student Union (renamed as Gay People's Union), 86;

University of California, Berkeley (*continued*) hosting "gay convocation," 83; Medieval/Renaissance Dance, 23, 71, 145n74; Student Legislative Council (SLC), 23, 38, 66, 87, 91, 157n51; Women's Music Collective, 53, 136n48. *See also* GSU at UC Berkeley

University of California, Davis (UC Davis): *California Aggie*, 146n4, 127n38; California Gay and Lesbian Student Coalition, 83; experimental college, 41; Gay Union, 114n91; National Gay Student Center, 152n71

University of California, Los Angeles (UCLA): administrators, 25, 28; Geoffrey Chancre, 66, 142n33; Coalition against the Dehumanization of Children, 89; community activism, 43, 55, 78; Larry Duplechan, 22, 71, 87–88, 114n84; experimental college, 42; Gay Awareness Week, 43, 52–53, 55, 58, 66; Gay '70s Dance organized with Cal State Northridge, 23; Dave Johnson, 49, 66, 87, 89, 153n11, 154n16; Powell Library, 23, 39; West Coast Lesbian Conference, 55, 68, 82, 132n86, 138n69; Joe Whitney, 56, 66, 142n30; women's studies programs, 44, 52. *See also Daily Bruin*; Gay Sisterhood; *Gayzette*; GSU at UCLA; Lesbian Sisterhood; Student Legislative Council at UCLA; Women's Resource Center at UCLA

University of California, Santa Barbara (UC Santa Barbara): Associated Students, 90; Black Students Union, 90; coming out program, 50, 134n18; *Daily Nexus*, 110n26; Gay Pride Week, 140n98; Gay Students Union (later People's), 6, 25, 70; Richard Robbins, 70, 91; Andy Rogers, 90, 132n94; Valentine's Day dance, 23; Women's Caucus, 50

University of California, Santa Cruz (UC Santa Cruz): Gay and Lesbian Alliance, 95; Rachel Harwood, 45; oral history project, 2; Zeisel Saunders, 41; student demands for and efforts to develop courses, 40–41; women's studies programs, 45–46; Kathryn Wright, 40

University of San Francisco, 77

University of Southern California (USC): Associated Students, 32; Larry Bernard, 29–30, 33, 47, 74, 122n58; Board of Trustees, 30, 32–33, 36, 119n20, 122n62; *Daily Trojan*, 33, 117n8122n62; dances, 35, 69, 94–95; experimental college, 120n23; Sal Licata and political caucus, 80; *ONE Letter*, 123n65; recognition legal cases, 33–34; trustees, 30, 32–33, 36, 119n20, 122n62; University Senate, 32. *See also* Gay Liberation Forum at USC

University Times (Cal State Los Angeles): archival access, 109n20

Valrajean, Rebecca: *The Lavender Troubadour*, 67
vandal, 27
Vanguard, 3
Vector (San Francisco), 36, 40, 103n2
Vietnam War, 93
Voice of the Gay Students Coalition, 78. *See also* Gay Students Coalition of the San Francisco Bay Area

Wallace, Matty, 18, 44, 46, 49, 52, 60, 140n2. *See also* Matrisha Person
Warwoop (El Camino College), archival access, 138n70
Weir, Joan, 16
Werner, Steve, 28, 33, 76
West Coast Lesbian Conference, 55, 68, 82, 132n86, 138n69
West Los Angeles College, 16, 18
Whitney, Joe, 56, 66, 142n30
Wilkowski, Jill, 16
Williams, Zelima, 20, 88
Women's Centers, 16–17, 39, 44, 93; alliances with GSU, 20
women's colleges, 7
Women's Resource Center at UCLA, 19, 23–24, 39, 44, 52, 54–55, 116n109, 126n22
women's leadership, 82
women's liberation, 15, 18, 75–76, 98, 125n7, 148n17; movement, 2, 5, 14, 38, 44, 90, 93; protest, 88, 154n20
women's studies programs, 1, 6–7, 9, 44, 86; Sacramento State College, 44–45, 68; San Francisco State College, 45; San José State College, 129n66; Sonoma State University, 46; UCLA, 44, 52; UC Santa Cruz, 45–46
women's weeks, 54–55. *See* awareness weeks
Word Is Out, 53
World War II, 3, 5, 7
Wright, Kathryn, 40
Wysocki, Paul, 21

Zenger's/Golden Gater (San Francisco State University), archival access, 111n38

Since 1970: Histories of Contemporary America

Jimmy Carter, the Politics of Family, and the Rise of the Religious Right
    by J. Brooks Flippen

Rumor, Repression, and Racial Politics: How the Harassment of Black Elected Officials Shaped Post-Civil Rights America
    by George Derek Musgrove

Doing Recent History: On Privacy, Copyright, Video Games, Institutional Review Boards, Activist Scholarship, and History That Talks Back
    edited by Claire Bond Potter and Renee C. Romano

The Dinner Party: Judy Chicago and the Power of Popular Feminism, 1970–2007
    by Jane F. Gerhard

Reconsidering Roots: Race, Politics, and Memory
    edited by Erica L. Ball and Kellie Carter Jackson

Liberation in Print: Feminist Periodicals and Social Movement Identity
    by Agatha Beins

Pushing Back: Women of Color–Led Grassroots Activism in New York City
    by Ariella Rotramel

Remaking Radicalism: A Grassroots Documentary Reader of the United States, 1973–2001
    edited by Dan Berger and Emily K. Hobson

Deep Cut: Science, Power, and the Unbuilt Interoceanic Canal
    by Christine Keiner

America's Other Automakers: A History of the Foreign-Owned Automotive Sector in the United States
    by Timothy J. Minchin

Public Religions in the Future World: Postsecularism and Utopia
    by David Morris

Goldwater Girls to Reagan Women: Gender, Georgia, and the Growth of the New Right
    by Robin M. Morris

Here Are My People: LGBT College Student Organizing in California
    by David A. Reichard

www.ingramcontent.com/pod-product-compliance
Lightning Source LLC
Chambersburg PA
CBHW031834230426
43669CB00009B/1340